D1259412

Legislature

Legislature

California's School

for Politics

William K. Muir, Jr.

The University of Chicago Press
Chicago and London

WILLIAM MADISON RANDALL LIBRARY UNC AT WILMINGTON

WILLIAM K. MUIR, JR., is chairman of the Department of
Political Science at the University of California, Berkeley. He is
the author of *Prayer in the Public Schools: Law and Attitude
Change* and *Police: Streetcorner Politicians*, both published by the
University of Chicago Press.

The University of Chicago Press, Chicago 60637
The University of Chicago Press, Ltd., London

© 1982 by The University of Chicago
All rights reserved. Published 1982
Printed in the United States of America
89 88 87 86 85 84 83 82   5 4 3 2 1

Library of Congress Cataloging in Publication Data

Muir, William Ker.
    Legislature : California's school for politics.

    Includes index.
    1. California. Legislature.   2. Legislators—
California.   I. Title.
JK8771.M84   1982   328.794   82-16128
ISBN 0-226-54627-6

JK8771
.M84
1982

To my mother and father,
whose interest and ambivalence
about politics began
my political education, and
to Jess Unruh and Leo McCarthy,
legislative leaders whose hope and vision
nurtured a good institution

235229

Contents

[By] the delegation of the government . . . to a small number of citizens elected by the rest . . . the effect . . . is . . . to refine and enlarge the public views by passing them through the medium of a chosen body of citizens, whose wisdom may best discern the true interest of their country, and whose patriotism and love of justice will be least likely to sacrifice it to temporary and partial considerations.

James Madison, *Federalist* no. 10

The greatest imperfection of popular local institutions, and the chief cause of the failure which so often attends them, is the low caliber of the men by whom they are almost always carried on. That these should be of a very miscellaneous character is, indeed, part of the usefulness of the institution; it is that circumstance chiefly which renders it a school of political capacity and general intelligence. But a school supposes teachers as well as scholars; the utility of the instruction greatly depends on its bringing inferior minds into contact with superior. . . .

John Stuart Mill, *Considerations on Representative Government*

The first of the duties that are at this time imposed upon those who direct our affairs is to educate democracy, to reawaken, if possible, its religious beliefs; to purify its morals; to mold its actions; to substitute a knowledge of statecraft for its inexperience, and an awareness of its true interests for its blind instincts. . . .

Alexis de Tocqueville, *Democracy in America*

Preface

Why write? Paul Robinson, a historian of ideas at Stanford, once wrote an essay on the motives of authors. He dismissed both money and audiences (each "embarrassingly low"). After admitting to writing for himself ("we are our own best audience"), he added a second reason:

> Sometimes we write to say thank you, to render gratitude to a member or a portion of humanity that has given us pleasure, elevated us and made us think better of ourselves. Such is the motivation we sense and find so moving in the opening sentences of Fernand Braudel's great study of the Mediterranean world in the 16th century: "I have loved the Mediterranean with passion. . . ." I discovered a similar motive in myself as I began my study of Verdi. Part of the energy for the project, I found, came from the wish to reciprocate. I have spent thousands of hours listening to Verdi. Indeed, measured in purely quantitative terms, no other human being has given me more pleasure. A writer is in the fortunate position of being able to acknowledge such a gift in a more fully satisfying fashion than those who don't write.

I clipped Robinson's piece from the 31 March 1979 *New Republic* because a motive for writing this book was my need "to render gratitude." I wrote for myself, with the narcissistic and the sound logic such a purpose would imply. But I also wrote to acknowledge a debt to "a portion of humanity"—to admirable politicians of the free world, men and women, ancient and contemporary, who have worked to neutralize the destructiveness that inheres in the human condition without destroying the creative energies that lie inter-mingled with it. Democracy (and its quintessential institution, the legislature) gives me the same pleasure Robinson derived from Verdi. I wrote this book "to say thank you" to the best of the architects and incumbents of the free world's legislatures.

What is the book about? It offers answers to three questions. What is a legislature? What do legislators do in one? Under what circumstances does a legislature make its members competent?

A legislature is like a school. It educates its members in the science of public policy and the arts of politics. Through its subject-matter committees it exposes legislators to a wealth of knowledge about human affairs. Through the bill-carrying responsibilities it imposes on authors of legislation, it teaches the art of negotiation. And through the division of labor, it invites its members to specialize and create a network of key persons who share an interest in a single field of public policy.

Service on committees, authorship of legislation, and specialization constitute the major elements of the legislative curriculum. Enlargement of intellectual horizons, improvement of negotiation skills, and cultivation of an expertise result. In a good legislature, most members acquire what James Madison called the three competencies of democratic leadership: patriotism, love of justice, and wisdom. By patriotism Madison meant an expanded empathy for all one's country-men, with their diverse occupations and hopes; by love of justice he implied a concern for fair play; and by wisdom he referred to the kind of enlightened statecraft necessary to achieve enduring improvements in the general welfare. When a legislature educates well and develops sympathy, equity, and mastery among its members, it functions as a school of their political capacity. It provides them an education in patriotism, love of justice, and wisdom.

Unlike the education offered in the conventional school, with its reliance on the schoolmaster's whip, the education provided in a good legislature depends on reciprocity. It results from numerous voluntary exchanges among the legislators. This point is important and worth an additional word. In virtually every American legislature reciprocity, not coercion, is the dominant form of behavior, because give and take is a happier way to deal with colleagues than threats and punishments. Legislatures differ markedly, however, in the subjects of their members' mutual exchange. Every legislative institution influences its members' "tastes"—their desires for money or power or votes or friendships or (and this is the important point) knowledge. A good legislature whets the appetite for knowledge.

How? In a good legislature certain practices make it less difficult for members to learn. Nonpartisan staff members and rules assuring fair partisan competition make it easier for legislators to understand how policy is developed and how laws actually make a difference. In the reciprocal community of a legislature, reducing the obstacles to learning stimulates demand for knowledge. That is, when an education in the competencies of democratic leadership can be had through reasonable effort, most legislators will take the opportunity to get one. On the other hand, if a poor educational environment makes becoming competent too troublesome, legislators will not make the effort to become competent.

The system of procedures determines whether most of a legislature's members will strive to learn. At least, that is the lesson I learned from examining America's best state legislature in the 1970s—California's. Because it was easy for California legislators to study the public business, most of them learned to value knowledge and to practice the reciprocal means of obtaining it—by teaching one another well.

The reader may wonder about the accuracy of detail and methods of observation employed in this study. During the 1975–76 session of the California state legislature I served as a staff member on two assembly committees, welfare and business. In 1977–78 I conducted interviews with twenty-eight legislators whom I selected for reasons of their eloquence, diversity, and availability, each interview lasting from two to four hours. The main theme of the questions was, "As a legislator, how do you make the legislature intelligible to the layman?" I made no effort to get a random sample of legislators because I was not interested in estimating the frequencies of opinions. Because my interest was in the early stages of individual political development, I concentrated for the most part on the California state assembly, its membership of eighty men and women, and the process by which they enhanced their skills and knowledge. They tended to be younger and less experienced than the members of the state senate. Once assembly members learned their elementary political p's and q's, they tended to "graduate" to the senate.

Many people participated in the making of this book, either through their instruction or criticism or both: Eugene Bardach, Kenneth Betsalel, Patricia Boling, Carl Brakensiek, Richard Brandsma,

Bill Cavala, Eric Davis, Thomas Fischer, Fred Greenstein, Jeannette Hopkins, Robert Kagan, Bill Kahrl, Eugene Lee, Frank Levy, William Lockyer, Virginia Magnus, Alister McAlister, Mike McCann, Nelson Polsby, Steve Spellman, Preble Stolz, Aaron Wildavsky, and Bill Zinn. Working with them was a pleasure. The late Jeff Pressman first convinced me of the significance of legislatures.

One last acknowledgment. More than a quarter-century ago four men taught me to look at the miracle of free people doing "ordinary" things. This book is a small repayment to those former teachers: Robert Dahl, Herbert Kaufman, Charles Edward Lindblom, and John Schroeder.

William K. Muir, Jr.

Connoisseurs of good sausage and lovers of good laws have one thing in common: they should never watch either being made.
American political folklore

Politics is perhaps the only profession for which no preparation is thought necessary.
Robert Louis Stevenson

Introduction:
What Is a Legislature?

Ask what a legislature is like, and you will hear it likened to an arena, assembly, back alley, balance, bawdy house, brokerage firm, bunch of horse traders, branch of a tree, butcher shop, card game, cash register, circus, citadel, club, cockpit, collection agency, conciliator, congeries of committees, dance hall, debating society, decision maker, engine, errand boy, factory, family, forum, group, house, inquisition, judge, jury, linchpin, locus of pressures, machine, magnet, marketplace, medium, mender of the social fabric, mirror, moral midwife, nightclub, organ of the body, porkbarrel, pride of lions, rat race, referee, sausage maker, school, seminar, small town, stage, struggle, theater, and zoo. Metaphors all, they recur in our conversations and reflect our different notions of what legislators do—and should do—in a legislature. The metaphor of legislature-as-sausage maker, for example, highlights the fact that lawmakers and sausage makers engage in the unpleasant enterprise of blending sordid elements into palatable compromises—and ought to.

Some metaphors rise to the level of analogy. Analogies, as the philosopher Abraham Kaplan once noted, suggest more than a few interesting likenesses: "they provide a systematic elaboration of resemblances," which leads to genuine intellectual discovery.[1] Two of our most original political theorists, James Madison (1751–1836) and John Stuart Mill (1806–73), were drawn to the analogy of the leg-

---

1. Abraham Kaplan, *The Conduct of Inquiry* (San Francisco: Chandler, 1964), p. 266.

1

islature as school. They both insisted that legislative institutions in a free society must teach their members to govern well. In fact, the preparation of political leaders was—or ought to be—a central event in a legislature.

II

Democracy's success depends upon legislatures' performing their teaching function well. Madison was the first American political thinker to make the point at length. In the *Federalist Papers,* he warned that the Achilles heel of a democracy was majority tyranny: if a democracy meant that government and its coercive power should be responsive to a majority of the people, could it be restrained from being responsive to a capricious majority? Madison's solution to the problem of democratic caprice was representative government: bar the public from direct rule, and delegate leadership of the nation to a popularly chosen house of representatives, which would "refine and enlarge"[2] the opinions and passions of the people. Passing the people's "temporary or partial considerations" through a "medium" of legislative representation would moderate the public views and synthesize them into "the true interest" of the country. This notion of a popularly chosen assembly buffering the nation's passions con-stituted the "republican genius"[3] of the United States Constitution.

Madison understood that this legislative medium needed to be carefully cultivated. He had no illusions about the low caliber of the individual representatives, selected as they would be from parochial circumstance, deficient in the theory and practice of public affairs, and lacking "due acquaintance with the objects and principles of legislation."[4]

> It is not possible that an assembly of men called for the most part from pursuits of a private nature, continued in appointment for a short time, and led by no permanent motive to devote the intervals of public occupation to a study of the laws, the affairs, and the comprehensive interests of their country, should, if left wholly to themselves, escape a variety of important errors in the exercise of their legislative trust.[5]

2. The quoted phrases all come from *Federalist* no. 10 unless otherwise noted.
3. *Federalist* no. 66.
4. *Federalist* no. 62.
5. *Federalist* no. 62.

Madison's object was to design a congressional institution that would not leave the representatives "wholly to themselves," but instead would motivate them to "study . . . the comprehensive interests of their country."[6] Legislative misrule, as he foresaw it, would stem more from incompetence than from a lack of "upright intention,"[7] from blunders of "the heads rather than the hearts."[8] To avoid such blunders, democratic legislators had to be made to master three fundamental competencies.

First, they had to be taught sympathy for the circumstances of all their constituents. They had to learn about the concerns not only of partisans and neighbors but also of opponents and strangers. *Patriotism* was Madison's term for this enlargement of identification. A legislator was patriotic if he regarded every constituent as one of his people. If a legislator lacked patriotism, if he were too lazy or too parochial to study the affairs of all the diverse individuals in his district—farmers and laborers, rebels and contented, young and old—then he would serve the legislature poorly. Representatives had to understand the hopes and dilemmas of all the citizenry if they were to avoid passing oppressive laws. If representatives were ignorant of particular circumstances in their districts, they could not anticipate the subtle consequences of applying general policies to a highly diverse people.[9]

Second, individual legislators had to learn to manage legislation and discipline themselves to do it fairly, openly, and in the face of opposition. This skill of public negotiation Madison called the *love of justice*, an ability to play the broker's part and negotiate a fair give and take with guarantees of due process to all interests. To do justice, Madison insisted, was to "protect all parties, the weaker as well as

6. See *Federalist* nos. 51, 53, 55, 56, 61, 62, and 63. The political scientist Robert Dahl, in his brilliant *Preface to Democratic Theory* (Chicago: University of Chicago Press, 1956), tends to minimize Madison's concern about schooling the political capacity of legislators. For example, while accurately stating the Madisonian solution to majority tyranny, he dismisses it as probably false: "The only remaining possibility, then, is that some specified group in the community, not defined as the majority, but not necessarily always in opposition to it, would be empowered to decide. But . . . any group in the community with such a power would use it to tyrannize over other individuals in the community" (p.24). But according to my reading of Madison, the House of Representatives, having been schooled to increase its enlightenment and virtue, was precisely the "specified group" Madison had in mind to buffer government from the majority's transient passions.
7. *Federalist* no. 53.
8. *Federalist* no. 62.
9. *Federalist* no. 53.

the more powerful."[10] Love of justice signified a representative's insistence on the integrity of the legislative process, so that "all parties" that were touched by a governmental policy would have a real say in influencing its design.

Third, legislators had to learn to take personal responsibility for a discrete segment of the legislative load. By specializing and giving "constant attention" to a particular area of public policy, each representative would develop an expert's competence. He would attain a vision of the public interest in that area more subtle than that of any generalist. Moreover, the specialist legislator would bear the primary responsibility for preparing "a succession of well-chosen and well-connected measures" in the area of his concern. In order to move this "train of measures" through the legislature, the specialist would have to bring together a number of informed and committed citizens who would persevere in enacting the whole program[11]. *Wisdom* was Madison's term for the specialist's capacity to conceive and realize an idea in a democratic society. Wisdom was the social skill of building enduring coalitions. A wise legislator understood the republican genius of representative government and grasped the fact that ideas and vision and hard work could prevail in a republic only by building agreement over time among a community of the truly concerned. Wisdom was knowing how to establish, and become the center of, a broad network of trustworthy individuals.

Madison's solution to the problem of democratic caprice consisted of designing legislative institutions that educated their members to become political professionals "whose wisdom may best discern the true interest of their country, and whose patriotism and love of justice will be least likely to sacrifice it to temporary and partial considerations." He saw one danger lurking in such a solution. A legislature would be a poor school if it played favorites among its students. Unless it was egalitarian in the best sense, unless all legislators had an equal opportunity to learn how to be professionals, "the countenance of the government [might] become more democratic, but the soul that animates it [would] be more oligarchic."[12] A legislative institution that contained only a few well-informed members while the majority remained ignorant not only muffed its chance to teach the educable; it also ran the danger of becoming corrupt.

10. *Federalist* no. 51.
11. *Federalist* no. 63.
12. *Federalist* no. 58.

A few of the members, as happens in all such assemblies, will possess superior talents; will, by frequent re-elections, become members of long standing; will be thoroughly masters of the public business, and perhaps not unwilling to avail themselves of those advantages.[13]

To prevent a "superior" few from "avail[ing] themselves of [oligarchical] advantages," a good legislature had to devise procedures to deepen the intellects of *all* its members and to place within their reach the mastery of public affairs necessary to discourage personal corruption.[14]

Madison saw a second advantage in increasing the competence of all the representatives. As legislators improved their skills in conducting the public business, their commitment to the vocation of politics would harden. As a result they would stand for re-election. Their competence, if they had taken the trouble to nurture it, would stand out boldly against the inexperience of any challengers. The electorate would discern the differences and tend to return incumbents to office, thus giving the legislature an institutional continuity. Madison was convinced that democratic government could be stable (and a good society possible) only if most legislators were veterans, were "members of long standing."[15] The ideal legislature was one in which "the bulk of the members"[16] were experienced political incumbents and in which the few new representatives entering the

13. *Federalist* no. 53.
14. The Federalist insisted on six minimal conditions for a good legislative school: (1) books and the time to read them, and a private "closet" for each legislator, (2) diverse colleagues and the motivation and the opportunities to learn from them, (3) lobbyists and the inducements to listen to their "oral" information, (4) specialists from government agencies from whom expertise for particular topics could be obtained, (5) records of the legislative history of matters treated by the legislature which would provide, among other things, the opportunity to avoid repeating previous errors, and (6) bill-carrying responsibilities, which would provide individual representatives experience by which their understanding and vision could be tested against results. See *Federalist* nos. 53, 55, and 56.
15. *Federalist* no. 62: "Another effect of public instability is the unreasonable advantage it gives to the sagacious, the enterprising, and the moneyed few over the industrious and uninformed mass of the people. Every new regulation concerning commerce or revenue, or in any manner affecting the value of the different species of property, presents a new harvest to those who watch the change and can trace its consequences; a harvest, feared not by themselves, but by the toils and cares of the great body of their fellow citizens. This is a state of things in which it may be said with some truth that laws are made for the *few*, not for the *many*."
16. *Federalist* no. 53.

legislature each term would be schooled, gradually and systematically, in the subtle arts of leading a democracy.

III

It was John Stuart Mill who elaborated on how legislatures might actually go about the business of effectively teaching leadership. In *Considerations on Representative Government*, Mill, like Madison, pondered the natural incompetence of democratic officials. A potential remedy for their shortcomings, he suggested, was the subnational legislatures (Mill called them "provincial assemblies"[17]), places where national leadership capacity could be cultivated. Local legislatures had the advantage of handling problems of lesser moment and scope than the national parliament. Hence, if local legislators made important errors—and mistakes were inherent in any good educational process—the harm resulting from them would be restricted and remediable.

Mill set down six circumstances under which a local legislature could be made into an effective "school of political capacity."[18] First, the legislators, or the "scholars"[19], as Mill liked to describe them, had to come from all walks of life. When assembled, they should constitute "a fair sample of every grade of intellect among the people."[20] Initial diversity was crucial, thus the principle of open admission had to apply.

Second, the education in the legislative school should be adversarial and oral. Rhetorical argumentation, practiced "in the face of opponents,"[21] should be the major pedagogical method. The representatives should be made to "work . . . against pressures,"[22] pushed to the Socratic hilt, thus coming to enjoy the testing of ideas by frequent controversy. Their minds were not so much to be filled as to be "exercised."[23] Constant classroom attendance must be required. A norm of sharp criticism must be established. Performance

17. John Stuart Mill, *Considerations on Representative Government* (New York: Liberal Arts Press, 1958; originally published in 1861), p. 248.
18. Ibid, p. 219.
19. Ibid. The quoted phrases all come from chapter 15 of *Representative Government* unless otherwise noted.
20. Ibid, p. 83.
21. Ibid, p. 82.
22. Ibid, p. 162.
23. Ibid, p. 76.

must be immediately graded, as a "means of making ignorance aware of itself."

Third, two classes of teachers must exist. One would consist of fellow legislators with "superior" minds. Educating as much by example as by precept, these model legislators would be the tutors of the legislative community. They would be drawn from the senior class of the legislative school and would be obliged to teach their "enlarged ideas" and "more enlightened purposes" to their pupils.

Fourth, as an incentive to teach, a norm of reciprocity would require that those who learned from these tutors teach something in return. As Mill foresaw, the "schooling of grown people by public business" would take place in characteristically reciprocal circumstances. Each legislator would give and take instruction, in marked contrast to the one-way, authoritarian methods of "the schooling of youth in academies and colleges."

Fifth, there must exist a faculty of outsiders not a part of the student body. Some might be part-time and temporary—"thinkers and writers," whose compensation would be nothing more than the pleasure of "pressing [their] useful ideas" upon the scholars. Others would be full-time and professional lobbyists—subject-matter experts whose jobs would be to teach the students a specific topic and a "defense"of a position concerning it, "cramming"[24] their students' heads with facts, arguments, and reason, preparing them for the tests of floor debate and negotiation.

Finally, overseeing the educational process would be a "schoolmaster," the supervisor and disciplinarian of the school. Mill quoted approvingly the old saw, "As the schoolmaster is, so will be the school." The schoolmaster's job comprised three tasks: to maintain standards and moral discipline; to develop procedures for effective teaching; and to assure that the subject matter in the classrooms was sufficiently diverse and challenging to stimulate the interest of the best students and stretch the less able to their utmost. Mill left it ambiguous whether the schoolmaster would be formally part of, or outside of, the student body.

Mill regarded these six conditions as necessary to a good legislative school. In sum, there had to be a diverse student body, testing by floor debate, some exemplary legislators, manners grounded in the

24. Ibid, p. 78.

norm of reciprocity, well-informed lobbyists working openly, and leadership concerned about process.

Mill did not forget that the analogy of legislature as school was only an intellectual construct. The "education of the citizens," he wrote, "is not the only thing to be considered; government and administration do not exist for that alone, great as its importance is."[25] A legislature was more than a school for democratic leadership. But for one's first encounter with a legislature, for an illuminating analogy, Mill insisted on emphasizing the academy-like qualities of the representative legislature. Think of it as a school, he might have said, and you will see it as individual legislators do. Representatives attend their legislative school to get a good education in public affairs. They do so to advance their personal political careers. Suppose that a public affairs education is their immediate purpose, and you will observe them getting one by using their resources, particularly their votes in committees and on the floor, their status as bill-carriers, and their political skills and acquaintance, to attract teachers to educate them. The legislative experience is an opportunity to gain a knowledge of statecraft.

IV

The educative notions of Madison and Mill may seem to turn matters on their heads. A good legislator, according to the conventional wisdom, is supposed to use his position as lawmaker to improve society by making laws. The analogy of legislature as school, however, reverses the implications of the more typical metaphor of legislature as sausage maker. Public policy, instead of being the *raison d'être* of a legislature, simply becomes one of several simultaneous concerns, the social byproduct of the legislature's schooling function.

The intellectual test of analogy comes in its application. What I propose to do in this book is to apply the analogy of legislature as school to the "best" state legislature in operation during the mid-1970s. At that time, the California state legislature fulfilled the six conditions Mill specified as essential to a good legislative school of political capacity. Whether a systematic elaboration of the school analogy will lead to any genuine discovery about democratic legislatures is the central question I attempt to answer.

25. Ibid, p. 228.

Part One

In looking at the California state legislature as it functioned in 1975–76, it is wise to keep one vital fact in mind. Political institutions, like people, are susceptible to cycles of invigoration and exhaustion. They grow vital, decline, and revive again. They experience eras of good feeling, when nothing seems to go wrong, and they undergo breakdown, when faith is shaken.

The session of 1975–76 was a golden age for the California legislature. Institutional self-confidence seemed to embolden individual legislators. Several factors contributed to the general sense of well-being. For one thing, there was a new governor in the statehouse. Jerry Brown was elected in November 1974, and he had a sharp and confident style that challenged others to do their best. He also brought into state government several talented persons as agency heads and staff. Moreover, there was a new legislative leader in the assembly: Leo McCarthy, a lawyer whose vision of the legislature as an intellectually challenging institution pleased most members. Furthermore, 1975–76 followed hard on the so-called Watergate debacle in Washington, as a result of which the integrity of governmental institutions in general was put into question. In the aftermath of this national scandal, California passed a strict political reform act, one effect of which was to force lobbyists and legislators to reassess their mutual relationships, now expected to be different and somehow better than before. Finally, the policy problems with which the legislature dealt in 1975–76 were manageable. A legislature has only so much capacity and energy. If it has to swallow too much, it may develop a case of indigestion. A moderate diet of relatively manageable problems, on the other hand, is likely to nourish a sense

9

of achievement, which in turn will enhance a legislature's competence. In 1975–76 the California legislative session seemed to be filled with particular, concrete accomplishments.

All this needs to be said because the California legislature has not always functioned well. Nor is it likely that its future will be perpetually rosy. William Buchanan's fine history of the California legislature from 1910 to 1960 describes the institutional ups and downs in phrases like "the frustration of partisanship," "the years of the lobby," "the revolution of 1951," "the passing of the senate strong men," and "the bifactional system."[1] Indeed, in the 1940s California's legislature was regarded as a negative model, a symbol of what a legislature should not become. Those were years when the notorious Artie Samish was lobbyist for liquor and trucking interests in the state. Samish was even bold enough to permit himself to be quoted in a national news magazine, "I am the governor of the legislature. To hell with the Governor of California."[2] The article helped bring about his downfall.

A historical perspective on the California state legislature serves as a reminder that political institutions improve themselves painfully. In governmental matters scandal is often essential to bring about reform. This book purposely neglects the detail of past abuses (and the sometimes violent corrective processes necessary to halt them) that led to improvements in the methods of conducting legislative business in California. For example, the assembly's housekeeping committee (the Rules Committee) became bipartisan because of a reform accomplished in 1951 to check the liquor scandals that came to light as a result of Artie Samish's downfall.[3] In another case, the professionalization of the assembly committee staff—the symbol and essence of a good legislature—was in part accomplished by abrasive and crude means that violate the scruples of most adherents of good government.[4] The golden age of 1975–76 was not born immaculate and fully grown. It evolved from conflicts and tragedies and acts of courage and vision nearly forgotten.

1. William Buchanan, *Legislative Partisanship: The Deviant Case of California* (Berkeley and Los Angeles: University of California Press, 1963).

2. Lester Velie, "The Secret Boss of California," *Colliers*, 13 and 20 August, 1949.

3. Eugene C. Lee, *The Presiding Officer and Rules Committee in Legislatures of the United States* (Berkeley: Bureau of Public Administration, 1952).

4. Lou Cannon, *Ronnie and Jesse: A Political Odyssey* (Garden City, N.Y.: Doubleday, 1969), chaps. 9, 10.

Moreover, the dialectic of human affairs does not come to a halt once a golden age is attained. After 1975–76 there was to be a downturn in California legislative fortunes. By 1980, the state legislature seemed shaky and fragile. An intraparty fight over the assembly speakership brought out the worst and meanest in legislative colleagues. In the assembly at least, the members' faith in their institution was badly shaken. Moreover, the massive job of reconstructing the fiscal relationships between state and local governments, made necessary by a radical tax reform (the Jarvis-Gann "Proposition 13" property tax initiative), defied quick accomplishment. Finally, abnormally high rates of inflation worked to depress the members' real salaries and to send campaign costs soaring, and both effects heightened opportunities for legislative bribery. Acute observers wondered whether the legislature could ever recover from the damage done. (It would, but not without tears and toil.)

Life is full of growth and death, healing and hurting. There are summers and winters in all things, even legislatures.

One

Well, I'll tell you what a legislature is: it's a cram course in economics, education, health, and the science of humanity.
Assemblyman Frank Lanterman, 1976

The California legislature . . . enables each member to be about as effective as his talents will allow.
Report of the Citizens Conference on State Legislatures, 1971

The California Legislature in 1975–76

I

California's legislature was the best state legislature in the United States. So concluded the Citizens Conference on State Legislatures in 1971,[1] and in the following half-decade the California legislature suffered no obvious decline. Quite the contrary. It actually effected some significant improvements. California's was also the busiest state legislature. After all, if in 1976 California had been one of the world's nations, it would have ranked thirty-first in population and eighth in the size of its economy.[2] It had governmental problems to match its size. In 1976 alone the state legislature authorized and oversaw the expenditure of about $25 billion—$16 billion in the governor's budget, $9 billion in off-budget items such as capital expenditures and numerous special funds such as the unemployment insurance account. In the two-year

1. Citizens Conference on State Legislatures, *The Sometime Governments* (written by John Burns) (New York: Bantam, 1971), p. 8. "The California legislature leads the list in our overall rankings. It comes closest to having all the characteristics that a legislature should have" (p. 8). "It is . . . both a 'citizen' and a 'professional' legislature; it makes informed decisions, and it makes them democratically; it listens to its public, and it leads it" (p. 36). "The kinds of reforms that the New York Assembly is just beginning to undertake have reached a more mature stage of development in the California legislature, which is, as a result, open to a greater diversity of people and enables each member to be about as effective as his talents will allow" (p. 140).
2. See *World Almanac and Book of Facts 1978* (New York: Newspaper Enterprise Association, 1978); Robert M. Williams, *What's Good about California's Business Climate* . . . (Sacramento: California Commission for Economic Development, 1978), p. 8 (based on data provided by the Security Pacific National Bank).

session of 1975–76, the state legislature enacted over 2,570 laws. Many of these were of minor moment, making small adjustments to existing legislation. But some were significant in consequence, magnitude of difficulty, or fiscal scale. Among them were the nation's first agricultural labor relations act; a complete restructuring of prison sentencing; public school teachers' collective bargaining legislation; a $600 million increase in annual unemployment insurance taxes; a significant tort and professional reform in the area of medical malpractice; a program to subsidize the construction of low-income, privately owned housing; a complex scheme for regulating all building construction within a thousand-mile-long coastal zone; a comprehensive reform of eminent-domain legislation; a pathbreaking and stringent nuclear energy safety act; the first euthanasia (or right-to-die) law in the United States; elimination of the oil-depletion income-tax deduction; a new basis for taxing timber; decriminalization of both marijuana use and private adult sex acts; and provision of unemployment insurance to farmworkers, not to mention numerous proposals considered at length but not passed, such as a statewide agricultural land-use law.

Being a state legislature, it did not deal with foreign affairs, military defense, or immigration, and it lacked the monetary power of the national government, which meant it had to balance its budget and could do little about inflation. Otherwise, its agenda was boundless. It made laws relating to every domestic matter except the post office.[3]

When one walked from the streets of Sacramento onto the grounds of the state capitol, however, the feeling was one of entering not a lawmaking factory but a campus. The grounds occupied fourteen city blocks, with the main building standing at the center. There

3. The California state legislature is a subordinate legislature in two senses: its legislation has to meet United States constitutional standards (principally the Fourteenth Amendment's requirements of "due process of law" and "equal protection"), and its laws cannot conflict with the laws of Congress or cover policy matters "preempted" by the federal government. The matter of preemption is one of the stickier constitutional questions. At bottom, the doctrine of preemption recognizes the danger of burdening citizens with multiple regulation by national and local government units. Typically, the issue arises at the state legislative level in this form: if Congress (or some federal agency acting by congressional authority) has set down certain standards of nationwide application—say, with respect to the pollution of air, the safety of nuclear power-generating plants, or the water content of a pound of flour—may a state impose different and more stringent standards? The answer depends on "Congressional intent" and "the burden on interstate commerce," to be determined by the courts in each case.

were gardens and open spaces. Runners jogged around the grounds. Music—Vivaldi, Bach, and Mozart mainly—floated down from speakers hidden in the palm trees and sequoias. In the main building educational displays, largely historical, were hung along the corridors. A changing series of art exhibitions occupied the public part of the governor's office. On bulletin boards were countless announcements of lectures, meetings, colloquia, films, musical events, and athletic contests. Enter on the "floors" of the two legislative chambers, and you would see eighty (for the assembly) or forty (for the senate) schoolchildren's desks, with hinged tops that concealed pencils and paperclips, gum and candy, and many books—looseleaf volumes, hardcover treatises, and paperbacks. There was a lecture platform at the front of each of the chambers.

II

Scurrying around the hallways were men and women burdened with books and briefcases, often looking like children late for school, snatching a last look at some hard-to-remember fact before being quizzed on it. Legislators and citizens intermixed; they rushed, talked, and rushed on again. There was laughter, gesticulation, concentration, energy, and interest.

Were one to ask the legislators what was happening to them, they might reply:

"This is the greatest education I've ever had."

"I've learned so much up here."

"My class—the class of '66—was the largest and the best they've ever had up here."

"Everybody is teaching here."

"Life here is nothing but a day in school."

"The whole thing in the legislature is a learning process."

"The legislature is the only cram course in the University of Hard Knocks which you can get, where you do or die on the instant recall of the key, salient points of a bill."

The legislators tended to see themselves as students and teachers. The "freshmen" wandered about, unsure and raw.[4] The "senior"

4. One of the more mature "freshmen," an internationally traveled lawyer with years of prior political experience at the local level, summed up the degree of ignorance he felt when he first arrived: "Although I was active politically, I had no concept of the legislative process. We had to learn the organization of the house, of the committee structure, of how to get a bill drafted, even where to introduce the bloody thing. We

members played pranks on them, ragged them in debate, and initiated them into the traditions of the house. Freshmen and seniors alike wrote papers and speeches, which they gave to each other for appraisal and improvement. And, like students, they constantly pondered the difficult questions of personal identity: Who were they? What would they do with their lives? What were their responsibilities to themselves? What role would they play in the world?[5]

It was a posh school, this California legislature, a special kind of school where the students were important, a boarding school like the one in *Tom Brown's Schooldays* or, to Americanize the simile, like the kind of school Fitzgerald and Auchincloss and Knowles and Salinger might write about, with the unmistakable air of the East Coast prep school to which the sons and daughters of the well-to-do went.

Like the scholars of Rugby and Groton, the legislators had left home and their families, and they were often lonely. Since the school year was long—from January to mid-September—they were on their own for extensive periods of time. Some had trouble adapting to their liberation from familiar domestic routine. Like students, a few caroused at first. But most of them soon found that their best and most valuable friends were their fellow students. Town-gown hostility existed, and rather than continue to face the resentments of the "townies," they associated mainly with one another, finding nearby apartments to share and reasonable restaurants to frequent. At night some even returned to the main building, the capitol, ostensibly to "burn the midnight oil" (their homework was never ending) but actually to engage in bull sessions with their colleagues, from whom much that was valuable could be learned. They also talked about their families, and their home away from home, and the legislature's isolation from the "real world."

It was a good boarding school, and the scholars enjoyed enviable academic privileges. They had individual private suites to do their

---

had also to develop an understanding of existing law. In my area of interest, I was well served by having a legal background, but I had no concept of the overall legislative process. It was a matter of trial-and-error."

5. One sophomore legislator expressed the legislator's identity crisis this way: "One of the tasks, and frustrations, for a freshman is to try to get some understanding of what these segments of policy are, and to find out what you are really interested in, and what areas are staked out already by others. These choices of where you fit are crucial to being happy here."

studies in—elaborate "closets," to use one of James Madison's quaint, eighteenth-century terms.[6] They were also all on scholarships, obviating the need to find part-time employment that would detract from their studies. Room and board and books were free, so to speak, thanks to a living allowance that came with their admission to the legislature; about $25,000 annually, plus $35 a day for each of the 200-plus legislative days they spent each year in Sacramento. It was a school to which many eager candidates applied. Like slots in the military academies of West Point, Annapolis, and Colorado Springs, places in the legislature were determined on a geographical basis: one scholar from each of the eighty assembly and forty state senate districts. The admissions and scholarships committee was the electorate, decentralized by district and applying standards of merit through a series of tests administered at service clubs, union halls, political gatherings, press conferences, and radio and television stations. Typically, the qualities examined for were rhetorical ability, digestion of knowledge, trustworthiness, and energy. The candidates for assembly slots were selected every two years, for state senate slots every four.[7]

The purpose and result of this decentralized and populist admissions and scholarships process were the selection of a rather diverse student body. Most were men, but some were women; several were elderly, but many were youngish; a few were intellectuals, but for the most part they were persons of action; some were self-taught, some elegantly educated; some were thing-oriented engineers, most were people-oriented humanists; some were rich, some not so. It included persons of different religious persuasions. There were blacks, Hispanic Americans, Asian-Americans, and whites of every European background. While they tended to share what the political scientist Louis Hartz called the liberal tradition in America,[8] their diverse backgrounds, schooling, and professional experience made

6. *Federalist* nos. 53, 56.
7. The legislative school was organized on a two-college system basis. As Oxford University comprises several institutions of learning—Bailliol, Magdalen, and so forth—with separate endowments and admissions policies, and with affiliated faculty devoting more time to the college than the university as a whole, so the California legislature contained two schools—the larger, more structured and disciplined assembly and the smaller, more exclusive senate.
8. Louis Hartz, *The Liberal Tradition in America* (New York: Harcourt, Brace, 1955). That tradition takes for granted the reality and desirability of "atomistic social freedom" (p. 62), that the individual is and ought to be free of any entanglements with state, church, place, guild, or class that he does not voluntarily assume.

them about as heterogeneous a student body as any first-rate American college could boast. In John Stuart Mill's words, they constituted "a fair sample of intellect among the people."[9]

III

If the legislators were the "scholars," who were the teachers? The outside faculty were the lobbyists. As one Democratic assemblyman put it,

> When there is legislation involving complicated matters which I don't fully understand, I call in proponents and opponents (separately, mind you), and in five minutes they describe very succinctly what the legislation does. I get the pros and cons very quickly. I can learn things which would have taken five hours of research if I had to assign staff to find out from scratch.

9. John Stuart Mill, *Considerations on Representative Government* (New York: Liberal Arts Press, 1958: originally published in 1861), p.83. One Republican assemblyman alleged that "the make-up of the legislature is reflective of the socio-economic make-up of the state-at-large: the ethnic make-up, economic status, racial make-up, people from different professions, and so forth. Of course, there are exceptions: women are underrepresented, and agriculture is too, now. Basically we're not too different from the twenty-one and a half million people who vote for us, however." The accompanying table may help the reader test that sentiment. Initially the reader may note the older and more lawyerly characteristics of the senators relative to the members of the assembly in 1975–76. The second matter one might infer from the legislators' educational attainments is their middle- and upper-class status.

Makeup of Legislature Compared with 1970 Population (Percent)

Category	Assembly	State Senate	California*
Black	8	5	7
Chicano/Hispanic	5	5	16
Asian-American	3	3	1
Lawyers	35	55	.3†
Teachers	19	5	5†
B.A. or B.S.	83	88	14†
Age: 50-older	28	50	42†
Women	4	0	52†

* *Source*: United States Bureau of the Census, *1970 Census of the Population: General Social and Economic Characteristics, California* (Washington, D.C.: U.S. Government Printing Office, 1972). The total population of California was reported as 19,957,715.

† The base figure used for these calculations was the population of California twenty-five years of age or older: 10,875,983. The number of lawyers, 31,467, was provided by the California Bar Association.

A senior Republican, who was just beginning to inform himself about the complexities of health insurance, had been using lobbyists in order to develop estimates of the number of Americans who were then unprotected from catastrophic hospital and medical bills:

> We have 700 lobbyists around here, and they are a needed ingredient. Most people don't understand what a lobbyist does and how important he is. The lobbyist is a great wealth of information. . . . Take this health insurance matter. Without the lobbyists we would have an impossible job just to find out the basic information.

The task of the lobbyist—"what a lobbyist does"—was to provide basic information "quickly" and intelligibly.

As a teacher, the lobbyist also framed the intellectual issues, pointed out subtleties in a situation, and implied a conclusion. All the teaching was done in an adversary context. To teach "the pros and cons" from their vantage point there were lobbyists for nearly everybody—the old and the young, the wealthy and the poverty-stricken,[10] the boss and the worker, the farmer and the rancher, the sailor and the mountaineer, the citizen and the immigrant.

Lobbyists represented not only private interests, but governmental interests as well: cities, special districts, the judiciary, public employees, executive agencies, and even the governor. But lobbyists, whether or not they were dubbed "legislative advocates" (as registered lobbyists were called) or "departmental liaisons and cabinet secretaries" (as the governor's lobbyists were called), were all professional educators of the legislature, and they roamed the corridors of the capitol day in, day out, on perpetual call to respond to their students' requests for "basic information" about the "real world" beyond Sacramento.

They could be teachers for the same reasons that any professor could teach a subject. Lobbyists specialized; they repeated the les-

---

10. For example, there was the "brown bag lobby," so called because its members met regularly in Sacramento over unpretentious lunches to discuss their mutual efforts to influence legislation affecting poor persons. The lunches were attended by full-time registered lobbyists who represented the following groups: American Civil Liberties Union of Northern California, American Civil Liberties Union of Southern California, California Rural Legal Assistance, California Tenants' Council, Los Angeles County Public Defender's Association, National Association for the Advancement of Colored People, National Association of Social Workers, and Western Center on Law and Poverty. See chapter 10 on the importance of this lobby.

sons over and over again; and they crammed beforehand so that they could stay a few pages ahead of their students.

Dick Ratcliff represented banks, for example. He and his two assistants knew next to nothing about energy, land use, public employees, unemployment, transportation, or any of several dozen topics on the legislature's agenda. He had not even opened the copy of the governor's budget in his office. He did not have to read it, because the relationship between the state and the banking industry was not a fiscal but a regulatory one. Ratcliff knew about banks and their situation in the financial world and had been teaching banking to the legislators for ten years. In that time he probably had appeared more than three hundred times before the major business committees of the legislature on more than eight hundred different bills. In those ten years the personnel of each of these committees had been constantly changing. For example, during his decade of representing banks, sixty-two different assemblymen had at one time or another occupied a place on the fifteen-member business committee of the lower house. Ratcliff had talked to every one of them, on almost every banking bill, often at length when the legislator was encountering the subject matter for the first time. Conversely, whenever a novel banking topic was brought up by a piece of legislation, Ratcliff would meet with his client, the California Bankers Association, and its members would cram him with the knowledge necessary to do his pedagogical job in the legislative corridors.[11] There were always new topics coming up, giving variety to the teaching task. New technology, for example, made for new banking possibilities, such as electronic transfer of funds, which in turn required new facilitating legislation. At the same time the basic notions about banking—of supply and demand, capital-formation and credit-extension, reserves, bank holding companies—had to be taught and retaught.

Specialization, repetition, early cramming: that was the formula of the legislative teaching profession.

11. On his education as a lobbyist, Ratcliff said, "At first when I started working for the banks, I scrambled like crazy, trying to learn the ropes. I relied heavily on the legislative committee and talked with all of the bankers on it all the time. Then the banks sent up a fellow to work with me, and we made a great pair. We got good teachers to instruct us about banking; then we would spend hours arguing about this point or that, until we really learned the stuff."

Ratcliff was engaging and accessible to his students.[12] With his handlebar mustache, he appeared genuine and informal. He was not reluctant to display publicly his personal disagreement with some of the positions asserted by his client when he thought it unreasonably stubborn. Had his students not liked and trusted him, the marketplace would have discarded him. An ineffective lobbyist—one who lied or "was not prepared" or did not get to the point of his students' questions or was boring—lost bills; and a lobbyist who failed more often than was necessary did not get his contract renewed by his clients.

One admiring legislator of considerable sophistication summed up Ratcliff:

He's completely honest. He is very well informed. He is very troubled regarding certain positions his clients force him to take. He is concerned that they may be wrong, both in substance and in the image they are creating. He projects complete frankness, yet never appears disloyal to his clients. And like any good lobbyist, he never lays to you the question how you are going to vote.

Ratcliff scored high in student evaluations, and his client—the Bankers Association—continued to endow his professorial chair as a result.

Bud Carpenter represented cities. He and his half-dozen associates knew a great deal about energy, land use, public employees, unemployment, transportation, and a dozen more complex topics because they related to urban life in California. Unlike Ratcliff, Carpenter had a heavily used copy of the governor's budget in his office because the cities he represented depended heavily upon the treasury of the state of California.

He had represented California cities for thirty-seven years. He had appeared before the local government committees nearly a thousand times and had dealt with possibly fifteen thousand different bills. Many of those bills repeated earlier ones, of course, but even these had to be taught to new legislators. Carpenter knew his subject

12. Ratcliff perceived his role as lobbyist this way: "A lobbyist has several ends. One is to be sure that a bill passes or fails. But he has, and I play, a role as popularizer: I feel like I'm Robert Ardrey, who takes all sorts of advanced scientific ideas and makes them accessible to people. That's the long-range objective."

matter in a way that legislators, generalists that they were, could
never know it.

The same legislator who admired Ratcliff's skills described Bud
Carpenter's abilities:

> He was the most astute lobbyist. When he sat in the audience
> of the Committee on Local Government, a question would come
> up that no one could answer, not the chairman nor the staff of
> the committee. Invariably the chairman would ask Bud how the
> bill would work. He always knew more both in extent and
> accuracy of his information. He always rose above his position
> and acted as the thirteenth member in the jury box. He had
> great integrity and great experience. Also he had a sense of self-
> worth combined with a discerning intelligence.

Then the legislator, drawing on his recollection of undergraduate
teachers, contrasted Carpenter with the formidable qualities of
Chauncey Tinker, a professor who had taught him English literature
at Yale University:

> Bud Carpenter would not have been a great college teacher
> because he had no dramatic flair. Being an educator of a
> legislature does require a different combination of traits.
> Chauncey Tinker would have been a poor legislative teacher.
> Carpenter, with what he had, could have become a great college
> teacher with a little flair. Bud infiltrated you; Chauncey
> impacted you. Who is going to buy something that impacts you
> unless he's on a podium or pulpit? Otherwise it does not seem
> appropriate.

Lobbyists, not being "on a podium or pulpit," were quiet teachers.
They capitalized on their different traits. Those who were comfortable encouraging their students by the warmth of their personalities did so. Others, no less effective, were cold, dispassionate, and
seemingly detached about the personal development of their students, yet their sustained attachment to their subject matter won
admiration. The realtors' lobbyist was a scholar of the law of property
who wrote scholarly articles and assigned them to the legislators for
reading. In committee or individually, he would introduce, say, the
topic of mortgages at normal levels of complexity, but if he found
he had tapped a legislator's interest, he went on, dwelling on the
topic and drilling further into it, placing it in a series of perspectives—historical, social, legal, ethical, commercial—until satiation

set in. When he realized that his student's attention had been exhausted, he usually stopped.

Lobbyists were of every description: dull and brilliant, inexperienced and veteran, slick and hard-working, friendly and detached, subtle and blunt. But the effective lobbyists all educated. "All the good ones do it with knowledge." That was the unanimous testimony of California legislators.

IV

The rule of the California legislative school was "the open door."No assemblyman or state senator would think of refusing to discuss a bill with a lobbyist or his client. That is, a lobbyist was welcome to enter any legislative office—unless he had lied, and virtually no lobbyist did that.[13] When freshmen legislators marveled at "the open place this legislature is," they were essentially remarking on the commitment to the policy of the "open door." The obligation implied by the privilege of being a legislator was inescapable exposure to the educational bombardment by lobbyists.

The lobbyists' formal classrooms, however, were "in committee." Scattered throughout the main building were several dozen smaller rooms—"committee rooms"—that looked like small lecture halls. Here the desks of the legislators were usually elevated above the lecture stand, so that the lobbyist stood at the center of a semicircle, in the style of a law or medical school instructor, speaking up to the students arranged in graduated banks, an arrangement that allowed their faces to be scrutinized more piercingly.

In these classroom-like settings the formal courses of the legislative school took place. The subjects were taught in the committees to which the legislators were assigned. In the assembly, for example, the normal load of each member was three committees, selected from an offering of twenty subject-matter committees. The courses dealt

13. It was the serial nature of the legislator-lobbyist relationship, an interaction that recurred over and over again, that prevented mendacity. Legislators and lobbyists ran into each other in the halls; they turned to one another for help; they needed each other's good will, not only for today but for tomorrow. Memories were long, and the grapevine never let an impression die: "Once you've been misled, you never forget it," said one legislator. "Integrity is as important among lobbyists as it is among legislators. If he misleads you, he prejudices his case the next time." However, not every lobbyist was perfectly forthcoming. Lobbyists had a hard time divulging the "downside" of their proposals. The "downside" of a bill was its indigestible or unfavorable aspects. The best protection against the hidden downside was talking with adversary lobbyists.

with every aspect of life: agriculture, business, labor, law, transportation; criminal justice, education, health, housing, welfare; energy, land, water; appropriations, taxation; elective politics, local government, public administration (which was enlivened by the topics of whiskey and horseracing), government personnel; and the management of the legislature itself.

Able legislators saw the educational possibilities of such a rich curriculum. As freshmen, they would take the courses open to freshmen—perhaps labor, transportation, and education might each have an opening. In their second terms, however, they might stay with education but shift from labor and transportation to business and welfare. In their third term, they might drop welfare and substitute government personnel. Thus, at the end of six years, they would have acquainted themselves with six topics, including a major, so to speak, in education.[14]

Not only would legislators learn the subject matter, they would also come to know the executive agency heads, the labor union representatives, the leaders of commerce, the welfare rights lawyers, the county supervisors, and other key people in the field.[15] As

14. Typically, one senior Democratic legislator described his pattern of course selection: "I always rotate one committee. So this year I've moved into government organization. Last year I was on housing rather than G.O. I do it just because of the idea of noticing what's going on in other fields. On the other hand, I like to stick with education and business simply because of the importance of the subject matters. This is my fifteenth year on education. And I like to know what makes the wheels turn, and you find that out on [the] business [committee]."

15. And when these guest lecturers came before the committees, they were pumped for information. Typical of the way a smart legislator got a "quick-study" from these experts was this interchange between Harry Hensley, director of the state Workers' Compensation Fund, and Assemblyman Beverly, minority leader and the most knowledgeable Republican on business matters. The colloquy occurred in the midst of a hearing on medical malpractice, the issue being whether the state should set up an insurance fund for doctors if private carriers were unwilling to provide insurance coverage for practitioners at a reasonable premium. The proponents of the idea argued that the analogue was in the workers' compensation field, where the state had set up a compensation fund for businesses that could not get coverage from private insurers. The introductory questions by Beverly went like this:

BEVERLY: When was the State Compensation Fund founded?
HENSLEY: 1914.
BEVERLY: When did workers' compensation become mandatory?
HENSLEY: 1917.
BEVERLY: Why was a State Fund deemed necessary then?
HENSLEY: Because of the uncertainty of private insurers about the no-fault concept in workers' compensation.
BEVERLY: On what principle was workers' compensation established with its notion of limited recovery for the worker?

witnesses recruited by lobbyists, these prominent and knowledgeable citizens would give guest lectures to the legislators sitting in committee and follow up with individual conversation.

V

Most of the pedagogy in the legislature followed the "problem method." For example, a constituent's letter or the testimony of a witness might contain a question like, "Fran Borden, a mother of two youngsters, recently divorced and living on alimony, has become very sick and in need of surgery and long hospitalization. Who pays her bill of $15,000?" Such a problem required an examination of the insurance and health laws of nation and state. It set a legislator to thinking about the historical development of health insurance, the nature of labor-management collective bargaining which determined the terms of so many Americans' health benefits, the changing nature of the family, the liberal judicial treatment of marital dissolution, the job market for divorcees, and the costs of health care. There was no dearth of such challenging and provocative problems. As a business school is fed suggestions for case studies by outside businesses, so the California legislature attracted provocative problems to nourish its members' educations.

To organize the teaching materials for this problem-based learning process, each committee engaged staff members, called consultants, who played the part of teaching assistants.[16] Their formal job was to "analyze" proposed legislation. In fact, their essential function was to maintain the intellectual integrity of the educational process.

HENSLEY: The right to sue was sacrificed for quick compensation.
BEVERLY: Do private carriers compete with the State Fund?
HENSLEY: Yes, and they have 77 percent of the business.
That interchange constituted a quick-study, chock full of information, that put the medical malpractice proposal in historical and analytic perspective.
16. In 1975 the California state legislature had a staff—both technical and clerical—of 1,800 and paid nearly $25,000,000 in wages. Some of the staff had permanent assignments to the nearly forty standing committees and were nonpartisan. However, others were assigned to the thirty ad hoc "joint" (two-house) or "select" (one-house) committees, created at the behest of an individual legislator who was given an appropriation and a professional staff to examine some particular topic with the goal of producing proposals for reform. Often these select or joint committees had no fixed volume of work, were loosely supervised, and were staffed by cronies. In 1975, after Leo McCarthy became Speaker of the assembly, he abolished sixteen of the lower house select committees, and no one seemed to miss them. (In 1980, however, in order to weather an intraparty challenge to his Speakership, he began to create new ad hoc committees to appease those who were discontent with his regime.)

Their job, if executed responsibly, was to make sure that each topic was taught fairly.[17] That meant that they solicited from each relevant lobbyist a contribution to the written teaching materials prepared for each problem. The usual form of these teaching materials was the "bill analysis," which contained a statement of a problem, a variety of perspectives on it (legal, historical, social, and philosophical), a solution (the "bill"), a statement of competing principles of assessment, some suggestions for technical improvements, and a "bibliography" (in the basically *oral* process of the legislature, the best "bibliography" was a list of the relevant groups and lobbyists who had taken sides on the matter).[18]

VI

Some of the courses were more complicated than others. The business course, for example, was intellectually challenging because commercial occupations are so various: insurance, banking, cosmetology, running a grocery, real estate, optometry, pawnbroking, plumbing, and telephone work. Some courses seemed complicated to a particular legislator because he had never encountered the subject before: the basic laws of welfare or educational finance, for example,

17. The procedure that held the staff accountable for fair preparation of these materials was called the Third Reading Analysis (TRA) (see chapter 6). There were moral controls as well, to keep the staff nonpartisan and fair. For example, in June 1975, Larry Margolis, a former staff member and later executive director of the Center for Legislative Improvement, addressed the staff at what was called Mice Milk, a monthly luncheon meeting for all assembly consultants. My notes of the meeting record Margolis emphasizing the responsibility of a good staff "to teach legislators how to be effective members of the legislature" and "to put the stamp of the institution on its members." He talked of the need to have classes, seminars, training, and orientation for members and staff. He pointed out that it was crucial to "ask basic questions: what is a legislature? a legislator? an effective staff person? What do we mean by a professional staff?" He warned that "a partisan staff destroys a legislature" because a legislature functions "to reconcile . . . to create a compromise, to work out a settlement"; "the failure of a legislature is deadlock, the failure to resolve," and a nonpartisan staff, by disbursing reason and fact to all parties, can ease deadlock and facilitate settlement. He advocated that the staff suppress their egos, switch around (i.e., don't stay with one committee), and remember who was elected—not the staff, but the legislators.

18. A typical bill analysis is given in the appendix. The bill analyzed is a simple one: whether auto insurance companies should be required to disregard on-the-job accidents in establishing the annual premiums of the personal auto insurance policies of certain state Transportation Department employees. The interest group lobbying for the bill was a state agency. In this respect, the proposed legislation was also typical: public employees actively utilized the legislative process. Incidentally, the bill lost in committee.

were outside the average person's experience before he or she entered the legislature. Some courses tended to the technical or parochial: local government and elective politics were usually seen as less intellectual and abstract in these respects. Some were wide-ranging in their intellectual sweep: the energy committee sent its scholars to books on nuclear energy and geology.

Courses also had different meanings for different members, depending on their backgrounds and outlooks. A city resident taking agriculture, a labor union member studying business, a young man exploring the health problems of the aged—each opened mental windows to new worlds. In the local government course a Republican with a belief in decentralized power saw intellectual implications that failed to arouse the interest of a Democrat with his notions about accountability through centralization. Conversely, the same Democrat with his determination to make the public sector function a bit better was stirred by the possibilities he encountered in the government personnel committee, which bored the Republican with his different notions of where salvation lay.

Furthermore, the courses varied in the quality of instruction. The business course was taught by some of the best lobbyists in town. Guest speakers, notables in the world of finance and industry, flew in and out of Sacramento to share their knowledge and experience. The energy committee's fifteen members spent the fall of 1975 in two eight-hour classes per week, for eight consecutive weeks, taught by Nobel scientists (like Edward Teller and Harold Urey), internationally known lawyers (like Mason Willrich), and eminent members of the environmental movement (like Jacques Cousteau). (The committee was then wrestling with the problem of safety in the generation of nuclear energy.)

Conversely, there were courses where most of the students were neither very interested nor very diverse; hence, some matters were not explored as fully as they might have been. There were also committees where teachers were inept or unavailable; the students felt isolated when no one of any caliber took an interest in them. Sometimes the teaching materials prepared by committee staff were shoddy or insufficient: housing, for example, with a subject matter much narrower than its title would suggest, was assessed by the students as a poor course partly for that reason.

Finally, and most important, there were both elementary and advanced courses of instruction on most topics. An elementary course taught the fundamentals; a follow-up course permitted an exploration of more subtle aspects of the material. These different levels of treatment reflected the difference between the policy (or technical) process of the legislature and the fiscal (or appropriations) process.

Briefly, most bills went through two committee examinations in a single house (which meant a successful bill would usually run through four committees in all, assembly and state senate combined). The first examination would raise such questions as, Will the bill work? Is it logical? Are the assumptions about cause and effect intelligent? Is there a real problem to be solved? At this level the bill and the problem would be examined technically: the policy committee would intend to design as good a remedy as it could. After the bill's technical efficiency was perfected, it was subjected to a second examination, the fiscal process. The proposal was appraised comparatively, relative to the competing merits of other perfected proposals.[19] Would the good results of this bill outweigh the good results of some other proposal that would have to be foregone for lack of funds, manpower, or energy? Was a technically good farm labor relations board more valuable than a necessary freeway or a vital land-use planning board? The fiscal committee had to decide whether the good "orange" designed by one policy committee was more desirable than the good "apple" developed by a different policy committee.[20]

19. Cf. Michael Bevier, *Politics Backstage: Inside the California Legislature* (Philadelphia: Temple University Press, 1979), pp. 219–20: "In my experience, though, the finance committees . . . did not attempt any sort of cost-benefit comparisons . . . rather, they attempted to confine the scope of inquiry to the kind and magnitude of impact each bill would have on the state's finances." Bevier's point about the Sacramento fiscal process, I think, was that the interprogram comparative appraisal was done individually and implicitly by each legislator, not explicitly, not with the help of staff analysis, and not collegially. So stated, Bevier's point was well taken. In 1975–76, however, the assembly appropriations committee devised a system of more explicit interprogram comparisons—the "suspense file." Bills with substantial financial costs were provisionally approved throughout the legislative year, then put "on hold" or "in suspense," and only at the end of each year, when the comparative merits could be assessed by the committee and its staff, were the "best" of the lot finally passed and sent to the floor for debate.

20. An eloquent legislator described the fiscal process of establishing priorities with this energetic metaphor: "Appropriations is where the action is. That's where major decisions are made on major bills, all of which carry appropriations. . . . The budget-making and budget-analysis process establishes the priorities which the administration or the committee or you possibly lay against all the major areas of governmental responsibility. Putting dollar signs on measures sharpens up the process. You've got education, health and welfare, environment, substantive programs in other

The technical process related to what Was, the fiscal process to what Ought to Be. The former was empirical in nature, the latter normative. Of course, the distinctions were not so clear, and each process encroached from time to time upon the other's territory. The policy committees anticipated questions of priorities, and the fiscal committees frequently touched up one technical aspect or another. But the important point was that there were two tasks to be done on almost every bill, and that the second task of "putting dollar signs on" two efficiently designed bills so as to choose between them required comparative focus and judgment, not just a limited technical skill.

The fiscal task of making choices was conducted mainly by one large committee in each house—appropriations, comprised of four subcommittees. To it came the handiwork of all the policy committees for review. The appropriations committee consisted predominantly of senior members. Most of its members had already mastered a half-dozen or so subjects by sitting on that many policy committees during their legislative careers. Attentive observers of the legislature could observe on the appropriations committee the same senior legislator they had seen earlier in the week at work on the education committee, or the same knowledgeable type who was earlier dominant on the local government committee, or the very same legislator who had played an important part in getting the developmentally disabled bill through the health committee. If there had been a senior honors seminar in the legislative school, appropriations would have been it.

The senior legislators sitting on appropriations were not the only upperclassmen of the legislature. Others, some of them equally competent, served only on policy committees. The course on appropriations was a time-consuming one because there was so much hard work to be done, and some highly regarded legislators elected not to take it. But, generally, the members who did take on appropriations seemed experienced and at home with the various topics, more so than the average legislator on policy committees.

---

areas. And you have to decide which are the most important. Dollars represent the kind of emphasis programs have achieved in the pecking order. Dollars are the gasoline in the tanks. Some programs may be inefficient, getting only 9 miles per gallon, and others may be efficient, achieving, say, 39 miles per gallon. But they all need dollars. Dollars are the fuel which asserts the importance of things."

VII

The legislative seniors talked often with the freshmen and younger members. The Speaker of the assembly systematically assigned desks on the floor to the older legislators so that they sat beside their younger brethren, in a friendly, older sibling program. Experienced and rookie legislators dined together and competed athletically and sat next to each other at party functions. Each senior member on appropriations had a chance to observe and question any junior legislators who were carrying bills being examined in appropriations and who were pleading for dollars for their particular proposals. And, finally, the several generations engaged in debate on the floor. Attendance at all floor sessions was mandatory. The seniors set high standards in these debates; they were not easily beaten. In these several contexts, informal and formal, the "enlarged ideas" and "enlightened purposes" (to use John Stuart Mill's phrases) of the seniors were handed down systematically to the newer membership of the house.[21]

VIII

To provide a little meat to the bones of the foregoing description of the legislative school, let us examine three assemblymen in the freshman Class of '74, which came to Sacramento in January 1975— Herschel Rosenthal, Gary Hart, and Bill Thomas. None had had previous legislative experience, and in a number of other ways they were representative of their twenty-four colleagues in the assembly freshman class that year.[22] None was a lawyer; in fact, only five of the twenty-four freshmen were attorneys.[23] All three were males;

21. One example from the Republican side of the aisle illustrates the process of enlightenment. A young assemblyman described the lesson he received from the twenty-six-year veteran, Frank Lanterman, known affectionately to his colleagues as "Uncle Frank": "I remember in my first term having a bill I liked. I lost the vote on the floor, something like 70–4, and I was fuming. And I sat down in the seat in front of Uncle Frank and began telling him my woes. At last he asked, 'Are you quite through?' I was a little taken aback, but I said yes, I was. He said, 'Remember one thing: no one is holding a gun to your head and forcing you to be a legislator.' I learned more that day than I have in a month of Sundays."

22. Twenty-two had never served in the assembly before. Two others were returned to the assembly in the November 1974 election after having been absent the previous term.

23. Cf. *The Sometime Governments* (see n. 1), p. 140: "California has an able and extensive legal staff. As a result, its members not only get excellent legal service, but 'being a lawyer' becomes far less important as a 'requirement' for legislative service than it does in a legislature where members are thrown back upon their own personal resources."

only two of the twenty-four were women. Their partisan makeup—
two Democrats and one Republican—reflected the fact that the electorate had admitted only three Republican freshmen that year.
In January 1975 Herschel Rosenthal had turned fifty-seven years
old, had never before held government office (either elective or appointive), did not have a college degree, was a printer by trade, had
no political ambitions beyond retaining his assembly seat, and was
a devout, kindly Jew from a heavily Jewish district which could be
expected to reelect him till hell froze over. In a legislative house in
which the median age was forty-five (and in which the freshman
median was under forty), in which Democrats tended to have had
substantial governmental experience prior to election to the Assembly, in which sixty-eight of the eighty members had a four-year
college degree, in which fewer than a dozen members had ever run
a small business, and in which only half a dozen were Jews, Herschel
Rosenthal hardly looked the freshman politician. While he had been
in the Democratic Club Movement[24] since 1958, his experience in
politics had not prepared him for the legislature. In Sacramento he
seemed initially out of his depth, inarticulate on his feet, and ill-
prepared in his homework. He was always suffering surprise. Typically, "It never came through to me—before I took the job—just
how hard people worked up here," he said. He knew nothing about
public policy. He admitted his lack of sophistication with a remark
that revealed the degree of his naivete:

> I confess, before I became a legislator, I always knew I had the
> answer to every question. Since I've been here, I've come to
> realize that there are no easy answers, sometimes no answers at
> all. It's because we all have our own self-interest.

But the speaker assigned him to three interesting committees—
health, energy, and governmental organization.

> I learned a lot in every committee I was on. I made it my
> business to be there. In the press I was picked as the one with
> the best legislative committee attendance. When I go into a
> committee, I rarely leave it. I'm usually there at the beginning
> and at the end. I've learned a lot. And the subject matters go
> from A to Z.

24. See James Q. Wilson, *The Amateur Democrat: Club Politics in Three Cities*
(Chicago: University of Chicago Press, 1962), chap. 4, for a description of the California Democratic Club (CDC) Movement.

The subject he liked best was health. He joined with the chairman of the health committee to investigate the governor's Department of Health and its problems with prepaid health plans—clinics to which persons paid a fixed annual fee that entitled them to all the medical care they needed. Moreover, Rosenthal threw himself into every aspect of health care, from education for health professionals to caring for the developmentally disabled. He worked with the state's Little Hoover Commission, a citizen-constituted watchdog for governmental inefficiency, when it proposed reorganizing the Department of Health. As a liaison with the health committee in the state senate, he found the senators calling him "the *ex officio* member of the senate committee."

His confidence was nourished by his learning. By delving into the area of health he began to grasp the importance of general notions such as "the budgetary concept" (by which he meant the hard task of adjudging priorities among meritorious programs), "the logrolling concept" (under which he subsumed all the dilemmas of how to vote despite inadequate information), the power of the subpoena (indispensable to a committee, he realized, in order "to ascertain whether things were true or not"), and the necessity of legislative oversight of the bureaucracy.

Meanwhile he continued in regular attendance at committee hearings. Diffident, kind, well-meaning, judicious, he went to each class meeting "with ideas of learning all that I can." His questions became more penetrating. His background knowledge became richer. Two years after he had first stumbled into the legislature, he was given the supreme accolade: Assemblyman Jack Knox, the Democratic legislator deemed by his colleagues to be the best appraiser of legislative talent, commented publicly, "Hersh Rosenthal is developing a real sense on health matters."

Gary Hart, though a Democrat like Rosenthal, offered a dramatic contrast in outward appearance. He was thirty-two, had degrees from Stanford and Harvard, had been part of the "Dump Lyndon Johnson" movement in 1967 (in which he was allied with his good friend and later congressman Allard Lowenstein), was an educator by profession (though his political career put a crimp in his classroom activities), aspired to a lifetime political career, and was an Episcopalian from affluent Santa Barbara, where many of the established citizenry suspected every "starry-eyed" liberal tendency in his makeup. But, like Rosenthal, Hart found certain aspects of the legislative job difficult. He lacked confidence, felt out of control in certain policy areas, knew that he didn't "know much," and fretted over voting decisions on even minor bills ("I'm too much hampered by a Hamlet complex"). He discovered, however, that he felt comfortable in the legislature when he "got to know the subject—that makes a difference." He was initially assigned to three committees—education, health, and energy—and his courses exhilarated him.

> To be able to question Jacques Cousteau, Edward Teller, and Harold Urey on nuclear energy matters is a real thrill. Here the Naders, the Governor Browns, and the Tellers come up all the time to talk to you. . . . To be able to write James Q. Wilson [a Harvard professor] about crime and get a response is fun. I've learned about "tort liability." I now know the difference between an optometrist and an ophthamologist. I've been taught about nuclear power. . . . A legislature . . . is a pretty unreal world.

By 1977, with his first reelection behind him, Hart was beginning to throw himself ever more eagerly into the "pretty unreal" legislative curriculum.

> This year I've been appointed to appropriations, and I'm looking forward to it because I'm really fascinated how the whole thing fits together. And on appropriations you get the overview. This year I'm going to spend more time in analyzing bills and learning to be as good at asking critical questions as I can be. I'll spend more time reading bill analyses, preparing myself for floor and committee sessions.

With his work on appropriations, Hart had found that he could fit all the pieces of his knowledge together into a pattern: energy, tort, crimes, health, education. He was "really fascinated" and gratified as he began to see himself "develop as a legislator."

Finally, Bill Thomas, a Republican from a rural, small-city district, aged thirty-four, a college instructor of political science, the only Republican to defeat a Democratic incumbent in 1974, resembled Hart in his sustained ambition to be a political professional, but, unlike Hart, was of the minority party. The Democratic leadership of the legislature did not assign him to the education committee (despite the fact education was his vocation) nor to agriculture (despite the fact agriculture was his district's major industry). Instead he was assigned to the three courses deemed worst by most legislators—housing, welfare, and elections. None of the subjects in any way related to the concerns of his district.[25] Regarding welfare, he turned away with chagrin: "I simply don't understand the relationships with federal, state, and local governments. I could know it, but I'm not motivated enough to master it enough to play with it."

But chance would have it that the elections committee turned out to be more interesting than he expected. Elections was the "dump committee," the course for the school's cut-ups, those Democrats and Republicans whom the Speaker thought of as disruptive. The Speaker found out too late that by concentrating them in one seemingly unimportant committee he licensed them to do what rejects at every school have tended to do: act up. In Bill Thomas's words, "They'd vote no on everything the Speaker wanted, or yes just to harass him. They had no responsibility. It was pathetic and funny at the same time."

Thomas helped salvage matters by contributing his own substantial knowledge of electoral politics and mechanics to the discussions and decisions of the committee. Perhaps out of gratitude, the Speaker changed one of Thomas's assignments to agriculture. Moreover, Thomas's Republican colleagues voted to put him on rules in his second term. Rules—the management of the legislature—was the exception to the general procedure that the Speaker appointed all committees. Rules consisted of three members appointed by the minority party, three members appointed by the caucus of the majority party, and a chairman selected by the Speaker. Rules performed two functions: it arbitrated procedural matters, and it was the landlord of the house, allocating (or at least approving the Speaker's decisions to allocate) staff and the money to pay for staff and other perquisites of legislative office.[26]

Rules was Thomas's first choice among committees. He explained why:

25. Thomas believed he understood why he got such bad assignments: the Speaker "didn't want me to get reelected. . . . Our committee system is controlled by plain power. It's politics, with the benign paternalistic influence of the Speaker (if he's so inclined)." Cf. chapter 8 on the Speaker's appointive power and its desirable and undesirable consequences.

26. On what the Assembly Rules Committee did and how it came to be appointed by the party caucuses instead of solely by the Speaker, see Eugene C. Lee, *The Presiding Officer and Rules Committee in Legislatures of the United States* (Berkeley: Bureau of Public Administration, 1952), pp. 43 ff.

I'm here in the assembly to see how this place works, what finances support what facilities, and so on. . . . I'm interested in things like the cost per mile of each kind of car. If the cost of maintenance and so forth is higher on one make more than on another, I want to notify members of it. . . . We have some very good staff. We have more than we need, and we pay more than we have to. Since the staff now exceeds the minimum number to perform the basics, it falls back into the Speaker's power to distribute the surplus. The perks go to those with the best power relationship. The number of staffers is reflected in pure power.

Thomas was becoming educated in institutional politics, in "pure power." As a holder of a seat on the rules committee, he found that his fellow legislators, often his seniors, had to come to him for parliamentary help and staff assistance. In putting requests to him, they taught him the ins and outs of being a politician—which was exactly what he was "here in the assembly" to find out.

IX

To know why most of the members regarded the California legislature with pride and affection, one had to understand its schooling effects. As students of government and politics, the California state legislators, for the most part, felt they were growing in political capacity. At least most admitted to being exposed to the best political education they could imagine. The Republican Thomas, looking back in 1977 on his three years in the assembly, appraised his legislative education in this way:

I would like to compare it to post-secondary school education. We live in that kind of climate up here. You can say that at any institution you can get an education. If you choose not to, you can get a degree still. The same is true up here. You can stay in office and perpetuate yourself. But you'll never be a worker, but only be worked on. It all depends on whether you're willing to work. In school you find the guy who makes you work and think. It may be that he's an SOB. But you stick yourself on him, and you learn. Same here: you pick a hard course of action to learn.

I've often said it was like going back to school. I have an apartment right across the street, and at night I used to come on campus, in the evening, to go to the hearings, just to watch the authors and the committee members and learn the subject matters. I've gotten enough of that education by now. I spend more time at Frank Fats Restaurant so as to watch that area of activity of the lobbyists. They say more business is done on the golf course than in business firms. Similarly, more legislation is written at Frank Fats. I've tried to be more social. I'm not one who readily goes to the Firehouse Restaurant for two hours at lunch. I've got to force myself to take these courses, but they're essential to my education.

Last year certain of the bills I introduced I did purposefully just so that I'd come before every committee, every one except the committees I was already on.

On the floor you can be superficially prepared, or you can know and understand why someone is trying to do something. You can sit in your seat on the floor, press a button, and go off and do your own thing: minimum participation. Or you can read all those forty bills, attempt to understand them, agonize, feel you are as informed as anyone on the floor, and then be pissed off because Willie Brown [a Democratic assemblyman widely regarded as without a superior in intellect or rhetorical skills] gets up and describes an impact you never thought of. Then you realize there will always be better people than you at doing the job. But you know you are valuable.

Knowing "you are valuable" and getting more so: that was the confidence bred by the educational effects of the best state legislature in the country.

Two

During the recess I went back to the district, and . . . my wife
. . . insisted that I take a look at a particular child day care
center. . . . Now some would say $2,500 a month paid to one
family amounts to really ripping off the system and the matter
has to be checked out. The fact is, it's just the reverse. Where
we are spending money is not on the lady providing the
services, but on the people up above who are checking on her—
nothing more. I didn't know about that stuff—wouldn't have if
I had wanted to even, until I decided to concentrate my
attention.
    Assemblyman Jerry Lewis, 1978

To enjoy politics one must enjoy people; it helps if one likes
them as well.
    Stimson Bullitt
To Be a Politician, 1959

How the Committee System Taught Patriotism

Legislators spoke repeatedly of the educational effects of the committee system. They insisted, however, on one contrast with the conventional school:

> You attend a committee like you do a class. But there is a major difference . . . : those who are educating you—because you have the vote—are subordinate to you in the temporary pecking order of things. They need you and have to give you what you want.

"Because you have the vote": the legislator's vote in committee and on the floor was the basis of the system of legislative education. It meant that interesting people with interesting problems and interesting things to say about them wanted to teach. It meant that the legislative students felt entitled to ask questions—endless questions about the consequences and the reasons and the vocabulary of things. It meant that the faculty had to give students what the students wanted. It meant that the students could say "Put it in writing," so that they could take the lecture notes home and study them. It meant that each teacher regarded his or her pupils as important. The vote made the legislature an unusually responsive school, "an unreal world," as Assemblyman Hart put it.

The drawing power of the legislative vote is so obvious in understanding a legislature that a close observer might—unwisely—overlook its magnetic effects. No lobbyist would take the time to educate legislators if they did not have the vote. Once individuals became representatives and were given the ability to say yes or no in a meaningful way, they were visited, importuned, enlightened, and encouraged by skilled teachers. The vote was the basis of the system of education in the legislature.

In that each member had legislative votes, the legislature was an egalitarian institution. Every member started with resources: each legislator received pieces of the franchise—like vouchers—to come to school with, to grant, withhold, and signal for attention. The dominating feature of the committee system in California was its egalitarian character. There was no poverty; no legislator was a have-not, for every member had a full load of authentic committee assignments.

But some committee votes were more equal than others. Lobbyists wanted more of certain legislative vouchers than of others and were willing to spend the time and the effort to get them. The worth of a vote—for educational purposes, at least—depended on five features of the committees to which the legislative student was assigned: their importance, busyness, size, balance, and openness.

Importance. The bills that came before certain committees were bigger in effect, cost, or complexity than the bills that came before other committees. These committees were thus more important. There was another sense of "importance," however. Some committees rewrote the work of others. Sometimes a bill passed through a policy committee and did not stop until it lay in the lap of the fiscal committee. The assembly's most active member summed up the extra importance of appropriations:

> I've often been asked why I did not go on the education committee. Why should I? . . . Anything of consequence the education committee deals with comes to appropriations, where I can get my hands on it.

In terms of ultimate responsibility the policy committees were often less important than the fiscal committee, and lobbyists discriminated accordingly. If appropriations could reshape "anything of consequence" after it had left a committee of origin such as education, then lobbyists had to make special efforts to "get their hands on" the members who sat on appropriations.

Some policy committees, however—notably business, taxation, crimes, and law—frequently developed important legislation that did not involve appropriations. The forbidding of supermarkets to computerize their checkout operations (a big labor issue), requiring health insurers to pay the medical expenses of complications of pregnancy (a big women's issue), and restoring the death penalty did not affect the state treasury. When appropriations was not in issue, the policy committees became important, and lobbyists' best pedagogical efforts were devoted to them.

Busyness. The number of bills a committee dealt with determined how many votes each legislator had and how many colleagues, lobbyists, and problems would present themselves for approval. Some committees required their members to meet twice a week to cover their bill loads; other committees averaged less than two meetings a month. The number of meetings a committee held was a good measure of its busyness.

Size. Some committees resembled small seminars; others looked like lecture classes. Each member of a committee of five had twenty percent of the action. Each member of a committee of twenty had five percent of the action. Class size affected how much time legislative teachers would (or could) devote to individual students.

Balance. Some committees hardly stirred up any commotion, their members all seemingly in dumb agreement with their chairman. Other committees consisted of lively and diverse disputants, students who loved to argue. If a committee was "predictable," if its conclusions as a class were always foregone because it lacked a healthy balance of viewpoints, then the lobbyists had no need to waste their time educating it. On the other hand, some committees always seemed to have several closely fought matters on the agenda, where a margin of one or two votes was the difference. For example, the energy committee had some members strongly committed to environmental concerns, some equally committed to business concerns, and a few in between. In the energy committee there was always a close dispute, always a degree of uncertainty, always a critical vote. Critical votes brought out the teachers. Balanced committees had critical votes, and unbalanced committees did not.

Openness. If votes did not count because they were not tabulated, if a committee chairman could nullify the worth of committee members' decisions by neglecting to count and abide by their vote, then the franchise would have been counterfeit, and the teachers would not have bothered to show up to educate them. Since the chairman would then have had the only authentic vote, he would be the only student to be served. The twin temptations—of a chairman to abrogate the votes of his committee colleagues—and of his colleagues to allow him to do so—were very strong. The effective check against usurpation of power was to open matters to public scrutiny, and a critical procedure in this regard was to take roll-call votes on every bill and require their publication. The procedure of published roll-call votes was only adopted in the assembly in 1966, in the state senate in 1975. Its importance cannot be overstated.

II

For a legislator the good news was that the vote was a resource that attracted the best pedagogical efforts of others. The bad news was that it was an asset terribly difficult to manage. The legislative vote required the giving or the withholding of assent, saying yes or no to legislative solutions to "real world" problems. And it was never easy to say no.

Why was it so hard to withhold assent? Good manners in the legislature permitted members to say no only if they had some comprehension of the proposal they were rejecting. No matter how personally concerned they were that the legislature might be passing too many bills, members felt obliged by the habits and expectations of their colleagues to justify the withholding of assent, and to justify meant to understand.

Sometimes the legislative proposals were so numerous or complex or remote that the effort required to grasp them was exhausting. As one fatigued legislator said late one term, "Sometimes—sometimes you get so damned tired of reading bills that you just want to vote for the next one without studying it." Offsetting the penchant "to vote for the next one" was the conventionally taught wisdom, "When in doubt, vote no." Legislators chuckled over the maxim and even applied it when the doubt was due to the ineptitude of a bill's proponents. A lobbyist's faulty presentation might justify the withholding of assent. When the doubt stemmed from other causes, however, when it arose because the world was an uncertain place, then the maxim did not apply. When some of the effects of a bill were unknown because the future was unknowable, decent members of the legislative school were expected to exercise their judgment, not to suspend it. Whenever the author of a bill had done his best, the burden of justification shifted to those legislators voting in judgment on committee. At that point they were expected to do their homework if they were to say no, if they were to insist on stopping a bill before it reached the governor's desk.

This expectation ruled the committee system and was known as the Buddy System Rule. "Vote no on the merits; otherwise vote yes."[1] That is, there was a reluctance to reject a legislative colleague's bill, and the burden was on the naysayer to overcome that reluctance by advancing a reason.

The merits of the proposed legislation related either to conscience or constituency. The individual legislator could invoke notions of philosophy or of what was locally offensive. If a proposal violated a member's view of what was right or of what was practical and he could express how it did so, withholding assent was perfectly proper. "Guys who say no and give reasons" were deemed well mannered because they hurt no feelings. Reasons were impersonal, and perceived as such. In order to give reasoned objections, however, a legislator first had to understand the proposal. Committee work required homework, and the achievement of sufficient mastery to survive politically amid controversy did not come easily. That was what made legislative students serving on committees "so damned tired."

The Buddy System Rule was the most important norm underlying the workings of the committee system. It prompted conversation and militated against the breaking off of legislative dialogue. The good sense underlying the Buddy System Rule was that, in order to justify a negative vote "on the merits," a legislator had to state his understanding of the bill, which in turn permitted its proponents to correct any misunderstanding of it.

The Buddy System Rule was taught every day through punishments that were inflicted within the legislative institution. The member who insisted on too many unjustified negative votes simply got ostracized. If he or she carried any legislation, a block was put on it. This sequestration of the ill-mannered colleague could be so devastating a sanction that it was never applied for long. It just hung suspended over the place, ominous and traditional.

1. An observant and sophisticated freshman recalled the first time he was apprised of the rule: "Take Walter Stiern as a state senator. I could not vote for a highway bill of his. He came to me and asked for my vote. I told him, if a legislature votes out a bill like that, it's doing the Highway Commission in. It's doing the Highway Commission's job. He said, 'I can take that. It's those guys who say no and won't give you any reasons whom I can't accept.' "

While the Buddy System Rule was simple and widely adhered-to, its application was sometimes problematic. Some proponents in the heat of combat sought to reinterpret it to mean political trade-offs, horsetrading, a personalized and clumsy version of reciprocity: "I'll give you a vote if you give me a vote, regardless of the merits." Then opponents had to be quick enough to reassert the real rule and draw distinctions.

On occasion it became difficult to give an explicit justification for a negative vote. There would be times when intuition simply outran explicit analysis, and the principled reasons for one's reservations eluded articulation. Then a legislator's justification would sound awkward and without merit, even though he had done his best to think through his position.[2]

The Buddy System Rule, however, had the support of the respected members of the legislature and retained its authority. In no way did it preclude the giving of "IOUs" for other reasons: the legislature was full of acts of gratitude.[3] Nor did it mean that legislators who voted for particular proposals always did so on the bills' merits. It did mean, however, that conscience and constituency were polite grounds for withholding assent. The formulation of the principles of conscience and constituency was within the exclusive personal control of any legislator with the wit to invent them. The Buddy System Rule protected personal autonomy.

Furthermore, lobbyists and legislators could resort to a legislative mechanism to force even the most acquiescent member to exercise his or her intellect. They introduced counterbills, thereby exposing the legislature to incompatible approaches to the same problem.

2. One sophomore legislator had watched some of his cleverer colleagues cope with the problem of the clumsy justification: "Some of the cleverest guys have worked out ways. They will say, I really want to help you, but I have this close friend back in my district who is upset about this bill, and if I voted for it, it would offend him."
3. Hard service and rare information earned gratitude especially. One Republican senator described an act of appreciated hard service: "An assemblyman had a bill banning secondary poisoning of predators. Terrible bill for my district. I have ranchers and farmers and sheep herdsmen, and they are hurt by predators. It was a rough bill to support, given my district, and he knew that. I helped him get that out of the Natural Resources Committee. Then I took it up on the senate floor. It was a bitchy bill. But I got it off the senate floor, much to his surprise. He's grateful. He's fought for that bill. He cares as much for his bill as I care for mine. I really worked that bill, and I work them all. It got to the point where some young senator met me at the clerk's desk and asked me, 'Don't you ever carry a noncontroversial bill for these assemblymen?' I said, 'No, I don't think I should. It's helping on close measures that gets appreciation.' "

Faced with competing proposals, legislators had to say no to at least one of the alternatives. In having to vote against one bill or the other, each member incurred the obligation to learn about the problem. Lobbyists understood the value of the mechanism. So did effective legislators. As a result, it was notable how often lobbyists prepared, and legislators introduced, counterbills when they sensed that the house was giving too little thought to a shortsighted proposal. On the subject of medical malpractice, one proposal limited patients' recoveries and lawyers' fees, another regulated the surgeon's discretion and the medical profession's habits of ignoring its incompetent members. When the issue concerned upgrading the skills of makers of eyeglasses, one proposal relied on an apprenticeship approach (under which the young optician had to serve as a journeyman's assistant for a period of years), while a second proposal opted for an academic solution (under which the tyro had to go to college). In an effort to improve schoolchildren's reading abilities, opposed bills presented a choice between remedial programs for the worst readers and enrichment programs for all readers. (As a matter of fact, the fiscal process was nothing but choices between bills that were incompatible—budgetary limits made competitors out of expensive programs.)

Counterbills, when combined with the Buddy System Rule, pressured the legislative students to take stands. In committee, as a result, they learned the skill of formulating principles of conscience and constituency. They learned to say no thoughtfully.

III

The legislative education in formulating principle and becoming comfortable in using it was never ending. But how was principle taught in committee? Here is an illustration.

The business committee was one of the larger assembly committees. In 1975 it consisted of fifteen members. Only four were Republicans, including the party leader, Bob Beverly. Among the eleven Democrats were four freshmen. The remaining seven members were important leaders in the assembly—six committee chairmen and the assistant speaker.

By assembly standards the committee promised an enlightening education for its members. It had a busy agenda: over six hundred bills a year, with diverse subject matters on complicated and topical subjects such as medical malpractice, no-fault auto insurance, bank holding companies, unemployment insurance, consumer protection legislation, and public utility regulation. Virtually none of its legislation depended upon substantial state funding, so that it, not the fiscal committee, was the committee of last resort (lobbyists had to "work it hard" because there was no tomorrow for them). While it was a big committee, a good part of its work was done in three five-member subcommittees that specialized in a particular subject. Finally, it was a balanced committee, with the four pro-business Republicans balanced by the four pro-consumer freshmen Democrats, the three more liberal veteran Democrats balanced by three more moderate veteran Democrats, and the chairman serving as the pivot.

The chairman was Alister McAlister, a formidable, taciturn Mormon lawyer—scrupulously honest, conscientious, hard-working, intelligent, and a student of politics. A good portion of his constituency was organized labor; a good portion of his conscience was Horatio Alger individualism. The mixture of social concern and private conservatism that resulted meant that no bill was certain to get his approval.

McAlister had been a law professor and had strong pedagogical concerns. He liked the fact that he had four freshmen on his committee, though he frequently despaired of their bumptiousness, their certitudes, and their intellectual blind spots.

Halfway through 1975 a bill was scheduled for a hearing, which afforded McAlister a chance to teach his freshmen some propositions about economics, particularly the principle of the free marketplace.[4] The principle shifted the burden of proof to those who urged economic regulation and could be summed up: When it is not necessary to regulate business, it is necessary not to regulate it.

4. See Charles W. Anderson, "The Place of Principles in Policy Analysis," *American Political Science Review* 73 (September, 1979): 711–23. He identifies as particularly central three principles of policy analysis—authority, justice, and efficiency. In the California legislature these three principles were formulated thus: "When it is not necessary to regulate, it is necessary not to regulate"; "When not all can be served, who shall be served?"; and "A solution should not overreach the problem." Anderson comes to an astute conclusion: "There are in fact only a finite number of kinds of reasons that can and must be given in justification of a policy recommendation, a logically delimited set of grounds that are appropriate to the appraisal of public policy. It is possible to set standards of comprehensiveness in policy evaluation, to identify those questions that must at least be addressed if a policy appraisal is to appear 'worthy of consideration' in our eyes."

The bill before the committee was a simple one. It proposed to regulate the interest rate charged by bank credit card issuers—principally BankAmericard and Mastercharge—on outstanding balances of credit card holders. In California law the so-called Unruh Act already regulated the interest rate that retailers, not banks, applied to outstanding charge account balances; the proposed bill would apply the same ceilings to bank credit card finance charges.

The parity of treatment made sense, once the principle was accepted that a legislature had a responsibility to protect the consumer by regulating credit-giving institutions and limiting them to a "just price" and a "fair profit." The common sense of the matter was that the banks were simply standing in the stead of the retailers, which accepted the bank credit card as payment for goods. Combine the common sense of the matter with two other facts, and one could readily see why the banks harbored no illusions about defeating the bill in a committee where Democrats outnumbered Republicans three to one. The first fact was that the bill was timely in its concern for the consumer: the proconsumer character of public opinion was never higher than in 1975–76. The second fact was that the bill's author was the assembly's expert on lending practices and institutions, a highly respected Democrat, a close ally of the Speaker, a member of the assembly appropriations committee, and a smart, resourceful, and experienced man.

Facing that prospect, the banks were ready to concede the notion that interest rates on bank credit card accounts should be regulated. The issue they would argue would be the matter of price. They developed an industry position that the allowable rate for bank credit card accounts should be above the rates applied directly to retailers' charge accounts (on the grounds of the banks' additional costs).

The banks' lobbyists conveyed this industry position to Chairman McAlister. He received it with impatience. He called their conclusions premature and ill advised and told them to come to the committee prepared to educate it on the topic of consumer credit.

McAlister's advice removed the banks' opportunity to concede that credit card interest rates should be regulated at all. In preparation for the hearing they hired an expert economist, a Purdue University professor, to prepare a sixteen-page essay in which he explored the nature of credit and analyzed the effect upon consumers of fixed rate ceilings on credit in a competitive market.

By the time of the hearing McAlister had read the analysis thoroughly. When the professor testified before the business committee, he began badly, repetitiously, carelessly, and off the subject. Like a well-prepared and impatient student who knew what was worth talking about, McAlister interrupted and let it be known that he, too, "used to be a professor" and hence he knew "how hard it is to be brief and on track." With that piece of equivocal solace to spur him to his task, the professor explained his argument to the committee point by point: the consumer credit market in California was competitive; bank credit card revenue was not notably profitable to banks; lowering the yield further on credit card operations would induce banks to switch some of their credit card funds to other operations; the banks would restrict the availability of credit to a smaller number of consumers; the consumers who would thereby be denied bank credit card privileges would be the lower income credit card users (because they were worse credit risks); and the sole beneficiaries of a ceiling on interest rate charges would be higher income consumers. Moreover, there would be another irony: unless the legislature was prepared also to regulate the so-called "merchant discount" applied by the banks to the retailers, the banks could recover the revenues lost to interest rate ceilings by charging the merchants more for the use of bank credit card services; the merchants would then have to charge more for the goods they sold; and consequently in the long run the cash customer would be subsidizing the higher income credit customers.

It was a complex discussion, but the systematic dynamics of the price system were articulated minutely and precisely. McAlister wanted to be sure that his protégés on the committee clearly saw the forest amidst the trees and took it upon himself to sum up the lecture, all the while looking piercingly at his four freshmen: "In other words, any kind of legislation limiting interest rates contracts the market, and the major effects are visited upon low income credit card users disproportionately!"

The committee voted no unanimously; not one member invoked the Buddy System Rule to vote yes.[5]

---

5. Legislatures are difficult institutions for news reporters to give good press to. The compulsions of journalists to personalize, to create a heroes-and-villains scenario, and to be brief overwhelm truth. Few papers in the nation cover state legislatures more astutely than the Los Angeles *Times*. Yet, typically, its report of the business committee's disposition of the credit card bill began, "A bill which for the first time would have placed legal limits on bank credit card finance charges was sent into limbo

McAlister used the expert to touch on what he regarded as "profound economic issues": Could government regulate the marketplace without creating costs that would ultimately fall on the consumer? Were good intentions sufficient to produce good results without skillful analysis? Would the consumer benefit more from competition or from comprehensive planning by the legislature? He wanted to make sure no member of his committee was left without a reasonable and fundamentally based defense on the merits of his no vote, for he knew that his committee colleagues would be asked to justify their no votes by the author of the bill, by its proponents, and by its adherents in the districts back home. To the liberal legislators, with their concern for the lower income consumer, McAlister molded the analysis so as to reconcile their consciences with their votes. To the conservative legislators like Beverly, with their concern for the overregulated entrepreneur, the analysis provided reasons to back up their intuition.

The legislature got a lot of legislators "thinking about" the principle of the free marketplace and the perverse effects of regulation. It taught the difference between intention and achievement. The legislators started thinking about the limits of regulation.

IV

Learning principles could not be done by simply memorizing some abstract rule such as, "When it is not necessary to regulate, it is necessary not to regulate." Rather, effective learning of principles consisted in achieving a felt understanding of the reasons for them and a confidence in their predicted effects. One lecture from a Purdue professor on bank credit cards, while useful, did not by itself make the principle of the free market meaningful to freshmen legislators. The principle could only really be understood by repeated use of it. Legislators needed the opportunity to test it in new applications and observe whether predictions based on it would be borne out.

Fortunately, in a specialized committee such as business there were plenty of practical issues to test the free marketplace principle. Pro-

---

Monday by an assembly committee after running into opposition from the banking lobby." (3 June 1975, part 1, p. 18). The article depicted the hearing as a defeat of the consumer caused by the "opposition from the banking lobby," by all the nefarious means that a phrase like "the banking lobby" implies. But "the banking lobby" was not initially in "opposition" to legal limits on finance charges. It was McAlister, the assembly's business expert, who opposed it and who prodded the banks to give his legislative committee a gratuitous course in economics. And it was ideas that defeated the measure, not "the banking lobby."

posals to substitute governmental controls in the place of allegedly defective market mechanisms were always making their way onto the committee agenda. Should the premiums of medical malpractice insurance policies be controlled? Should the fees of harbor pilots be set by the legislature? Should public utilities be ordered to provide telephones and energy to old people at below-market rates? Should banks be prohibited from redlining certain city residential areas, even though the risks of forfeitures on home loans were greater within those areas? Should auto insurers be denied the freedom to "experience-rate" automobile insurance lest city dwellers pay more than suburbanites because car vandalism was greater in cities than in suburbs? Each of these matters provided legislators the chance to apply the reasoning that underlay the principle of the free marketplace. Each exercised their ability to predict and observe the effects of price changes on consumer and producer behavior in a new setting. By the end of the two-year course in business, the four freshmen who sat on the assembly business committee (and their eleven experienced colleagues as well) had many public policy problems to analyze in terms of economic fundamentals, and they gathered abundant evidence from which to conclude whether the principle of the free marketplace were "true" or not.

From these experiments in principle and practice, these fifteen legislators on the committee developed their own economic theories. They learned how to use principles to focus on markets. Their theories enabled them to see recurrent and universal patterns of economic behavior. As a result, they developed a confidence in anticipating economic events: they believed they knew what to look for and where to concentrate their attention in order to see it happening.

The legislators' committee education changed the habits of their eyes. They learned the theory of things. They became principled thinkers about social processes and institutions. From their vantage point in Sacramento, the world began to look more orderly.

V

But the legislative scholars left their boarding school of politics on weekends and vacations. They went back to their districts, leaving the academy behind. Theirs was an exhausting regimen back home. Typically, they spent all of Friday in appointments in their local offices. Moreover, Saturdays and Sundays, from dawn to dusk, were filled with ceremonies, breakfast conferences, luncheons, and more meetings. Evenings brought obligatory social events—cocktail parties, retirement galas for local dignitaries, fund raisers, and the inevitable prize of making the rounds, chicken dinners.

Going back home made them uncomfortable. Just as the college student immersed in Renaissance studies, the army sergeant preoccupied with his leadership responsibilities, and the Peace Corps volunteer exposed to peasant starvation all have trouble reentering into home life, so the legislator was disoriented by the change in roles brought on by his going home. In Sacramento he had been an abstract thinker, exhilarated by his principled insights into the world. Back home, among his constituents, he was an agent of his citizenry, subordinated to the job of protecting his constituents by virtue of his practical knowledge. His constituents felt that they were footing the bill to send him to his Sacramento boarding school in order to safeguard their district. With his improved governmental know-how, he was expected to stop a highway (or build one), close down an intolerably noisy airport (or obtain one), and put a neighborhood child care center back on its financial feet. The constituents' expectation that he would protect them invariably forced the representative to adjust his way of defining himself, and that was uncomfortable.[6]

Nevertheless, he met endlessly with the folks back home, who told him of their troubles and asked him what he would do for them, with their health problems, their livelihoods, their homes, and their ingrained and effective habits. As he talked with his constituents, certain disparities became obvious to him between the abstract notions he had developed in committees and the concrete problems of the people he was elected to protect. The kid from Sacramento discovered back home a shadowy fallibility falling upon his brilliant theoretical expectations.

Anomalies occurred. For example, despite the principle of the free market, a bank credit card user told of an experience in which a bank had mistakenly placed a stop-order on his credit card account, leaving him abandoned out-of-state without any funds for a much-needed vacation. A widow told of how her bank had revoked her credit card on the death of her husband. A workman showed him

---

6. To use the terminology of John Wahlke and his coauthors, *The Legislative System* (New York: Wiley, 1962), chap. 1, the legislator played the role of "trustee" in Sacramento, but was put in the role of "delegate" when he returned home to his district.

an incomprehensible letter from the bank explaining a new method of calculating finance charges. To their particular complaints the principle of the free market, so elegantly taught back in the legislature, seemed to offer neither solace nor explanation. The theory was fine as a general matter, but it did not fit the concrete problems. The poor fit between theory and practice increased his discomfort all the more.

If a legislator were lucky, however, he learned to use his intellect profitably. He began to apply the procedures he had learned in committee to formulate general principles to subsume a variety of particular instances. In the credit card case, he saw a general theme in the variety of instances brought to his attention. Individuals were having trouble making big enterprises responsive to small problems. Ordinary people lacked equality of bargaining power when their problem was an isolated one. While the price system gave them as consumers the collective power to influence producers, it did much less well in helping the isolated consumer with a particular and parochial problem. Neither the out-of-state vacationer, the grieving widow, nor the financially illiterate workman was capable of focusing the necessary attention on tiny problems unless the government weighted the consumer side of the balance of power.

The legislator formulated the observations he made in his district into a general principle called the balance of power: Regulation is necessary to correct an imbalance of bargaining strength. As the principle of the free market had helped him gather together a larger picture of society, so the principle of the balance of power enlarged his understanding of the small problems of his individual constituents. The two principles, of the free market and of the balance of power, were polar opposites, but contemplated simultaneously they worked together to avoid surprise. Their combined use confined their predictions about the effects of regulation to appropriate areas and thereby prevented the mistake of excess application of either one.

A legislator's realization that there were polar opposites to the theoretical principles he was learning in Sacramento was intellectually invigorating. He began to see that the dialectic between legislature and district could be counted on to generate useful pairs of principle and counterprinciple, a "social slant" and an "individual slant."[7] One pair of principles, in particular, turned out to be a valuable intellectual tool. The need principle ("to each according to his needs") and the incentive principle ("to each according to his contribution to productivity") always seemed to be working against one another. They made a splendid tool for dealing with many tax, welfare, and business decisions. In liability insurance matters, for example, the twin concerns of compensating the accidentally injured and encouraging others to avoid injurious accidents could be grasped in the counteracting thrusts of the need and incentive principles.

Legislators became wary of unopposed general principles as a result of the clash between the lessons learned in the legislature and those learned in the district. Freshmen legislators began to send new proposals back to the districts for comments, to get the competing slant on matters. Hart, the Santa Barbara liberal, for example, used his conservative constituents in order to help him grasp the "real world" effects of liberal proposals:

> One of the best ways to get a handle on a problem is to relate it to my district. I take the concept back and talk with a doctor or a teacher and let them tell me how it would affect them practically.

Getting a handle on a problem: it was a marvelous metaphor for conveying the necessity and use of polar principles. Like a pair of ice tongs, with its two arms, one from the left and one from the right, connected at a pivot, permitting force to be applied by one hand and thereby effecting the force and counterforce necessary to grasp an unwieldy chunk of ice, so a knowledge handle, with its

---

7. In this sense we could say that there was an "intellectual connection" between the legislative district and the legislature. If constituencies do cause legislators to think differently, then we ought to inquire into the intellectual effects of reapportionment. Parenthetically, I might note that with regard to some of the legislators in Sacramento the cognitive repercussions of reapportionment appeared to be extraordinary. For example, the Democratic assemblyman John Foran had originally represented a conservative, working-class, largely Irish district in San Francisco, but reapportionment gave him a district with a startlingly different constituency, comprised of the gay communities in Castro and Noe Valleys, Asian-Americans in China town, blacks in Hunters Point, and Chicanos in the Mission district, the last an area very responsive to the radicalism of an influential Roman Catholic priest named Father Boyle (after reapportionment Foran knowledgeably carried legislation to prevent employment discrimination against homosexuals, an issue, it would be fair to say, in which he had shown scant interest as representative of his former district).

liberal and conservative slants, could close in intellectually on sprawling, messy policy problems.

With an intellectual handle, a legislator suddenly understood
"what the real issue was." Once the issue was comprehended within
a polar framework of familiar principles, he knew in his heart what
people were fighting about.[8] Once he had forged an appropriate
handle of countervailing intellectual principles, not only could he
deal with a problem without surprise, but he was excited by the
diversity of human affairs existing back in his district and the big
ideas they represented. He could often anticipate the differences of
opinion he was going to encounter in the "real world," and what he
could anticipate, he could esteem. His intellectual handles, his tools
of polar principles, enlarged his capacity to like his people. He would
fondly call them "my bosses," "my flock," "my employers," "my
neighborhoods," "the 250,000 people who depend on me."[9] They
were a never-ending source of, and testing ground for, his ideas.

8. Polar principles were not necessarily arrayed along conservative/liberal or social/
individual dimensions. As long as they framed the collision of competing considerations or values, they sufficed as a handle. For example, some kinds of insurance
policies tended to be "community rated," some "experience rated": that is, some
coverages were provided to everyone at the same price, some at rates differentiated
by some criterion or another, such as age (life insurance), sex (annuities), longevity,
safe driving records, proximity to fire hydrants (fire insurance), and employment
(workers' compensation). From the point of view of spreading the risk of social
accidents as widely as possible, experience rating looked inequitable and community
rating looked just. But from the point of view of providing incentives to reduce risks,
experience rating looked much fairer and community rating looked demoralizing.
The legislator who remembered the two principles of socialized risk and accident-
prevention incentives was not likely to jump to hasty conclusions, but rather to learn
about details. It also meant that he could categorize, intellectually and impersonally,
the advocates on either side of an issue.

9. The most affectionate statements regarding constituents came from assembly
members who had previously had careers in local government. Their sense of the
importance of grass roots made them appear less aggressive in developing state social
programs and more defensive of local autonomy against tendencies of centralization
and uniformity. Yet, to my surprise, a strong sense of personal responsibility for the
business of their districts was present in most liberal, programmatic legislators as
well. The personal, district-focused sense of responsibility of two liberals (Assemblymen John Burton and Willie Brown) was stressed in a story told by an observant
Republican moderate. He was discussing the very tough negotiations over welfare
reform between the Republican forces representing Ronald Reagan and the Democratic opposition: "We were negotiating the Welfare Reform Act of 1971. John Burton
and Willie Brown would not get off our backs about a restaurant allowance for those
poor people who were housed in hotel rooms. There had been a series of fires in hotel
rooms where these men cooked suppers. It was important to Willie and John to get
these restaurant allowances recognized. To us . . . it was a rip-off, but to John and

Thus he learned to be skeptical of unopposed certitudes. He grew to mistrust simple ideologies and to love ideas full of paradox and tension. And, most importantly, once he developed handles with sufficient explanatory power to comprehend the experiences of all his constituents, he no longer found them intellectually uncomfortable. Able to tolerate contradictory evidence, he learned the true meaning of patriotism, the kind that a democratic leader had to acquire—a concern for all his constituents, irrespective of their political beliefs, because they were "his" people.

Willie, those winos were their constituents." Winos in hotel rooms were the "flock" of two assemblymen, part of the quarter of a million individuals who depended on them.

Three

We all like to point to something we built. If we're a contractor, to the houses we built. To the faces we rebuilt if we are plastic surgeons. To the highways we made if we build roads. To the gardens we've made if we are landscapers. To the pictures we've painted if we're artists. Well, legislators make laws, and we're no different. . . . It's the creative aspects of your life. . . . Although the longer you're here as a legislator, the more you realize that your importance may lie in being responsible for the things you killed. But it is hard to draw dignity from the babies you abort rather than the ones that come to full term.

Assemblyman Walter Ingalls, 1977

[A legislator should] feel all the passions which actuate a multitude, yet not . . . be incapable of pursuing the objects of its passions by means which reason prescribes.

James Madison, *Federalist* no. 48, 1789

How the Author System
Taught a Love of Justice

I

The committee system was the curricular framework within which
the legislators were educated. All legislators learned within it. Some,
however, were more active participants than others. They "moved
out," as one member put it, assuming a more creative role in which
they built courses of study for others and taught as well.

In any good school students tend to be transformed over time
from sponges of knowledge to communicators of it. They tutor their
friends, take responsibility for preparing a topic for class discussion,
and write research papers on various matters. In crossing the line
from passive absorbers to active presenters, students test the ade-
quacy of their understanding. The prospect of having to teach invariably exposes gaps in knowledge and motivates strenuous
preparation to cure them.

Thus good schools always give students a chance to play the teaching role. The political boarding school in Sacramento was a very fine
school, and it utilized a curricular device that was especially effective
in the transformation of students from sponges to speakers of political
knowledge. The particular pedagogical mechanism the school employed was called the author system.

II

The author system was a simple idea. Every legislator controlled
his or her bills, from inception to the governor's desk. It meant that
any legislator—from senior to freshman—offered as many bills as
he (and I shall use the male gender for brevity rather than accuracy)

wanted, was entitled to a committee hearing on any matter he wished to take up, had the opportunity to go as far with it as his colleagues would tolerate thereafter, managed each bill without interference or preemption by the committees or their chairmen, dealt with both the policy and fiscal aspects of each proposal, and negotiated personally the compromises that had to be made among groups and bureaucracies. The author system obliged each author to solicit legal, informational, and analytical assistance from whatever quarter, determine the timing and tactics of each move, obtain publicity, organize witnesses, "mark up" his own bills, lead debate on the floor, marshal his forces, and defend his bill against the governor's veto.

The author system of the California legislature generated the content of each committee curriculum. Topic selection for the classes was not left to the committee itself, its staff, or its chairman. Rather, the courses were determined by the individual members of the legislature, who acted like a band of itinerant teachers wandering in and out of the committee classrooms. Responsibility for the topics that the committee members had to study was delegated to the individual bill-authors.

In no starker way did the Sacramento legislature contrast with Congress than in the critical importance of the author system. In Congress only senior legislators carried big legislation, and although infinite numbers of bills could be introduced, most never were heard. The congressional leadership decided which bills would pan out and were valuable enough to get legislative time. The rest were washed away without a hearing, without a chance to be examined. Moreover, in Congress the committees took over the bills from the individual bill-carriers and "marked them up," adding amendments with or without the authors' concurrence and negotiating the necessary compromises. Hence, the lobbyists tended to deal with the chairmen, the staffs, and the members of the committees, not the individual authors. Furthermore, in Congress the policy aspects of a bill were separated from its fiscal aspects, and different committee chairmen took responsibility for carrying its separate aspects. Finally, each legislative committee wrote its own report about bills, defended the merits of its own legislation in the other house, and protected its own offspring from the presidential veto.

The difference between the author system of Sacramento and the committee system in Washington, D.C. was very important with regard to the education each provided. Sacramento's author system was individually exhilarating; the Congressional system, on the other

hand, being collective, seemed oppressive by comparison. The freshman legislator who enjoyed playing the role of teacher could do "his
own thing" in Sacramento. In Washington a similar legislator would
be advised to keep his eyes open, his mouth shut, and wait.
Both systems have merits and defects. The author system would
be unthinkable in a legislature of 435 members: to revert to the
academic analogy, there would be too many topics to cover and too
many papers to discuss to make the system worthwhile. The committee system, on the other hand, would be unnecessary in a legislature of only eighty (or forty) members. Because of political party
strength or a tradition of legislative centralism, one might still find
a committee system in a small legislature, but it would not be essential. Nor in my mind would committee control under such circumstances be as invigorating. In comparison with an author system,
committee control is about as exciting as when a seminar teacher
insists that he lecture all semester long on topics of interest only
to him.

III

Five basic notions are crucial to an understanding of the author
system as it was practiced in Sacramento.

The first is that legislators monopolized bill-carrying. No one else
in the state possessed the right to author a bill that might become
a state law. Neither the governor nor his Department of Health nor
General Motors nor the Teamsters Union nor the Los Angeles School
Board had the smallest right to hand a bill to the house clerk, an
action that began the educative process of the state legislature. Those
outside the legislature participated essentially as invited guests of the
members of the house. The real participation of the sponsors of a
bill, however, was more complicated and more important than the
phrase "invited guests" might imply,[1] yet the essential feature of the

1. Under some circumstances legislators simply lent their names to bills; the legislative work would be planned and executed entirely by the sponsor. For example,
the State Employment Department wanted to introduce a package of legislation. The
department lobbyist chose a senate author, Al Rodda, because he was smart and
principled, and was also obliging enough to help the department out. The lobbyist
explained: "After all, most legislators at this point in the session have twenty-five or
thirty bills and don't want any more. So any legislator would normally say, 'Give me
one' if they would agree to carry any. But we wanted them introduced as a package.
That's why I went to Rodda, because he would say to me, 'I don't even want to read
them. Put them across the desk [of the clerk]. I'm trusting you, and I'm going to

California legislature was that legislators had a monopoly of the bill-carrying privilege. That meant that no matter how exalted a citizen's status, he or she needed the active assistance of at least one legislator to trigger the lawmaking process of the state. If the Department of Corporations, the State Bar, the Chamber of Commerce, and the federal government's Securities and Exchange Commission all agreed upon a particular revision of the Corporations Code, they still had to entreat some legislator to author a bill embodying their proposal. Even the governor was powerless to get his specific ideas on the legislature's agenda without a legislator's cooperation. In that sense the students of Sacramento were the ultimate arbiters of what they wanted to study.

An allied, and second, notion is that bills derived from sources. Whether a legislator was an inactive author or a busy one, whether his bill load was twenty or a hundred and twenty, a legislator rarely introduced a bill exclusively of his own devising. Typically bills were thrust upon legislators by sponsors. Bills were carried at the request of "the interests" such as the governor's office or local governments or industry associations. Slightly less frequently, the initiative came from a constituent with a problem,[2] but even when that was the case, the legislator would seek out an agency or a private association to sponsor the proposal as evidence that its interests were allied (or at least not incompatible) with the constituent's needs. Rarely, a bill with neither a sponsor nor a constituent problem behind it sprang full-grown from a legislator's imagination. It usually went nowhere—"for lack of a push," as one astute member put it. Legislators got plenty of suggestions about urgent or fruitful topics; "it was a question of culling rather than finding legislation to carry," Senator Peter Behr, a Republican, remarked.

---

leave it up to you to decide whether any of them go against my philosophy, whatever it is.' I will also assure him that we will bear the workload, except in those situations where hearings drag on seven or eight hours, and then he'll have to do the job. Also, we have to jack up the governor to decide his position on these bills. I don't want the governor at the last moment to come out opposed to the bills we have asked Rodda to carry for us."

2. A liberal assemblyman said of the physically handicapped access bill he authored: "A guy brought it to my attention, Milton Miller. He's a lawyer in Los Angeles. He had read Gene Chappie's bill, which had given the physically handicapped access to all public buildings. So Miller told me about the bill and that it did not apply to private buildings. . . . So it was a friend of mine who turned up the problem."

A third notion critical to understanding the author system is that of the local bill. Many proposals for legislation had only local significance. They were popularly called "district bills" and dealt with problems such as joining separated parts of a freeway, acquiring land for an urban park, reorganizing a particular school system, establishing a particular bike path across a county, closing down a noisy airport runway, or paying the rent for a site for ornithologists. District bills were introduced by legislators in their capacity as protectors of their constituencies; they were frequently necessitated because some locality lacked effective home rule over some matter.[3] Usually the locality also lacked money, and the job of the legislator was, as one member liked to say, "to favor his particular area with such legislative largesse as he can manage to rip off, so to speak, for his constituents." A district bill was important to an individual legislator in his role as advocate for his district; it was likely, however, to be quite unimportant to the rest of his colleagues.

There was a double aspect to district bills. On the one hand, carrying them was the exclusive prerogative of the home legislator: each legislator abided by an understanding not to "mess with" the district matters of his colleagues. On the other hand, legislators would give their assent to each other's district bills, not on their merits but out of indifference. A district bill, almost by definition, had no adverse effects outside of the local district. On district bills the Logrolling Axiom applied: "You help me roll my local project; I'll help you roll yours." District bills did not get the careful committee attention given to "legislation," i.e., important bills. Their costs individually did not amount to much, otherwise they would have had extra-district effects and transcended the classification of a district bill. As a general rule the legislature had historically delegated most decisions susceptible to logrolling to bureaucracies and commissions independent of legislative influence. In California it was a matter of legislative policy whether the state would build highways, plant parks, and establish schools. But where particular highways, parks, and schools would be situated and who would construct and

---

3. See V. O. Key Jr., *Southern Politics* (New York: Knopf, 1949), particularly the chapters on Virginia and South Carolina, for a depiction of the centralizing effects of a political system that provides little home rule. California, in contrast, enjoyed strong local government, a high level of home rule, and a constitutional ban on "special legislation." Relative to many other states, the need for and appropriateness of local bills were considerably less in California.

staff them was a matter of executive administration. The governor liked matters that way and was jealous of his prerogatives. He could be counted upon to resist district bills that encroached too much on his "turf."

The general notion of a "district bill" was fuzzy at the edges. A bill to clean up Lake Tahoe was not a district bill, even though the lake was situated entirely within a single legislative district. Lake Tahoe was an asset of statewide importance; thus any legislator could author legislation to protect it without being regarded as a trespasser.

Sometimes a truly local problem could not be solved except by a proposal of general application. For example, one legislator submitted a bill to waive university tuition for all children of disabled veterans, but all he really wanted was tuition assistance for the two sons of a needy constituent (who was a disabled war vet). He had a local problem, but had been unable to craft a purely local solution to it. Because the proposed solution overreached its local purpose, it became more than a district bill.

A final cause of confusion over what constituted a "district bill" stemmed from the different perceptions of individual legislators. Some legislators saw dangerous precedent or broad implications in essentially what the author thought was a parochial matter. Nevertheless, if agreement could be reached that a particular proposal was a district bill, committees took care of it, not as an educational matter, but as an administrative one, something equivalent to housekeeping chores.

A fourth notion is the concept of "learning the ropes." There were written procedures that governed the course through which bills progressed. They were scattered like monuments on a battlefield, to function as obstacles or shields according to the wit of the tactician: the thirty-day rule (no bill could be heard until it had been published and in circulation for a month), the four-day rule (four days had to elapse between the time when a committee reported favorably on a bill to the floor and when floor debate could begin), deadline rules (bills had to be passed favorably out of committees by certain dates or they were dead), extraordinary majority rules (some bills, among the most important of which were those involving the expenditure of state funds, required extraordinary majorities for passage, fifty-four votes in the assembly and twenty-seven in the state senate), conference committee rules (a house of origin could refuse to accept the other house's amendments and commit a bill to an ad hoc joint committee with the authority to develop a compromise version acceptable to both houses), rules regarding suspending the rules, and governor's veto rules (the governor could veto any bill and could adjust any appropriation downwards, and only an extraordinary majority in both houses could override such actions).

There were also unwritten procedures relating to the influencing of people, principally adversaries. They ranged from how to approach a particular legislator to general political folk wisdom ("When you can't persuade a legislative opponent directly, get one of his constituents to talk to him").

Using these written and unwritten procedures to increase one's effectiveness looked easy when practiced by legislative masters. To the average freshman they loomed as hindrances. To assist in the mastery of them, the Sacramento school had a freshman orientation. It worked like this:

Freshmen were especially allotted the services of a pool of special tutors, called party consultants. (The relatively small staffs allotted to the Republican and Democratic caucuses played a vital part in the intellectual process of the legislature, as we shall see in chapter 8.) One of their incidental functions was to take responsibility for their parties' newcomers, teaching them how to write press releases, prepare legislation, develop a public opinion survey, and run a district office. One "service" the tutors provided—often unbeknownst to the freshmen legislators themselves—was teaching them the ropes of the author system. The tutors would suggest to each of their charges that there was a "terribly important piece of controversial legislation" that needed to be carried into law. Practically everybody but the unwitting freshman believed that the suggested bill was a "turkey" or a "dog"—a proposal so worthless or impractical that it had little chance of gaining ultimate passage. For that reason the republic usually had little to fear from the exercise the authors were set; it was as close to a harmless calisthenic as breathing deeply, yet the freshmen got experience in the system of influencing others. They ran through the author system and, once in awhile, did it so skillfully as to convince others that the proposal was really not so harmful or impractical as originally believed.

Typically, one such "turkey" proposed that life insurance contracts be "readable" to a person with a sixth-grade education. (It was regarded as a "turkey" because the bill attached greater importance to the contract as consumer product than as a legal document

to be judicially construed in light of legislation and precedent.) In
the course of taking responsibility for carrying the bill, a freshman
author would discover how to do a great many things, from finding
the location of the clerk's office to learning how to tap the resources
of information available in the insurance and academic communities
of California. By the time the bill was finally slain, its carrier had
begun to learn the ropes of the author system.

The fifth and final notion is that being an author of a bill was
quintessentially a social experience in the sense that it brought the
legislative scholars into working contact with a lot of people of varied
character and background. In providing the legislator an opportunity
to choose what he wanted to study, the author system also permitted
him to choose the people he wanted to study with. He might choose
a bill because he would thereby acquaint himself with interesting
lobbyists, important sponsors, proud people, brilliant experts, masterful politicians, or stubborn adversaries. The chance to learn what
made them all tick made carrying bills exhilarating. Testing one's
strength in competition with formidable opponents was just as re-
vitalizing as having the opportunity to associate with worthy allies.

The opening paragraph of Stimson Bullitt's brilliant primer on
what it is like to be a politician begins with an emphasis of the
personal nature of politics:

> To enjoy politics one must enjoy people; it helps if one likes
> them as well. A politician wants and tries to like people. He
> must be with them, and a friendly relationship makes it easier
> for him to satisfy and please. He meets and works with every
> kind. He is enabled to associate with the best, and compelled
> by duty and circumstances to spend time with some of the
> worst. Near the centers of government, which has come to
> reach us all, he is invited to open almost any door.[4]

The author system of the legislative school gave the politician the
occasion to "open almost any door." It was his opportunity "to
associate with the best."

IV

Learning how to deal with adversaries was the knowledge politicians acquired through the author system. Three cases of successful

    4. Stimson Bullitt, *To Be a Politician* (New Haven: Yale University Press, 1977),
p. 3.

authorship illustrate the three modes of dealing with opponents: in the first case the author successfully persuaded; in the second case the author successfully bargained; and in the third case he successfully assaulted.

In reading these case studies, keep in mind that the three bills being discussed were among more than one thousand pieces of legislation that were actually passed in the California legislature in a typical year. They constituted a tenth of one percent of the 3,500 proposals that obtained legislative consideration annually. They were controversial bills, and they were important, but they were neither the most controversial nor the most important.

One frequently heard an able legislator say that the workload was manageable because "only two percent of it was really difficult"— that is, was controversial and important. But two percent of 3,500 bills turned out to be seventy bills, not including the backbreaking Budget Bill, whose complexity and size devoured the energies of that quarter of the membership of each house who served on appropriations.

All this needs to be said because the reader must put the battles over the three bills in perspective. The legislature had a lot going on; it was a "ten-ring circus." Focusing on the making of a single bill tends to distort the picture. By rendering the larger context invisible, it blinds us to the relationships between bills.

With that warning, let us turn to the three case studies: the elimination of the oil depletion tax exemption, the Venice Child Care Center Bill, and the Wild Rivers Bill.

V

The oil depletion tax exemption permitted oil well owners in California to exempt from their state income tax about twenty-five percent of their net revenues. The state depletion allowance paralleled a similar provision in the federal tax codes, which was originally legislated in 1924. The federal provision had been passed partly on the grounds of the substantial equivalence between mineral depletion and the allowance for depreciation on capital goods, a provision that permitted an investor to recover the cost of his investment without paying tax on it. Depletion was nothing more than real estate depreciation, it had been argued. In fact, however, it permitted the oil well owner to recover far more than his initial investment. That was what upset its opponents, the liberal coalition of labor and urban groups, who saw it as an unjustified loophole (the defenders of the depletion exemption, on the other hand, urged that this "bonus" was necessary to encourage entrepreneurial investment in a risky business).

Efforts to rescind the federal oil depletion allowance had long been resisted successfully. To labor and urban groups in 1974 the California state income tax provision looked more vulnerable. Governor Brown, in his 1974 campaign, had promised to eliminate it. In fact, it appeared that the tail might wag the dog: the liberals hoped that if California abolished the state loophole, Congress might be encouraged to eliminate the federal one. The rescission of the state provision thus became a symbolic goal of a liberal coalition of labor leaders, city mayors, and intellectuals. It was seen as a tax reform with far greater significance than the $70,000,000 of additional tax revenue it would generate annually.

In 1974, in the wake of Watergate, fifty-five Democrats were elected to the state assembly, many of them young, liberal professionals. None better typified them than Bill Lockyer. He came from urban Oakland, was thirty-four, had made politics his life since he was a youngster, and had won a seat in the assembly in a special election to fill the seat held by his late boss, who had been killed mid-term in an auto accident.[5]

Lockyer found the oil depletion bill extremely interesting. As a politician with a reformist bent, he was interested in taxes as a topic of study. Not being an attorney, accountant, or economist, he lacked formal education in the subject, however, and he knew no practitioners, officials, or scholars in the tax field. He was, however, a member of the taxation committee, and he persuaded the Speaker and the tax committee chairman that a member of that committee should carry the oil depletion legislation and that, by elimination, he was the right member to assume responsibility as author.

The oil depletion bill represented the popular stereotype of legislation. It was partisan: by and large Democrats and Republicans took opposing positions on it as a matter of constituency. It had an ideological appearance: legislators seemed to take principled positions on it as a matter of either egalitarianism or entrepreneurial risk-taking. It seemed to be an either/or proposition: a legislator had to

---

5. All California legislative vacancies were filled by special elections, in contrast to California judicial vacancies, which were filled by the governor's appointees.

be for it or against it; a middle ground seemed to be lacking. And it pitted big business—individuals who were resourceful, powerful, committed to self-interest, and knowledgeable—against big government with its economists, public servants, and political movers and shakers. Because of the governor's support and the oil companies' opposition, the author of the oil depletion bill could open the door to every government office in Sacramento and every oil mogul's executive suite in Los Angeles and San Francisco.

Procedures made passage of the bill highly problematic, however. Legislation that changed the rates of taxation required an extraordinary majority to obtain favorable passage through the assembly and senate. Lockyer's oil depletion proposal changed the rates of taxation; thus fifty-four assemblymen and twenty-seven senators had to give the bill their affirmative vote.

The necessary votes to gain passage in the assembly were easily obtained. The Democratic caucus agreed that its members would support the bill unanimously. Caucus votes were taken rarely in California, so rarely in fact that they were of negligible importance except on the Budget Bill. But in the oil depletion matter the exceptional occurred. The measure came up for a vote early in the year; the Democratic governor and assembly Speaker had supported the bill strongly; it was Speaker Leo McCarthy's first major policy stance since coming to power; many of the Democrats were freshmen with little inclination to cross the leadership; and the veteran mavericks on the Democratic side who would have had the temerity to buck the Speaker were liberal ideologues who liked the bill.

Getting twenty-seven votes from the senate was another matter, however. Simply on the principle that unnecessary tax exemptions should be abolished, Lockyer found that he had nineteen senate votes. That left him with twenty-one adversaries, eight of whom he would have to persuade to support the legislation. Some of the senators opposed to him stood their ground on principle; others based their stand on constituency, for they had oil wells in their districts, whose owners were bound to be hurt if the depletion allowance were to go.

Lockyer chose to work on senators with constituency problems. He compromised the provisions of the bill so as to keep the depletion allowance for small producers, the so-called mom-and-pop oil interests. He drew a line separating the big producers from the producers who pumped relatively small amounts of oil, and exempted those falling below the line from the new taxes. Thus in the districts of eight of the original senate opposition, every oil-producing constituent retained the oil depletion allowance. Lockyer told the story this way:

> Eight votes had to be gotten from amendments to exempt the small producers. So then we undertook to inform each swing legislator about the interests of his constituents in oil. We developed a packet for each legislator on each district as to the oil reserves there, a little map and list of holdings. And they went out to each of the forty senators. Through talk I had found out who would be giving a flat yes or no, and I found out who was interested in exemptions, and the size of the exemption which would satisfy that member. When we got to a line where we could get eight of them, we knew where the line had to be drawn. That was a lot of work, because most of the legislators did not know anything about their district in these terms. They were more likely just to say which company they knew about and that it had to be eliminated, exempted from the bill. I got a lot of help from the Department of Finance on this matter and from the Tax Board. I must have read a dozen books and a hundred articles on the matter, preparing.

The upshot of this work was passage of the bill. But several important implications of the author system became visible from this case.

First, because of the procedure requiring an extraordinary majority, Lockyer had to appeal to members outside his own party. On this unusually partisan bill, he had to swing some Republican senators to support his bill, and it appeared to him that he would have to do it on the bill's merits.

Second, the bill was at an impasse. To negotiate the bill's passage through the senate, Lockyer ferreted out all interested adversaries to find out the sources of their opposition. Lockyer discovered by listening to every side that some opponents were knowledgeable and some ignorant. He also became confident that some opposition would swing to his side if he could resolve their uncertainty about their own constituents. Here was a case in which knowledge was power. Lockyer could make the knowledge accessible to his colleagues by collecting the bits and pieces of information lying scattered in that agency, this office, that file, this census. He eventually succeeded because he became expert in packaging knowledge.

Things can go wrong in complicated undertakings, however, and Lockyer's tactics were extremely complex. He calculated too finely, it turned out, and jeopardized his bill. One senator who had earlier promised to vote yes backed out of his commitment, leaving Lockyer one vote short. Governor Brown came to Lockyer's rescue. By blandishments and careful cultivation, the governor changed the negative vote of one susceptible senator. Yet note that while the governor's play on the hopes of a single legislator for a judgeship got the last vote, it was Lockyer's intellectual proficiency that had earlier swung around seven senators. The governor's influence on one man would have been worthless had not Lockyer already persuaded twenty-six senators to vote yes. The arousal of hopes (or the threat to trample on them), while a dramatic and terrifying part of politics, never played more than a marginal part in the state legislature.

Third, as a result of participating in the author system, Lockyer learned the nature of the state senate. In searching out the location, size, and ownership of oil resources district by district, he discovered much more. He came to grasp the economics, politics, demographics, and psychology of each of the forty state senate districts. While he was cramming his research on natural resources into packets consisting of "a little map and a list," at the same time he was mapping for future use the forces that underlay all the policy deliberations of the senate. He charted the background and susceptibilities of the individuals in the senate. He got to know their human nature.

There was more involved in Lockyer's authorship. For one thing, he telephoned the journalists in the districts of swing legislators to teach them the substance of oil depletion policy, and he succeeded in getting them to apply local editorial heat for his bill. For another, he cultivated and taught a senate collaborator to lead the debate on the senate floor (from which Lockyer as an assemblyman was prohibited during debate); because it was important legislation, Lockyer found it easier to interest an astute and effective senator in helping him. As a result Lockyer learned more useful things about how to be effective in the senate than he might have learned from a lesser collaborator.

Lockyer also noticed that the lobbyists for the oil companies were uneven in quality. While several were surprisingly inexperienced in legislative matters and hence were arrogant and prone to lie to cover up their ignorance, there were others who had been around, were good, and had a reliable store of knowledge. That taught Lockyer which doors to the oil industry were worth opening—invaluable information about the private sector for a man whose vocation was politics.

Finally, he learned about timing. He began to understand about the tides of popular feeling, that mixture of ideas and moods which in this case had put the oil companies on the defensive. To the journalists Lockyer spoke with, the crowds he addressed, the agencies he cultivated, the intellectuals he consulted, and the colleagues he approached, it seemed right that oil producers should pay their fair share of taxes. Tides flowed and ebbed; perspectives on what was fair and arbitrary altered with time. Lockyer could feel the power of the temporary consensus as it put the oil producers on the defensive. For perhaps the first time, while he was carrying the oil depletion bill, he sensed how time could momentarily erode (or make invincible) an opposition. He struck a quick compromise in order to exploit the accident of timing, and he would never thereafter forget the lesson of seizing the moment to break an impasse.

VI

Alan Sieroty was a liberal, too, and came from a liberal west Los Angeles district. He had both undergraduate and law degrees from Stanford University. He was the son and grandson of Jewish financial entrepreneurs, a product of the California Democratic clubs, and financially well heeled enough to devote himself full time to his legislative work. He focused his energies on civil liberties (free speech and the rights of criminals and prisoners, principally) and fair financial practices.

Education and welfare were not matters of particular interest to him. Some of his constituents in west Los Angeles, however, wanted a child care center and "the legislative largesse" to construct one. Since their need for a center was a district matter, it was his legislative responsibility to try to meet it. He enlisted the sponsorship of the Los Angeles School Board to support the proposal. The key provision of the bill Sieroty submitted involved an appropriation of three million dollars to be matched by the local school district.

In developing the bill Sieroty also conferred with representatives of the State Department of Education and the State Department of Finance, the governor's bureau of the budget. The talks proved fruitless. Despite Sieroty's arguments about the community's pressing needs, both state departments were opposed to the proposal, and eventually the governor reinforced their opposition. As was typical with district bills developed outside the state agency process, the governor perceived Sieroty's child care center bill as an encroachment on the principle of executive administration. Moreover, the Department of Education objected on grounds of priority: there were communities in greater need of such centers. And, finally, the Department of Finance objected on the grounds that preschool child care facilities were exorbitantly expensive and the state should stay out of the business of funding them.

Sieroty's problem thereafter was that he could not get the governor even to think about a compromise. The administration's answer was an absolute no. As long as the governor was sure that the bill would never reach his desk—in which case he would have to take local political heat for niggardliness were he to veto it—he would not confer further on the matter. Sieroty knew that the governor stood his ground confidently; he occupied a position of power where he was protected by a legislative redoubt of invincible strength. The fortification was a majority of the senate appropriations committee, which supported the governor's principled objections to Sieroty's proposal. As long as the committee majority would not pass Sieroty's child care center bill out of committee, the governor was not interested in compromise.

Sieroty's tactical problem was to devise a way to finesse the senate appropriations committee so that he could get the bill to the governor's desk. The solution lay in the advantages that certain legislative procedures could give to a really concerned author. The most useful pro-author rule was the conference committee procedure. If Sieroty could get his version of the bill out of the assembly and then just keep the bill alive in the senate, no matter what emasculating amendments he had to accept to do so, then the two versions could be sent to a small ad hoc conference committee for reconciliation. The result of the conference committee would then be sent back directly for senate and assembly approval, without further reference to any committee, particularly the "booby trap" of senate appropriations.

A device for exploiting this procedure was to submit simultaneous bills. In this case, Sieroty introduced his bill in the assembly, and in the technical and fiscal committees developed a workable bill— tight administration, guarantees of community participation, and so on. When the assembly passed the bill to the senate, the appropriations committee killed it because it contained an appropriation of three million dollars. Meanwhile a senate colleague of Sieroty's introduced a bill to enable the Los Angeles School District to establish child care centers, but it was skeletal. No money was requested, and senate objections to it were stilled by its fiscal insignificance. It passed out of the senate to the assembly. As soon as it was referred to the assembly committees, the provisions of the defeated Sieroty bill, both money and policy language, were amended into it. This completely altered version was then passed by the assembly. When the senate objected to the desecration of its original handiwork, the bill was referred to a conference committee. With the assistance of the Speaker, who negotiated with the senate leadership, Sieroty succeeded in packing a six-person conference committee with himself, his friendly senate colleague, and two favorable assemblymen. It seemed inevitable that the version approved by a majority of the conference committee would look very much like the Sieroty proposal.

The governor's Maginot Line had been breached. Sieroty's bill was now past the big guns of senate appropriations, whose barrels were now silent and powerless. From this position of practical strength, Sieroty approached the governor anew and found him more amenable to discussion and compromise. Sieroty and the governor struck an agreement to decrease the appropriation from three million dollars to one million, in return for which the governor withdrew his opposition. With all parties sharing command, the bill triumphantly marched through both houses, and the governor acclaimed it.

In political conflicts parties do not begin with equal power to influence one another. If one side is to be effective, an adverse balance of power has to be diminished. Such an imbalance initially existed in the case of the child care centers.

At the outset Sieroty had the support of his own house. He was a respected assemblyman by virtue of his intellectual and political skills. He was a loyal member of the Speaker's coalition. And he was carrying a "district bill." In his own house the governor's opposition would not have prevailed. Despite such support, however, he was vulnerable in the senate, and the governor was not. Moreover, Sieroty was subject to the threat of the governor's veto, which, if exercised, meant the nullification of all his and his constituents' hard work. Therefore, if he were to be effective and not wasteful of great legislative effort, he had to consider the governor's wishes and principles. On the other hand, the governor initially exposed no weaknesses to Sieroty: as long as the bill could be killed in the legislature, Sieroty could not lay the blame at the governor's feet. And as long as senate appropriations provided the governor a shield to protect his reputation as a responsive public official, there was little need for him to consider Assemblyman Sieroty's wishes and principles. That was an imbalance of power that Sieroty had to correct before the two men could confer productively on a compromise. Until each was in a position to threaten the other, the balance of power was such that the governor could stand deaf and blind to Sieroty's entreaties.[6]

The author system gave legislators lots of exercise in practicing the balance of power. Small problems, with small stakes, like a district child care center, provided just as much experience in the games of aligning the balances of power as big problems with big stakes. The author system was an apprenticeship in the techniques of coercing human nature. This apprenticeship was necessary for those practicing politics because mistakes were easy in playing with extortionate power. And much was learned from mistakes and the redemptive experience of enjoying a second chance.

What had to be learned? The fundamental mistake in practicing mutual coercion was to overreach. The temptation to exploit momentary strength was terribly difficult to avoid. Euphoria, vindictiveness, confusion, and the crowd's applause all urged a legislator to press to the mark, to seek unconditional surrender. The critical skill was to abstain from driving such a hard bargain that the other party was turned into an unnecessary enemy.[7] The goal was to strive for a bargain on such mutually beneficial terms that the foundation for mutual trust was built and rebuilt.[8] In Sieroty's case, previous exercise in the author system had already taught him that while he

6. A deft and eloquent Republican, Dixon Arnett, phrased the matter thus: "The process is based on the political premise that you gather political power and that gives you a position where you cannot be ignored. You have a right to debate the bill legitimately, and if you can gather support, you can then negotiate provisions of the bill."

7. To quote the legislator Lockyer: "One thing you learn in politics is the fluidity of coalitions—that an opponent today is going to be an ally the next year."

8. In their unique and compelling textbook, John C. Livingston and Robert G. Thompson characterize legislative restraint as "brokerage," whose "cardinal rule will be inoffensiveness. . . . The basic rule of the game is that no important interest may be adversely affected without its consent" (*The Consent of the Governed*, 2d ed. [New York: Macmillan, 1963], p. 88). I think they neglect to make the case for the value of mutual trust among contending social interests.

might finesse the governor's defenses today, he was going to be dependent on the governor tomorrow. For that reason he never stopped talking with the administration about its concerns, strove to do it favors in return, and honored his bested but worthy adversary with true dignity.

VII

A third interesting bill, the Wild Rivers Bill, was authored by a Republican. It was an important bill, regulatory in nature, that forbade hydroelectric development on three major northern California rivers: the Eel, the Klamath, and the Trinity. Its author was an environmentalist, a transplanted New Yorker, and an Ivy League lawyer in his sixties named Peter Behr. Like many of his Republican colleagues, and in contrast to most Democrats, he came to politics and the legislature late in life. While his age gave him savoir faire and the assurance of a veteran, he had no experience in the legislative process. He got his basic education in it because the Wild Rivers Bill was a key piece of legislation on the agenda of the Sierra Club and other environmental groups.

The trouble was that the rivers Behr was seeking to protect ran through the legislative district of Senator Randy Collier. Collier was a politician of the old school, and represented a rural district whose geographical extent exceeded the area of half the states of the union. He resented the environmental thrust of the bill, the temerity of its freshman author, and the fact that a colleague was poaching on his turf. Besides, he was the chairman of senate appropriations, a senator of thirty-five years' experience, and an astute student of human conflict.

Behr summarized the heart of the battle:

> It was in the second year of the session, and Collier held the bill in senate appropriations to the point where I then risked the bill dying simply because time had run out. The problem was, How do you get him to put the bill out in time? How do you object to his actions and his delaying the time for its hearing so that it outrages the consciences of everybody, but not so late that you endanger the bill? Finally, I called a press conference—to protest the conduct of the old man and his unfair handling of the bill. The next day he set it. Collier called a conference of his own and said he was surprised at all the hue and outcry and that these "amateurs" had thought that he

would not set the bill, when he had intended to all the time. He was wonderful; he really shadowboxed and made it look like he was wonderful. But I had already gone to the president pro tem, and he would not help. So our timing was really crucial.

The Wild Rivers Bill, once past the committee Collier controlled, went on to be passed.

Several matters about this case should be noted. First, the bill did not require appropriations, and hence it could pass the senate with a mere majority. It did, twenty-one to nineteen. In California authors who pressed for state regulation had an easier procedural course to run than authors who pressed for spending programs.

Second, even though the Wild Rivers Bill called only for regulation, it still had to run its course through appropriations as well as the relevant policy committees. The parliamentary rule was that if any bill imposed additional duties on any state agency, appropriations was to look at it. Since this bill gave some new tasks to the Fish and Game Commission, the bill had to survive at least seven points of decision—three in each house and the governor's veto decision. Failure at any one of them amounted to a permanent defeat. Senator Collier wanted to stop the legislation in the committee he chaired because then the bill would never reach the floor despite the wishes of a majority that it do so. If, however, Collier missed in his own committee, he had several more points where he had a chance to defeat the bill. To Behr, Collier seemed to lurk everywhere—in the assembly committees, on the floor, and in the governor's office, seeking to undo Behr's work if Behr were not constantly alert.

Third, managing the Wild Rivers Bill imposed significant responsibilities on Behr. He was the general in command of every organization behind the bill, from the Sierra Club on down. He marshaled his forces, which meant getting lots of "amateurs" to appear in Sacramento, contacting influential friends throughout the state, and compelling the media to support his efforts. He applied his pressure at the right time, creating popular support that obliged Senator Collier, one of the most formidable political figures in the state, to "put the bill out in time."

The ultimate dependence of a legislator on popular support was the most important lesson of the event. Persons in democratic politics like Behr could make progress, but only if they brought their people with them and worked to unite them. Leadership in a democracy, above all, implied doing things publicly, with all the pain and sweat such openness entailed. Secrecy did not work, because when formidable political opposition materialized, there was no knowledgeable popular backing to neutralize it. If in the legislature the weaker were to be given as fair a deal as the more powerful, as Madison observed, then the weaker had to unite and gather public support. The price of public support was public scrutiny. Scrutiny kept legislators fair, for it let opposition be heard, but it also provided an opportunity to make oneself heard. The job of a democratic politician was to teach and persuade, and there was often no tomorrow if he failed to persist in that never-ending task.

Behr summed up what he had learned from his encounter with Senator Collier:

> I have always thought that if a bill is truly worthwhile it will never win the first time. You first have to create an outside constituency. That's what the first time through is all about. Then that constituency must begin to create an inside constituency, and as that strengthens and grows, your chances improve. But it takes persistence and wisdom to understand this.

A democratic leader is only as strong as the focused strength of his people's convictions. He therefore has to build entire coalitions.

VIII

In the author system legislators learned what I have called a love of justice—of negotiating fairly through an open, conflict-ridden process. They absorbed the art and science of managing human conflict. They practiced three major skills, and they digested the reasons for the necessity for them. The first skill related to the exercise of pressure. We have seen that reducing adverse balances of power and extending honor to a defeated adversary were important to Sieroty's success. Lockyer had to overcome the oil producers' feelings of invulnerability. Had he been incompetent and lacked the governor's support, the oil lobbyists and the state bureaucracies might simply have ignored him and his need for critical knowledge about oil—knowledge that proved essential to the passage of this bill. Collier considered Behr an adversary unworthy of notice until Behr's skillfully called press conference imperiled Collier's reputation. Each author fought against opposition and won. In contrast, there were legislators who never won. A bill in their hands could be ignored; they floundered, and they never learned how to even out unfavorable balances of power. Often only those outside the legislature could apply the necessary pressure on a bill's adversaries. Thus, uniting outside constituencies and focusing their force, as Behr did, was a second crucial skill. Mobilizing trade association leaders, journalists, and fellow legislators was important not only to gain victory but to secure it. Legislative advocacy was not like winning a case in court, where a particular jury verdict convicts or acquits once and for all. Even after a bill like the Wild Rivers legislation was signed into law, nothing prevented destructive amendments from being introduced the next year. In controversial legislative matters it was the development of a favorable public opinion that would finally give a democratic leader occasion to rest from his labors.[9]

And finally there was compromise—the compromise that consolidated a legislative advance, materialized hopes into law, secured honor for adversaries, and gained the time necessary for outside constituencies to test their confidence in the handiwork of their democratic leaders.[10]

The author system thus supplemented the skills of patriotism learned in the committee system. While the committee system educated legislators in analytic skills[11] and empathy, it did not teach

9. The best legislators always pressed this point: "But the answer is, no matter how difficult it is to work with the public viewing everything you do, I think the rabble eventually does do a good job in making up its mind. They affect us in strange ways—directly and indirectly—and you had better bring them along with you."

10. See T. V. Smith, "Compromise: Its Context and Limits," *Ethics*, October 1942, pp. 1ff. See also T. V. Smith, *Discipline for Democracy* (Chapel Hill, N.C.: University of North Carolina Press, 1942) and *The Legislative Way of Life* (Chicago: University of Chicago Press, 1940).

11. Of course, an effective author had to have analytic skills and had to be ready to use them extemporaneously. He had to listen for the unstated assumptions of the opposing interest groups. I remember a meeting in which the industrial and labor lobbyists confronted one another over the issue of eligibility for unemployment insurance. The legislative author of the bill at issue perceived the stereotypes in the two lobbyists' minds. On the one hand, the business lobbyist, without saying so, was envisioning the in-and-out housewife reaping an unemployment insurance bonanza: in his mind was a woman who worked in a cannery for two months and then returned home to her family household, drawing in unemployment benefits for the succeeding ten months. The labor lobbyist, on the other hand, was imagining a Chicano employee working under sweatshop conditions, someone whose boss carefully calculated the day he would fire the employee in order to avoid incurring unemployment insurance obligations. As long as these stereotypes remained unstated, no agreement was possible. A legislator who was a good author could uncover those beliefs and make them proper subjects for mutual discussion. As the stereotypes faded, the parties frequently found that they were not so far apart as they had originally thought.

the three political skills of employing pressure, building coalitions, and securing a compromise. The author system did that. It taught how to practice human justice in a free society—how to play the broker's part, how to negotiate a fair give and take with guarantees of due process. It exercised what the political scientist Eugene Bardach has called "the skill factor in politics."[12]

12. Eugene Bardach, *The Skill Factor in Politics: Repealing the Mental Commitment Laws in California* (Berkeley, California: University of California Press, 1972).

Four

It can't be overemphasized, the significance of the specialist.
Assemblyman Bill Lockyer, 1976

It's not money that determines a man's place in the government
sun; it's what he *knows* that nobody else does.
Governor Edmund G. (Pat) Brown, 1967

How the Specialist System Taught Wisdom

Assemblyman Jerry Lewis, a Republican from southern California, looked out his office window, and he smiled as he recollected:

When I first came up here, we were just building a new movement and eliminating the old guard. Even then it was not accepted that new members spent time with old senators. I went over and watched senate transportation committee meetings, and I got exposed to the well-known senior member of that committee, Randy Collier. At that time he was having problems with his personal life, and he was spending lots of time in his office in the evening. And every night he would have ten to twelve people—highway people, lobbyists for truckers, people like that—in his office to talk. And I got in the habit of going down the hall and entering in. I just watched, and soon I had an open invitation to come anytime. One night we were by ourselves; no one showed up, and that night he felt open and expansive.

He turned to me. He said, "I assume you intend to stay around here and that you intend to do more than just get re-elected. I would hope, Jerry, that you will choose not to have answers to all the problems, that you will find maybe two or three problems which affect your district and go to work on them.

"Imagine that this wall is a huge mural," he said, "and you have a responsibility for a part of that mural. You want to make a puzzle out of your part of it. Every bill you introduce is like a piece of that puzzle. You want to think five and ten years down

81

the line so that, one piece at a time, that puzzle gets assembled. I hope you will select two or three areas which affect your district and slowly become the master of them so that you know more than some of those smartass young consultants of the committees. You've got to do some homework over the long haul."

II

"Over the long haul" the legislature led some of its members into specialties and gave them an individual responsibility for one area of California's public policy. Like students majoring in a discipline, legislative specialists concentrated their attentions on a few problems so that they might "slowly become the master of them." They made their expertise available to the membership of the legislature if it was wanted. They were also continuously contributing a train of measures into the legislative educational process. As they introduced one piece after another to complete their "puzzle" of public policy, they taught their colleagues the real importance of their specialty. The legislature as a whole was thus leavened by an elite of leading legislators, who gave the institution its confidence and its special character. They populated the specialist system, and it was the specialist system that permitted an individual to learn how to make a real difference in the world wisely.

III

Five basic ideas are essential to understanding the specialist system as it functioned in California. First is the notion of "turf," the area of specialization. There were big and little turfs. A specialist might ramble about in a vast expanse like social welfare or sit happily within the esoteric confines of the Improvement Act of 1911. Moreover, some turfs were jealously guarded, "staked out," with No Poaching signs posted all over them, while other turfs were governed by more than one sovereign, usually from different parties or generations, and seemed to offer unlimited access. Some specialists had only one turf; most had more than one in which they were expert, and many expanded the bounds of each a little bit each year. Specialists were not "whirlwinds," hopping from turf to turf; rather, they expanded into adjacent areas—from energy to energy and environment, from jobs for the able-bodied to jobs for the totally disabled. The basic limits on the size and the number of turfs a specialist had depended on his own intellectual abilities. As one specialist put it,

> There's no way you can roam the field and have any proficiency. Take education and educational financing. It's a complicated area of the law. I don't believe there are more than five people in both houses who really understand it. There is just no way I could carry legislation in that area and work in local government and work in water at the same time.

Turfs were self-defined by individual capacity.

The second critical notion is that of mastery. Mastery related to the level of knowledge a specialist had about his turf. We might call these different levels first-degree, second-degree, and third-degree, from the superficial to the profound. A first-degree level of knowledge came from legislative sources—a lobbyist or "one of those smart-ass young consultants of the committees," as Senator Collier referred to them. The sources themselves were not direct observers of government and society. Rather, they had read the works of others or had been told by direct participants. We saw that the bankers' lobbyist Ratcliff was prepped by real bankers. Likewise, committee consultants crammed their heads quickly with the observations of others. First-degree sources analyzed the knowledge of others. They might be—and often were—excellent. They taught the vocabulary of the policy area and framed the big issues. Their knowledge, however, was vicarious, based on experiences remote from their immediate lives. First-degree knowledge was the grist of the committee system's educational process.

Second-degree sources were organizational. Knowledge from second-degree sources came from and largely concerned the bureaucrats of government and industry, the persons on the administrative firing lines. They knew directly the problems of implementing government and corporate plans. They had the capacity to teach how dollars translated into personnel and effective operation. They knew the functioning of nurses and teachers and regulators and highway snow-removers and contractors who rebuilt old cities. Second-degree sources knew about shortage of money, about laws and their effects on an organization's efforts to perform. A legislator could get second-degree knowledge from immediate observation of the organization as well as from talking with people who made such observations themselves, and with second-degree knowledge one could get a feeling for the skill or corruptness or confusion of administrators. Second-degree knowledge gave a legislator a confident feeling for organizations that could not be obtained from an exclusive dependence on lobbyists' and consultants' glosses on reality. Second-degree knowledge was often divulged through the author system.[1]

Finally, there was third-degree knowledge, which legislators described as "an understanding or feeling for the people affected by the services." Third-degree knowledge came from and concerned the citizenry. It spoke not to how smoothly organizations were operating but to the real effect of those organizations. The sources of third-degree knowledge stemmed from direct observations of society. The legislator actually observed the lives of people, whether they were silent or assertive. Mastery was having all three degrees of knowledge, but especially the third degree.

Jerry Lewis, the young assemblyman whom we quoted at the beginning of the chapter, gave an example of third-degree knowledge of disabled children:

> To have an understanding or feeling for the people . . . affected by the services, or of how the money was spent and with what effect, you have to concentrate yourself. . . .
> During the recess I went back to the district. My wife [who is a psychiatric social worker, had me] take a look at a particular child day-care center for disabled children—one that was organized in a home. This home day-care program was an effort to avoid institutionalizing the handicapped child who for some reason had been abandoned by his or her family. Well, this home had six children being cared for. It was a beautiful home, and it was clear that the owner was really caring for these children. They were all home the first time I came. There was one little girl, exceptionally pretty, I remember. She obviously enjoyed the love she was receiving there. She was mentally retarded, and she also had some physical handicaps.

1. Assemblyman Jack Fenton gave an example of the importance of second-degree knowledge. In the wake of a tunnel construction accident, Fenton conducted an investigation of how the state industrial safety agency actually made its decisions to prosecute safety violations or to drop charges. He discovered that "each decision to prosecute was reviewed by the next highest layer; if the decision was not to prosecute, that ended it." With second-degree knowledge of the agency's actual practices, Fenton could legislate an appropriate remedy: "We turned it around. If any layer *disapproved* of criminal action, then the decision would go right to the top. When prosecution was turned down, that would trigger review by the higher-ups."

Another child was a five-year-old who weighed eighty-five pounds and just lay on the floor.

There were also three emotionally hyperactive children. The woman who cared for these kids was an exceptional person. For the last eight years she had worked seven days a week, twenty-four hours a day, 365 days a year. She was always on call. If she wanted relief, she had to have a registered nurse to give the care and medical attention that she gave every day. In those eight years she had never had a holiday, even Christmas and Thanksgiving, because the competent help she would need was not available. For this she got paid $440 per month per child, out of which she paid all the expenses of the children's care. Yet every month she had four social workers who came by to check on her. They all come by every month, yet essentially they do the same things—to check to see things are done properly. One comes all the way out from Los Angeles County. She checks on the littlest girl. Apparently her mother works, and her father was a lawyer. Well, after the child was born, the lawyer went over the hill when he found his girl was a limited child. The mother got the county to send the child to a private home in Los Angeles, but apparently it went bankrupt, and the little girl was transferred to this lady out in Riverside. It's been eight years, and Los Angeles still sends a social worker one day a month to check on the child. Here's a case where in the law there is not enough flexibility to permit the transfer of the child outside the county line to a really good home.

There are twelve other agencies involved with the six children as well. OSHA, the whole kit and caboodle. Now, some would say $2,500 a month paid to one family amounts to really ripping off the system, and the matter has to be checked out. The fact is, it's just the reverse. Where we are spending the money is not on the lady providing the services, but on the people up above who are checking on her—nothing more. I didn't know about that stuff—wouldn't have if I had wanted to even, until I decided to concentrate my attention.

Mastery was a knowledge of the interstices of policy, the microprocesses and their relationship to the big issues. It came from focusing one's attention on the world outside the capitol's corridors.

The third notion necessary to understand the specialist system is the idea of legislative subpoena power. In preceding chapters we discussed the importance of two of the three great resources that legislators had—the vote and the bill-carrying privilege. The third and last of the three powers on which the legislative education depended was the subpoena. The subpoena enabled legislators to compel any citizen to give testimony and to disclose physical evidence, on pain of imprisonment.

The subpoena was the legal basis of the "oversight function" of the legislature. It enabled legislators to supervise governmental bureaucracy and to find out why, in one legislator's phrase, "government does not function the way you'd like it to run." The subpoena power was the legal right to obtain information that would otherwise have remained hidden.

As a formal matter the subpoena power rarely had to be invoked to compel persons to tell their stories truthfully. It simply lurked in the background to ensure habits of cooperation and forthrightness.[2] No one in California, except the governor, could legally resist the legislative subpoena.[3] Everyone else was fair game and knew it.

If a legislator was brassy or aggressive enough, there was no escape from his inquiry into a mine disaster, corrupt administration, the way in which departmental funds were spent, or the reasoning behind a railroad fare increase. To the specialist with an interest in gathering accurate second- and third-degree knowledge, the subpoena was the equivalent of the scholar's stack privilege in a fine library. It made available rare sources of reason and fact.

The subpoena used the threat of imprisonment to uncover private matters. For that reason, in a free country, the subpoena was granted judiciously, eyed jealously, and used sparingly. The California Constitution made it available to only five groups: (1) criminal defendants; (2) the Public Utilities Commission; (3) the grand jury; (4) the legislature; and (5) legislative committees. Others—presidents, governors, judges acting on their own initiative, ombudsmen, county supervisors, city council members, large corporate executives—were

2. Republican assemblyman Dixon Arnett, the most acute student of the subpoena power in the assembly, remarked: "The subpoena power is rarely used. When we did hearings on the Southern Pacific rate increase, Southern Pacific would not send its chief counsel. So we started by calling everyone in sight, and the next day there was the chief counsel, ready to testify."

3. At the federal level a recent practice has been to protect the presidential staff—maybe seventy-five assistants in all—through the doctrine of executive privilege. Members of the Domestic Council and the National Security Council, for example, have no obligation to respond to congressional subpoenas. No such practice has been instituted in California regarding the governor's staff.

not privileged to exercise the subpoena power unless the legislature gave it to them.

Since subpoena powers were granted not to individual legislators but only to legislative committees, specialists who needed the subpoena tended to want to be chairmen of committees. As such they could initiate any reasonable use of the subpoena power without raising objections. Of course, in standing committees with large memberships, a chairman's power was subject to considerable scrutiny and, theoretically, to a legal check. In the small, special committees, appointed ad hoc to pursue a particular subject matter, however, this kind of external restraint on the subpoena power was weakened, and there was much greater reliance on the integrity of the specialist.

The fourth notion essential to understanding the specialist system is that a specialist pulled a "train of measures" slowly through the legislature. Year after year a specialist would introduce bills in the same specialized area. Problems never disappeared completely. If state funding were required, for example, the annual appropriations process required a specialist's constant attention lest his area of concern lose legislative support. Any legislator who specialized in education no sooner had secured this year's funding than he was immersed in next year's budgeting. Solutions to problems, especially big solutions to big problems, created new matters to attend to. Every proposal had an "upside" and a "downside." Once a bill was legislated, the specialist's job was to devise ways to minimize the downside with follow-up legislation. ("The major cause of problems is solutions," said the commentator Eric Severeid, not cynically, but in recognition that public policies were chosen not because they were panaceas but because the good they did outweighed the bad.) Finally, legislative proposals quickened expectations: the remedy accomplished in one area highlighted the needs in adjacent areas. By concerning himself with a woman's right to adequate pregnancy care, for example, a legislator soon found himself wondering whether pregnant women should get fully paid leave from their government jobs during the immediate pre- and postnatal periods. Lobbyists were attracted to this sort of specialist.

The short of it was that legislative specialists, by choice and by necessity, were the workhorses of the legislature. They dominated the author system. They wrote whole sections of the statute books, often in bits and pieces, often over a decade, adding a part here, a part there. Legislatures gave public policy a stability and a continuity because specialist legislators often served a long time.[4]

The fifth notion is expertise. Unlike mastery—the intellectual understanding of the social consequences of legislation—expertise meant political skill in building enduring coalitions within and outside of the legislature.[5] Expertise consisted of practical knowledge, not theoretical knowledge. It was the proficiency of an executive, for specialists were coordinators of others. The specialist's expertise did not lie in knowing more physics than the scientist Edward Teller, more about the environment than the Sierra Club, more economics than Southern California Edison, more demographics than population scholars, or even more vocabulary than a committee consultant. His expertise was knowing that all these things were related, and his special competence lay in relating a host of experts to one another. Over the long haul he played the role of communicator. He was like the famous telephone switchboard in Chester Barnard's book on the functions of the executive.[6] Standing at the center of a network of

4. The average number of years served in the state legislature by senators holding office in 1975–76 was twelve and a half years, and by members of the assembly seven and a half years. Twenty of the senators had fourteen or more years of legislative service under their belts. Twenty-eight members of the assembly had spent ten or more years in the assembly. Another indication of the longevity of California state legislators was that sixteen legislators, nearly fifteen percent of the entire membership of the legislature in 1976, were serving in the legislature in the 1950s.

5. Compare David S. Broder's comment on the importance of coalition-building skills: "what has been most conspicuously lacking at the federal level and in most of the states, as well, during the past decade has not been conscientious and capable performance by individual officeholders, but rather a government capable of delivering on its threats and promises. . . . What we need . . . are people in government who understand the need for coalition-building. We need people who have the skills of negotiation and compromise, the insights, the articulateness, and the boldness to overcome the centrifugal forces tugging government in this hyper-pluralistic age" (*San Francisco Chronicle*, 28 November 1979).

6. Chester I. Barnard, *The Functions of the Executive* (Cambridge: Harvard University Press, 1938), p. 178: "For the function of the center of communication in an organization is to translate incoming communications concerning external conditions, the progress of activity, successes, failures, difficulties, dangers, into outgoing communications in terms of new activities, preparatory steps, etc., all shaped according to the ultimate as well as the immediate purposes to be served. There is accordingly required more or less mastery of the technologies involved, of the capabilities of the personnel, of the informal organization situation, of the character and status of the subsidiary organizations, of the principles and action relative to purpose, of the interpretation of environmental factors, and a power of discrimination between communications that can possess authority because they are recognizably compatible with all the pertinent conditions and those which will not possess authority because they will not or cannot be accepted."

individuals, whom he was always connecting with one another, he built large and enduring coalitions of people who would otherwise have been strangers. He recruited talent, translated messages, brokered need and supply, designed strategy, elicited social reaction, and communicated matters. He was always a highly visible switch by means of which the public might galvanize this network of experts.

It is crucial to get a feeling for the importance of the specialist system and how it educated legislators to take on a "responsibility for a part of . . . the whole legislative process." This can best be done by listening at length to the premier specialist in the assembly, a Republican named Frank Lanterman, in his account of his experiences—keeping in mind the five notions of the specialist system: turf, mastery, oversight, workhorsemanship, and expertise in coalition-building. Here was democratic statecraft at its best.

IV

Imagine a fifty-year-old bachelor businessman, head of a small, family-owned water company, who was so provoked by harmful governmental action affecting the water supply of his community that he ran for legislative office in order to undo the damage. Picture him, this Don Quixote of private water companies, astride a laboring, creaking passenger train crawling over the Tehachapis and up the great valley and bringing him to Sacramento for the first time. All the while he was dreaming of tilting at the windmill of state and liberating his people from the burden of feeding its vanity and appetite.

Such was the picture Lanterman drew of himself as he reflected on what he was like in 1951 as a freshman legislator. "I did not come up for politics. I came here fighting politics." At the beginning of his sophomore term, however, the chairmanship of the welfare committee opened up, "a dog of a committee" then as now, which he took because

> at the time I was a conservative, and I voted no on everything that had a dollar sign on it. I wanted no expenditures of public funds . . . programs costing hundreds of millions of dollars every year passed through the scrutiny of the committee, and I thought it needed someone who had an eye for the buck.

The committee chairmanship gave him the authority to issue a subpoena and enabled him to oversee the welfare bureaucracy.

Unfortunately "for the buck," however, the very first witness to appear before Lanterman's committee was the state director of mental hygiene. Lanterman recalled the moment.

And he said, "I plead with your committee to give the persons committed to our hospitals some nutriment. The people in our mental hospitals get nothing to eat other than surplus food—beans and what have you. There is an utter lack of variety. If we could just give them some fruit or fruit juice, just once in a while, something to give hope to these people, even that would help." That was my first exposure to the problem of the mentally ill. I asked, "You mean it?" It gave me a jolt. "You mean there are still insane asylums?" "They changed the name," he said, "but little else."

Getting a glimpse of the nutrition problems of the mentally ill prompted Lanterman to take a second look at the broader problems of their existence. He was transformed from a conservative ideologue who wanted to stop spending no matter what the consequences, to an ardent advocate for the mentally ill: the issue for him ceased to be the level of expenditures, and became rather whether the state got its money's worth. His concern "for the buck" was transformed into seeing that the mentally ill got maximum assistance for the buck.

Respected friends and informed exposure transformed him. The process began with a hearing on a bill to transfer most of the responsibility for funding welfare from local to state governments.

Then up showed Charles Schottland. He was a retired New York Jew, affable, looked like a refined Kissinger, a fine grade human being, nice sense of humor. He brought in a totally disabled bill on behalf of the governor. Now that kind of bill was anathema to the tax boys. Well, Charley persuaded me that this would give county taxpayers some money. It would take the totally disabled off the indigent rolls of the county. I said to him, "Let me look at the bill." It was the kind of bill that had no controls in it and could end up as an endless drain. But I worked at it, and cut it clean down to the Wisconsin model, to which we could attach the Wisconsin regulations, which were very tight, and then I made it a pilot program. Well, we got it on the floor, and the Taxpayers Association and the Chamber of Commerce had kittens. I simply got up and said, "This will

save county taxpayers millions of dollars if it works. And we'll
learn from a pilot program whether that's so or not." Well, it
went sailing through the assembly. . . , but it was killed in the
senate. But, nevertheless, we had learned a lot as a result. It
happened this way: I had the director of charities, Arthur Will,
look at the totally disabled bill. . . . His son was superintendent
of hospitals in Los Angeles County. I went down to see him on
the totally disabled bill to get some support for it on the senate
side. He told me, "I wouldn't touch that thing with a ten-foot
pole." "Why not?" I asked. "Getting involved with the totally
disabled means you will get involved with the mentally ill, and
that's a sink. You can't deal with the mentally ill in this state.
You have a code which is barbaric and inhumane. You are
looking into a bucket of worms. The welfare code is
consequentially irrelevant, inhuman, reprehensible legislation,
jerry-built with unrelated and contradictory provisions. It has
never been rebuilt or recodified, and it never will because it is
acceptable to the judiciary and the legal profession and the
medical profession." "You mean it's a legal tool to cover up
mistakes?" "That's right." "Then, get off your butt, and come
up and talk about it yourself. We'll get something set up to look
into it, an interim committee hearing."

Thus began a complete revision of the welfare and institutions code
that would take many years to complete.

Interim committee hearings in California were held from October
to December of each year. They permitted legislative committees to
go into topics in depth. Staff usually developed substantial background papers; witnesses were invited to testify on matters on which
they had admitted competence; and written transcripts of all the
proceedings were kept. Lanterman described the effect of the hearings on the legislators:

As chairman of the welfare committee, I got a resolution
through Rules for an interim hearing. And out of it came a
study from Los Angeles County. At that time the county was
way ahead of most counties in that its officials did not indulge
in committing seniles under the guise that they were psychotic.
. . . Well, Los Angeles, through their resolute and active county
counsel, Harold Kennedy, agreed to put a chief deputy and two
assistant deputies to work to do a recodification of the welfare
and institutions code. They formed a committee, and how they
worked. They organized symposiums of judges, doctors, nurses,

social workers, everyone involved in the field, and when it was done they had come up with a bill—a monumental bill, AB 3300. Boy, it really hit the fan. All the bill said, in effect, was that for local health care there would be a screening device, and people with emotional storms would be brought to a psychiatric ward and processed and would be given medical and nursing care, and if they responded, they could be released and allowed to return home without a commitment. People with emotional storms would be treated no differently than any other person with an illness that was curable. If it was possible that nursing and medical care could reduce their troubles, then they could go home, and no yellow ticket would be filed in the record [to indicate] a mentally incompetent person.

In the bill itself we had to put the old welfare and institutions code, and that meant that all the brutalities of the old code were there to be seen. We had to show them what the old law was. At that time we had a bunch of witch-hunters in the legislature who were always looking for communists under every desk. And they looked at the bill and shouted, "Berea and Russia: people knocking on the door at night and taking people away without a hearing." They thought that we were trying to put this over on them. I eventually said, "You assholes, that's the law already. We're trying to change it." They never understood, I guess. It was quite a hilarious situation.

At that time Dr. Lowrey was head of Mental Hygiene. He had just come out from the east to run our Department of Mental Health. He had great credentials, and I remember he came to appropriations one day on a little bill. Waldie [later Congressman Jerome Waldie] and [State Senator Nick] Petris were there, and so after Dr. Lowrey had talked about his matter, I said,"Dr. Lowrey, may I ask you a question? In your estimate, how many laws are on the statute books which inhibit a person being committed from exercising his rights to protect himself?" "Oh, a dozen, I would say." "Well, can you get me a résumé of them? And what would you do with them?" "I'd have every one abolished," he said. "All of them?" "All of them." Waldie leaned over to me and said, "Did you hear that?" "Of course, I did, you nitwit; that's why I asked it." And Dr. Lowrey did. And out of it came a study which would curl your hair. It was called *Dilemma of Mental Commitment*. It was the first breakthrough on the problem. It was an attack on the system of mental health care. And that was the genesis of the Lanterman-Petris-Short Act. I'll never forget asking those

men—judges, lawyers—how commitment occurred. "Do you
mean to tell me that you can decide without evidence?" One
public defender said to us, "Everybody knew he was nuts."
"How did you protect the rights of the man while he was being
adjudicated that he was nuts, as you so delicately put it? How
long did it take you to figure out that he was nuts?" "Oh,
about three or four minutes." . . . That's how we got the
Magna Carta of the mentally ill. That's the term of Judge
Karesh from San Francisco. I had invited him earlier to come
up and testify before our committee on commitment problems.
He really got his catechism. We were seated in the judgment
seat, and we asked him a lot of embarrassing questions. Finally,
he got really emotional. "I admit it. I admit I have committed
people illegally because there was nothing else to do with them.
But I swear to you that after I leave this room, I'll never do it
again. If this bill is passed, it will be the Magna Carta of the
mentally ill." It was a very emotional moment.

Thus the state legislature developed Frank Lanterman into a specialist in mental health, a man who devoted a quarter of a century
to reshaping a huge part of California's public policy. Against his
every expectation, Lanterman took up the challenge of a single citizen
to take charge of the legislative turf on which the institutions for the
mentally ill were established. He sank deeper and deeper into an
understanding of the area. At first ignorant even of the vocabulary
of the mental health profession ("You mean there are still insane
asylums?"), he plunged into an examination of the practices of the
bureaucracy administering the welfare code ("You mean, it's a legal
tool to cover up mistakes?"), and thence into third-degree sources
of knowledge, seeing the policy from the perspective of the mentally
ill ("a study which would curl your hair"). Obtaining evidence by
cooperation and compulsion, he chaired legislative committee after
legislative committee to rebuild the system into one that would provide better nutrition, better financing structures, better judicial commitment procedures, better medical practice, and more appropriations.[7]

7. For example, in 1975, a year when the governor effectively beat back every other
legislative effort to augment a very meager budget, Lanterman, a member of the
minority party, succeeded. As chairman of the appropriations subcommittee on the
health and welfare component of the budget bill, Lanterman persuaded the full
committee, the assembly, the senate, and finally even the governor himself to augment
the original budget proposal by (1) $65.2 million for welfare grants to the aged, blind,
and disabled; (2) $15.7 million for local mental health services; (3) $11.6 million for
the homemakers/chore program; (4) $10 million for Medicaid rate increases so that

The more reforms Lanterman initiated, the more unfinished business he created. Pieces of public policy, like parts of a puzzle, had to be joined to adjacent pieces. To avoid consigning "people with emotional storms" to the oblivion of state mental hospitals, he had to establish in law both the concept and the actuality of outpatient clinics to which upset citizens could go to receive medical and nursing care without being committed. Furthermore, in sprawling cities like Los Angeles he had to propose and implement community clinics, ones stationed away from the main office downtown—a new concept of decentralization in the field. He also had to induce the state to develop inpatient services in local hospitals for those who needed them temporarily. He had to adapt the professional practices of doctors and psychiatric personnel to work in the unorthodox system of temporary care facilities. He had to make judges aware of the availability of the new community mental health centers, and in correcting judicial ideas about commitment, Lanterman found that the practices of probate conservatorship, which dealt with the property of the mentally ill, were so slipshod as to provide little protection against the greed and negligence of the conservators. And so on. The problem of the mentally ill was a true "sink," a hollow in need of boundless legal fill—enough of a task to consume a legislative lifetime.

All the time Lanterman was standing prominently at the heart of a team of good persons—welfare reformer Schottland, the governor, welfare director Will, the superintendent of the Los Angeles County hospitals, Assemblyman Waldie, State Senator Petris, County Counsel Kennedy, State Mental Health Director Lowrey, Judge Karesh. Lanterman prodded, encouraged, coordinated, and galvanized them into active contributions to the program.[8]

---

nursing homes could implement the higher standards of care mandated by Lanterman legislation; (5) $5 million for the developmentally disabled; (6) $1.7 million for crippled children's services; and (7) $300,000 for nutrition services for the elderly. As Lanterman said of his decision not to retire: "In my seventy-fourth year I am . . . a little worried with my decision to run again, that they must be asking, 'Do you have to shoot the old geezer to get rid of him?' But I just felt that we had to keep an eye on Jerry Junior [Governor Brown]. He made me realize there was some unfinished business—keeping established programs from being desecrated by the governor. . . ." There was always "unfinished business" left for the specialist.

8. Like most chroniclers of historical events, Lanterman revealed only a part of the story about mental commitments in California. But his hyperbole, selective vision, and delicate treatment of personal mistakes notwithstanding, Lanterman's account does not appreciably differ from the sensitive observations of Eugene Bardach, who adjudged the assemblyman's job of implementing his vision as "superlatively"

V

The specialist system had important consequences, five of which are worth mentioning briefly.

First, a specialist who could prove his competence became a person to respect. The news of his prowess entered the legislative grapevine, and other legislators took cues from him on how to vote on proposals within his specialty. There was a lot of cue-taking in the California legislature, and the cues came, in large part, not from the political leadership or from lobbyists, but from someone within the specialized intellectual leadership (because, as former Governor Pat Brown said, such a person "*knows* [what] nobody else does").[9] The specialist system provided what James Madison had hoped for, a buffer of intelligence that cooled the passions of society before they disrupted the organs of government.

Second, a competent specialist freed his fellow legislators to concentrate their energies and to develop specialties of their own, in large part because they had no fears about "going along" with a legislator reliable in his area.[10] Thus a division of labor developed, each specialist exchanging his specialized skills for the disciplined learning of others. As a result, the legislature did a lot of work intelligently. It processed, as I said earlier, 7,000 bills in two years, enacted 2,500 laws, approved annual expenditures up to $25,000,000,000, policed large bureaucracies, accommodated constituent problems, got its members reelected with all the public education electoral success implied, and still avoided substantial pitfalls and mistakes. An unspecialized legislature could not have been so successful.

---

done. I have always loved Bardach's working definition of "implementation" as what Lanterman did: "he 'oversaw,' 'intervened,' 'followed up,' 'corrected,' 'expanded,' 'overhauled,' 'protected,' and so forth." See Eugene Bardach, *The Implementation Game: What Happens After a Bill Becomes a Law* (Cambridge, Mass., MIT Press, 1977), pp. 297, 31. See also Eugene Bardach, *The Skill Factor in Politics*, chap. 5.

9. Cue-taking was epitomized by Assemblyman Knox's remark about his vote on juvenile justice legislation: "Whatever Julian Dixon says, I'll go along." Governor Edmund Brown's remarks appeared in the Los Angeles *Times* of 27 February 1967.

10. Trusting one's colleagues not to do something improper or inferior permitted specialists to give complete attention to their own domain of public policy. In this respect the comment of an astute freshman legislator took on added meaning: "It's also beneficial to the legislature, especially if that individual with the expertise goes about building trust and confidence in his colleagues, if he can establish the faith that he knows what he's doing."

Third, the specialist system made for better popular understanding of governmental policies. The test of the specialist was the "backgrounder": could he explain matters clearly to the layman journalist? If he could, the press would return to him whenever it was ignorant or uncertain. The specialist benefited from the publicity, and the public gained from the dissemination of his explanations.[11] The press, then, came to the specialist, not for an opinion, but for an understanding of the field. Because even the most inexperienced journalist could write a fairly accurate article if he talked with a specialist like Lanterman, popular understanding was likely to improve.

Fourth, the specialist system made possible the effective overseeing of the massive California state bureaucracies. Max Weber, the great student of bureaucracy, once made a gloomy prediction that as modern bureaucracies became more competent, bureaucratic politics would increasingly determine policy.[12] That is, the preferences of bureaucrats, not the interests of the public, would set policy. Bureaucrats, Weber worried, would become more powerful than the politically elected official because of their superior competence in their specialties. A legislative specialist like Lanterman, however, could offset the bureaucratic edge: an expert legislator could play the knowledgeable critic.

Legislative competence alone was not sufficient to assure effective surveillance. Courage, intelligence, a sense of decency, and perseverance were indispensable ingredients. But without legislative knowledge, all the other virtues would prove ineffectual to check the intellectual, and hence the political, advantages that bureaucracies possessed.

Finally, the advantages of federalism materialized through the specialist system. California's "leading legislators" participated in an interstate network of fellow legislative specialists. The education

11. The Republican Arnett talked of the pedagogical function of the specialist: "it does give you some exposure in the way of publicity. . . . The press comes to you. Journalists interview you in matters of [your specialty] . . . you get a broader exposure, and if you are a political person who loves the challenge, who likes the action, who aspires to higher offices, that's a good thing."

12. Max Weber, *Wirtschaft und Gesellschaft*, part 3, chap. 6, in H. H. Gerth and C. Wright Mills (eds. and trans.), *From Max Weber: Essays in Sociology*. Weber writes, for example: "Under normal conditions, the power position of a fully developed bureaucracy is always overtowering. The 'political master' finds himself in the position of the 'dilettante' who stands opposite the 'expert,' facing the trained official who stands within the management of administration" (p. 232).

expert in California regularly communicated with his counterparts in the Florida, New York, and Oregon legislatures.[13] Thanks to similar interstate networks of specialists, the California legislature discovered Massachusetts' system of prenatal examinations to help prevent retardation in infants; found out about Minnesota's experiments in pooling tax revenues from industrial properties, no matter in what local district they were situated; and (as in Lanterman's case) made use of the Wisconsin experience in shifting welfare funding for the mentally ill from local to state government. The function of state legislative specialists in a federal nation was to discover what could be learned from other states' experiences and then teach the lessons to their colleagues.

VI

Not all the specialists were as skilled and flamboyant as Lanterman, but there were many good ones. There were young members like Julian Dixon, a black legislator with a working-class constituency in Los Angeles, who attempted to reform the true trouble spot of criminal law, the juvenile justice system. Like Lanterman, Dixon was sucked down into a sink of related problems. Once he began to try to do something about violent youngsters, he found that the adjacent pieces of puzzle needed to be added—guardianships, custodial institutions, children who were neglected or battered, juvenile sanctuaries, probation departments, personnel training, police priorities, judicial due process, welfare, runaways, extradition, schools, and, of course, the annual appropriations to fund the new programs.

There was Gene Gualco, a freshman in 1975, who by taking on the responsibility for water resources was already on his way to becoming a specialist. A three-year drought made obvious all the interrelated problems of water—irrigation, water systems, ranching, sewage, rivers, polluted lakes, recreation, dams, hydro power,

13. Typically, according to the legislative specialist in primary education, "What happens is that you meet a senator from Florida at the Education Commission of the States, either at the annual meeting or at the steering committee, which meets three times a year. Well, the senator from Florida asks me about our statewide assessment program [a proficiency testing scheme that California had adopted]. I send him our legislation with advice on what not to adopt and what to add. Then I need help on the bingo bill [a bill to legalize the playing of bingo games under specified circumstances]. I ask about the status of it from Florida, New Jersey, Colorado, and New York. I get a laundry list of features, select some, and omit some. That process helps me get some ideas."

growth, land use, and so on. Citizens and bureaucrats recognized his competence, and he welcomed their confidence in him. Soon he began to coordinate them all.

Specialists like Lanterman, Dixon, and Gualco shared one characteristic. They were cross-pressured: they endured internal conflict, which paralleled the combat between groups in the outer world. As one legislator put it, the respected specialists "were not completely in step with their party" or with any single interest. Lanterman, a fiscal conservative by constituency, background, and inclination, was sensitive to the human values of those in need. Dixon, a civil libertarian by origin and professional training, had concluded that undue leniency was the problem of the juvenile justice system and that some kind of retribution was essential. Gualco, the business lawyer who was suspicious of governmental incompetence, was developing a sense of the uniqueness and fragility of the California environment. Each of these three men, by virtue of his temperament, stood in a kind of no-man's-land between contesting parties: Lanterman between libertarian Republicans and liberals who were overly confident about government's abilities, Dixon between aggrieved and suspicious minorities and law-and-order hardhats, Gualco between developers and daisy-pluckers, as extreme environmentalists were called. Each specialist experienced inner conflict as well, harboring an emotional attachment to polar intellectual principles of practicality and need, insight and indignation, short-run and long-run. As a consequence, the specialist identified to some extent with adversaries on every side.[14] He was the trusted truce-carrier running between the trenches—but with two differences. He had a subpoena power to compel the parties to talk and a bill-carrying power to compel them to listen, and, used skillfully, the two powers made the specialist's role more formidable.

Not all specialists were torn intellectually as Lanterman, Dixon, and Gualco were. Not all were balanced in the emotional grasp they had on matters. The higher education specialist in the assembly was John Vasconcellos. He dealt with universities, four-year colleges, and community colleges. A fine university has to balance the tension between its teaching and research demands, between its moral and scientific functions, and between its personal and intellectual char-

14. Peter W. Sperlich, *Conflict and Harmony in Human Affairs: A Study of Cross-Pressures and Political Behavior* (Chicago: Rand McNally, 1971), contains interesting suggestions about the usefulness of cross-pressures.

acters. The state was filled with interests who demanded that the university save the world solely by one means or the other. Vasconcellos in 1975 lacked the internal balance to deal with the external conflict. A young, ambitious legislator, educated in the Jesuit intellectual style and disenchanted with it, Vasconcellos had converted to an exclusive perspective of "humanism," as he called it. Instead of harmonizing the polar traditions of teaching and research, he had embraced the former and grown intolerant of the latter. He took up arms himself, and instead of promoting accord, attacked without remorse. He was, however, the only assembly member around who was willing to specialize in and oversee the higher education bureaucracy. In the assembly he alone immersed himself in the details of university matters, knowledge of which was legislative power. As a result of his hard work, he knew what nobody else did. In the absence of a challenger to Vasconcello's claim of "turf," the assembly allowed him to monopolize his specialist responsibility, but with a misgiving that was not typical of the specialist system. As one astute Republican observed:

> You know, we tend to get an awful lot of people coming up here who fall on the ends of the political spectrum. They tend to be strongly motivated to save the world in one image or another. Well, if they . . . stay here long enough, they tend to moderate their views and at the very least they certainly tend to tolerate other needs. But there are worrisome exceptions; John Vasconcellos—he would make a study in himself. For the last year and a half he has become increasingly uptight. He has gotten very unhappy with the way things are going for him. A person can be so thoughtful about things, so idealistic, so concerned about making the world a tolerant place to live, that his own intolerance grows. He becomes intolerant of people he feels are intolerant, and he grows bitter.

A "bitter" legislator in the specialist system was "worrisome" because the legislative division of labor delegated so much of its work to its leading legislators and thereby exposed itself to instability if its specialists ceased to grow in wisdom. And John Vasconcellos, at least in 1975–76, appeared to be a little too "uptight" to be wise.

VII

What was wisdom? To begin with, wisdom was the patience to see matters through to completion. After all, the experience of committee work had taught the legislator that men's ways and natures were sometimes sensible, often conflicting, and always diverse. The experience of the author system had taught him that fairness and a sense of timing could induce workable accords. Now the experience of the specialist system taught him that in the constant movement of the legislative process, persistence and time assured the popular acceptance of an idea. Experience taught the specialist the interconnectedness of things and convinced him that a train of measures was necessary to accomplish his goals. In the perspective of the five or ten years it would take to complete the puzzle pieces of his idea, defeat on any one measure was hardly soul-shattering; compromise to keep an action alive was nothing to be ashamed of. Part of wisdom was the realization that matters were always in process. To a specialist with purpose, triumph and defeat and compromise were imposters, as Kipling warned they were. Defeat might be necessary to galvanize support. Compromise might be necessary to induce the opposition to moderate a defiant mood.

Wisdom, then, was a sense of statecraft. It was knowing how to build a consensus around a good idea. The wise specialist had both the patience to wait for the consensus to form and the skill to build the coalition necessary to hurry it along. Wisdom dampened what legislators disparaged as the temptation to "die on every issue." A wise legislator knew not only how to work for, but how to wait for, the accord that would give impetus to vision. Wisdom therefore whetted his enjoyment in observing the play of today's events on the shaping of the mood of tomorrow. If, as Senator Behr expressed it, the specialist loses, he

> loses without rancor and malice. He knows how time will change matters. He puts in the same bill three different times, and each time it gets vetoed. But the fourth time the governor signs it—for some reason. It may be because his constituency changes, or he has grown aware of the need for the bill, or he just gets tired of vetoing it.

In the perspective that wisdom gave the specialist, temporizing took on a new meaning. Being patient and persistent about a special problem, consolidating agreement whenever possible with compromise and legislation, and using time and experience to build alliances, were indispensable means to govern a free people.

Part Two

Thus far I have described how legislators learned the elements of political capacity—patriotism, love of justice, and wisdom. Part Two explains why the legislators learned as much as they did in Sacramento and why the legislators taught so effectively.

In any causal explanation, as the late Karl Popper pointed out, there are two main ingredients:

> To give a *causal explanation* of an event means to deduce a statement which describes it, using as premises of the deductions one or more *universal laws*, together with certain singular statements, the *initial conditions.*[1]

Part One set out the initial conditions, the particulars of California's legislature, the committee, author, and specialist systems. Part Two elaborates the universal rules, the general principles about mankind and society, that governed the legislative systems so as to produce a superior education in political competence.

You may recall that John Stuart Mill insisted that a legislature was like a school, but not like an authoritarian school where the schoolmaster could whip the schoolchildren into mastering their lessons. The legislative school that Mill envisioned depended on reciprocity, on a give and take between individuals who were at once teachers and students. Part Two makes explicit the "universal laws" of reciprocity and uses them as premises to explain the operations of the California legislature.

1. Karl R. Popper, *The Logic of Scientific Discovery,* 2d ed. (New York: Basic Books, 1958), p. 58, as quoted in Robert E. Lane, *Political Ideology: Why the American Common Man Believes What He Does* (New York: The Free Press, 1962), p. 349.

Theorists of reciprocity, like the sociologist Peter Blau, have found the terminology of the marketplace unavoidable in describing and illustrating the nature of reciprocity in social life. Likewise, in this part much of the description of the general notions of reciprocal exchange will be couched in the economist's vernacular—monopoly, currency, customer, exploitation, and the like. Such marketplace terms are not used to equate the legislature with an economy. Rather, they are being employed to describe the nonauthoritative dynamics—the reciprocal regime, so to speak—of the legislative school.

I have attempted to apply the more abstract principles of reciprocity to answer the following four important questions:

1. If legislators could be reelected without working hard on legislation, what institutional arrangements within the legislature compelled them to increase their knowledge and work hard nonetheless?

2. If knowledge was power, why did legislators share knowledge with one another, and so liberally?

3. If the support system of the legislature evenhandedly distributed information to all legislators, why did a status hierarchy emerge, and did it serve any function?

4. If any members happened to be elected who were incompetent or unscrupulous, why did they refrain from exploiting their legislative authority to personal advantage? Similarly, if there were venal or threatening forces outside the legislature seeking to assert themselves, how did the legislature protect its intellectual integrity against them?

Five

To enter politics costs a person little in his vocational progress.
The return is the rub. . . . On returning a person often is set
back further in his private career than if his time away from it
had been spent in some neutral occupation such as the armed
forces.
Stimson Bullitt, *To Be a Politician*, 1959

The legislature is a magnificent internship, and it provides
invaluable knowledge for almost any future which any individual
might wish for—government, policy-making, even in the private
sector if that's where you're inclined to go.
Assemblyman Jerry Lewis, 1977

Why Legislators Desired
to Acquire Knowledge

I

Among observant legislators there was a noteworthy consensus: democracy was *not* sufficient to prod legislators to work hard in the California legislature. The fear of being defeated at the polls did not effectively goad legislators into doing their committee work well, carrying complicated legislation, or specializing. To support their point, legislators would cite the reelection of lazy colleagues, though they malingered in Sacramento, and the defeat of conscientious ones, though they contributed richly to legislative life. They believed that it was rare for an electorate to bounce a legislative slacker as long as he "worked" his district, and they worried that if they became legislative workhorses, they would have to sacrifice attention to the details of constituency work upon which electoral support was built.

Bud Collier, for example, was returned from Glendale for thirty years, despite the fact that in his later years he served on only two policy committees, never carried legislation, and was bypassed by lobbyists and legislators alike. By responding to his constituent mail, faithfully attending his district office hours, and appearing at social functions back home, he achieved virtually permanent tenure in his legislative seat. He rocked no boats, made no enemies, and aroused no opposition by playing hooky on the Sacramento golf links every sunny afternoon.

On the other hand, a workhorse was likely to make political adversaries. There was no surer way of getting on someone's "enemies list" than by doing a hard-nosed, negative analysis on some group's pet bill, or by authoring wild rivers legislation to prevent the construction of an important hydroelectric project, or by precipitating real change in probate practices regarding the assets of the institutionalized mentally ill.

Senator Behr, for one, saw little incentive for assuming heavy legislative responsibilities:

> After all, each bill is working against the Establishment, almost by definition. It creates conflict, and conflict is stormy water in which to go fishing. A bill may cause the author to risk political suicide. Your enemies just may end up outnumbering your friends.

There were easier ways to be reelected than fishing for trouble. While it was pleasant for an author to get fulsome testimonials, he was wise to remember that the hidden resentments of his enemies were likely to smolder far longer than the visible contentments of those who benefited from his good deeds. Active legislators were always getting burned. The heat of controversy seemed to excite rivals in one's own party as well as in the opposition.

That is not to say that democracy was a shuck. Democracy made legislators highly responsive. Without the threat posed by the constituent's vote, it was inconceivable that legislators would have labored so long and so promptly over constituent matters. Without the prospect of possible political defeat, legislators would have been unlikely to go back to the district every weekend and sacrifice their personal lives to one more Kiwanis luncheon. The need for votes was sufficient explanation of why they sought to keep their constituents happy.

But democracy alone could not explain hard legislative activity in Sacramento. The Rosenthals, the Lockyers, and the Lantermans worked responsibly and frenetically in the state capital. Despite the lack of democratic competition in their safe legislative districts, they made persistent efforts to master an area of public policy, and otherwise contribute to the legislative process.

Some other dynamic than the coercive force of democracy compelled their involvement. The force came from within the legislature itself. The controls were in the hands of their fellow legislators, and the influence they wielded was reciprocity.

II

Reciprocity. What is it? Two children exchange baseball cards, the Yankee rooter giving up his rare "Jackie Robinson" to get the

Dodger fan's extra "Joe DiMaggio." The children separate, each pleased by the trade. This transaction of voluntary give and take is an act of reciprocity. Each child looks forward to further exchanges with the other. Next time they may even complicate their trading by dealing across time, by developing credit so that "today's giving will be recompensed by tomorrow's taking."[1]

Each day countless acts of reciprocity occur. So pervasive is exchange that we identify it as the essence of civilization. Its best institutionalized embodiment is the marketplace, but reciprocity occurs outside the marketplace as well. Reciprocity is a universally employed means of power whereby individuals influence one another to do "desirable" things that they would not otherwise do.

Reciprocity is not the only means of personal influence. Coercion, controlling others by threats, and the manipulation of morality, which governs others by shaping their self-governing mechanisms of mind and conscience, are the two alternative forms of interpersonal power. But reciprocity—getting one's way by giving way—is a distinctively different method of influence. It accomplishes cooperation without the "whip of authority"[2] or the oppression of conformity.

Reciprocity enables people to get what they want. What people want depends on a culture, for culture justifies—gives meaning to—particular desires. In turn, these culturally determined desires shape the character of the exchange system; they create particular kinds of scarcity, and each scarcity disciplines a society to cultivate specific capacities and talents and resources to cure it.[3]

To understand a regime of reciprocity, then, one must begin with the elementary questions, What are the things that people desire and pursue? and Why do they believe they need them? Accordingly, in

1. Karl Polyani, *The Great Transformation* (Boston: Beacon Paperback, 1957), p. 51. My notions of reciprocity largely derive from these five social scientists: Peter M. Blau, *Exchange and Power in Social Life* (New York: John Wiley and Sons, 1954); Robert L. Heilbroner, *The Worldly Philosophers*, 4th ed. (New York: Simon and Schuster, 1972; originally published 1953); Albert Hirschman, *Exit, Voice, and Loyalty* (Cambridge, Mass.: Harvard University Press, 1970); George C. Homans, *Social Behavior: Its Elementary Forms* (New York: Harcourt Brace, 1961); and Frank H. Knight, *Risk, Uncertainty, and Profit* (Boston: Houghton Mifflin, 1921).

2. Heilbroner, *The Worldly Philosophers*, p. 17.

3. The longshoreman philosopher Eric Hoffer recently reflected on the importance of changing notions of scarcity: "To maintain social discipline, an affluent society must know how to create a new kind of scarcity—a new category of vital needs that are not easily fulfilled. . . . In an era of general abundance [societies] have to know how to induce a ceaseless striving for the realization of individual capacities and talents in order to preserve their stability and health. And by passing from an economy of matter to an economy of the spirit a society enters a world of incurable scarcity."

analyzing California's legislative school as a regime of reciprocity, we start by asking, What did the individual legislators most desire, and why did they desire it?

III

To answer these questions, it helps to look at an unusual occurrence. Let me provide a bit of background:

At least twice a week each legislative house assembled on the floor of its chambers. At such times the membership as a whole reviewed and voted on the bills handed it by the committees. Attendance was mandatory: only members with valid excuses were permitted to be absent from the day's business. (On the average perhaps one assemblyman out of eighty might be missing.)

One day a milk-price support bill came to the assembly floor. It permitted retail markets to sell milk and dairy products "below cost" (as defined in the bill). The real effect of the proposal was to drop a "fair pricing" requirement then in effect, freeing retailers to sell milk at prices below minimum levels established by state regulators. Since the depression of the 1930s, the state had established the price of milk sold at retail, that is, in the groceries and dairies that made direct sales to the public. The purpose of the minimum price regulation had been to restrict what its adherents liked to call cutthroat competition. The proponents of deregulation, on the other hand, claimed they were simply restoring normal price competition.

Legislators found the bill confusing because, for one thing, everyone was so divided on it. Consumers, farmers, and grocers were distributed equally among the proponents and opponents of the legislation. But a simpler explanation of the legislative difficulty with the bill was that it was a farm bill, and most legislators came from urban and suburban districts, knew nothing about farming, and hence did not understand the bill or its context. They had no feeling for the effect deregulated retail prices would have on wholesale prices (which would be left regulated); they did not know the difference between dairy cooperatives and milk pooling arrangements; they knew so little about public health regulation of the milk industry that they had no way of assessing how it would be affected by price deregulation; and the interrelationship between federal rules regarding milk marketing and the state rules under discussion was bewildering.

In the middle of the milk bill debate, a short recess was called for an unrelated reason, leaving most of the legislators on the floor with too little time to return to their offices. They stood up from their desks and chatted with one another. To the uninitiated observer viewing the movement on the floor from the spectators' gallery, the assembly members, conversing in low tones, appeared furtive, conspiratorial, and plainly up to no good. In fact, however, they were asking such questions as, "What's this bill all about?" and "What do you make of all this?" and proffering such unilluminating answers as, "I haven't got a clue about the real effects of this bill, much less how I'm going to vote on it."[4]

The milk-decontrol bill was an issue about which practically every member was ignorant. When the session resumed and the vote was taken, many members simply took their lead from the chairman of the agriculture committee, a rural legislator and a dairy farmer himself, who supported the bill.

This was an atypical case because the ignorance was so universal. No legislator seemed to vote with any certainty at all. After that session Julian Dixon felt dissatisfied. A legislator serving his second term in the assembly, Dixon was a lawyer from Los Angeles; he had a heavily black, urban constituency. He was, as was mentioned earlier, the assembly's specialist in juvenile justice. He also served on appropriations and two major policy committees and was chairman of the Democratic caucus. He was busy, very busy. His marriage had already broken up because of the demands politics placed on it. Even divorced he had insufficient time. As he put it:

> Between the work of the house and political demands, there is no time to think. I don't know how to solve it. . . . But as for time for a lot of research and a lot of reading, there is just no time.

Yet, despite the fact that there was not enough time, and even though he was not on the agriculture committee and had neither personal nor constituent reasons to be curious about milk pricing, he decided that he must do something about his ignorance in that particular area of policy. He recalled:

4. In *Member of the House* (New York: Charles Scribner's Sons, 1962), the late congressman Clem Miller described two incidents very similar to the milk-price deregulation debate. See pp. 108–9.

Does anybody really understand some issues? For example, milk price supports? I went a long time without understanding what the issue was. So I finally asked Joe Gonzalves to explain it to me. Joe Gonzalves is a good lobbyist. He is now representing the dairy people. Just look at his background: ten years as chairman of the assembly taxation committee, and also on rules. He has a sense of the house. He has a background as a dairy farmer. He is well prepared. Well, he sat down with me for two or three sessions on milk pooling. By the end I was just beginning to understand what the controversy was about. The whole trip about milk-pooling has been relatively clear since then.

Here was a busy legislator with very little time for research and reading, already a specialist in a well-defined and urgent field, making a quick-study on a remote subject. What good did it do him to take "two or three sessions" to learn the economics of milk? Why did he desire knowledge of the subject?

One possible answer is the Buddy System Rule, "Vote no on the merits; otherwise vote yes." Under the rule, Dixon could not vote according to his own familiarity on milk price bills because he lacked such familiarity. He was thus not in control of his vote—unless he could master the merits of the matter.

This answer, however, does not explain why there was a Buddy System Rule in the first place, a rule that tolerated, even invited legislative independence in any legislator willing to pay the price of learning about the merits of a bill. Why had the rule come into existence and been so widely accepted, instead of an alternative formulation like "Vote your party" or "Vote your friends"? Thus the Buddy System Rule cannot provide a real explanation.

A second answer is that without knowledge Dixon could not participate in floor debate on the bill. A frequent butt of ridicule was the legislator who made noises with his mouth without making sense to his colleagues. But then another question arises: Why was debate considered so important that attendance at floor debates was required and that the legislators demanded that sensible use be made of the time given to debate? One could attribute it to the "ethos" of the legislature.[5] To be sure, many legislators did feel an almost palpable obligation to be knowledgeable, to participate in debate, and to vote

5. Cf. Michael Rutter et al., *Fifteen Thousand Hours* (Cambridge: Harvard University Press, 1979) in which the authors established that schools differed appreciably

by their own lights, and those who did not do so felt guilty and demeaned by their lack of understanding of legislative subjects. Yet explanations in terms of ethos are always unsatisfactory because the origins of it are so vague and unclear. Ethos begs the question.

We might then begin by asking, What made the legislative ethos possible? What made it practical to require legislators to be knowledgeable?

For one thing, the legislature had created support systems that made the attainment of knowledge extremely easy and inexpensive. The educational processes of the legislative institution reached such levels of efficiency that legislators who valued and needed their time felt they were saving it by getting "two or three sessions" of clear explanation. Dixon, for example, simply went to Gonzalves, a former assembly member and "a good lobbyist," who tutored well and without requiring "a lot of researching . . . and reading." Gonzalves tendered his educational help regardless of whether Dixon was pro or con, powerful or not, on the agriculture committee or off it, Republican or Democrat.

But why were there good, nonpartisan lobbyists like Gonzalves around, and what was the relationship between their educational skills and the legislators' desire for knowledge? Did the legislators' desire impel the outside world to provide good lobbyists? Or did good lobbyists first come and quicken the thirst for learning?

Both explanations appear convincing. Yet the logic of the legislative world tends to point primarily to the first explanation—that the legislators' expectations determined the quality of the lobbyists. The members who had been on the scene long enough to observe the marked changes in the operations of the Third House, as the lobbyists were called, said that was the case, that changes in the desires of most of the legislators forced business interests to send better representation up to the legislature.

The savings and loan lobbyist described how lobbying operations were having to be organized differently:

> It used to be that we could get our way up here with one part-time lobbyist. Now we have three full-time representatives up

in their "ethos," which in turn affected significantly how the students performed. Ethos referred to the nature of the academic atmosphere, serious or careless. Interestingly enough, the other major factor that affected students' performance was the schools' "balance of intake": i.e., whether a school had its fair share of high-ability students.

here, and we are still being run ragged by the things we have
to do.

The insatiable educational demands of the legislators ran the lobbyists "ragged." When most legislators were content with money,
booze, and women, and only a relatively small number had to be
educated, only a part-time lobbyist was necessary for interests to get
their way. The freshman Hart was genuinely astonished when it
dawned on him how lobbyists might have worked if legislators had
not desired knowledge:

> I'm amazed at people who are pointed out as being powerful
> lobbyists of the past. They seem so ineffectual now, when the
> $10 limit on wining and dining is in effect.[6]

Why did legislators' desires change? What made them replace their
past priorities with their current craving for knowledge? As far as
I can see, an important cause of their appetite for knowledge—for
facts and arguments that met exacting standards of excellence—was
the Office of the Legislative Analyst.

IV
The Office of the Legislative Analyst was created in 1941. By 1975
it had a budget of more than $1,500,000 and employed forty-four
"technical" staff members, most of whom were economists. Basically, the office functioned as the legislature's agent to oversee the
executive. Each staff member specialized in a specific area of state
government. The most significant staff effort was devoted to analyzing the governor's proposed budget and participating in committee hearings on that document. As a basis for these hearings, the
staff prepared a written *Analysis of the Budget Bill*. This annual
document exceeded 1,200 printed pages and was available to the
legislature within a few days after the governor presented his budget
message. The timing was possible through a long-standing arrangement under which the governor's budget staff made available to the
analyst's staff, on a confidential basis, the preliminary drafts of the
proposed budget as it was being developed.

6. Proposition 9, the so-called "political reform initiative," was adopted through
the initiative process in California in June 1974. Among other things it required
monthly itemized disclosures of all payments to, and disbursements by, professional
lobbyists.

The legislative analyst was hired, and the cost of his office was authorized, by the Joint Legislative Budget Committee. By tradition key minority party members were always accorded seats on the committee. The tradition of the committee and of its staff operation was strictly nonpartisan. As a matter of policy, the budget recommendations of the legislative analyst were presented to the legislature and its committees without recommendation by the Joint Legislative Budget Committee. In this way the analyst presented his own conclusions without in any sense precommitting members of the committee to a particular position.

Through 1976 there had only been two legislative analysts, one who served from 1941 to 1949, and A. Alan Post from 1949 onward. As the analyst's office liked to point out in its public relations flyer:

Staff turnover in . . . the office has been limited over the years with the result that a substantial accumulation of experience is available to the legislature on a continuing and expanding basis. This experience, combined with working files and reference materials gathered from many sources, represents a valuable and immediate resource to the legislature on almost any question which affects the operations, organization, cost or revenues of state government.

If knowledge is power in a legislature, the Office of the Legislative Analyst was a powerhouse. Because of its nonpartisan character, however, its "valuable and immediate resource" was available to any legislator, no matter what his political connection or his ideological bent. Its duty was, in the language of the legislature's rules, "to provide all legislative committees and Members of the Legislature with information obtained under the direction of the Joint Legislative Budget Committee." And the analyst's office did its duty.

For each element of the governor's budget, for example, the written analysis provided a description of the program, its history, its legal and social context, economic data, and the budgetary assumptions about the future used in preparing that part of the budget. It provided detailed accounts of changes proposed by every agency in employment, workload, and practices. It made both major and minor recommendations, from specifying the salary increase for state employees to reducing by $3,000 the travel expenses of the state fire marshal. It made large purposes and small details understandable in a long and lucid narrative. If any matter was left unclear, the responsible member of the analyst's staff was always available to answer questions. Fred Chel, a freshman legislator who had left behind a sophisticated international law practice to come to Sacramento, commented: "I spend more time with the analysis of the Budget Bill than I do with the Budget Bill itself."

Alan Post, the legislative analyst in 1975–76, embodied the office. He read and rewrote every section of the Analysis, and legislators of every persuasion admired his intellectual and analytic powers. A liberal Democrat said:

> Post is impeccable because he has an impeccable reputation for approaching problems in an impartial manner and for being willing to step on anyone's toes. One time he'll make favorable comments about an agency's proposal, and the next moment he will be pointing out a shortcoming in the same agency.

A conservative Republican said much the same thing:

> Credibility is the key to his position. He has not played partisan politics. He's burned everybody. When he says this will be the effect, it usually is.

While the office was nonpartisan and in that sense nonpolitical, no legislator was under the illusion that Post lacked a point of view or that he started without particular assumptions that had to be questioned. However, the impartial character of the analysis ("he says that this will be the effect") invited rebuttal formulated with an equal level of care and attention to reason and fact. As his analysis proved to be correct sufficiently often to warrant the attention of the members, the analysis taught the members that problems were amenable to measured, thoughtful approaches.

At the same time that the office elevated the intellectual standards of the legislators, its surveillance of the governor's budgetary processes prevented executive agencies from making unjustified claims. Thus bureaucrats began to give more useful and lucid explanations to the analyst and his bosses.

Legislators were prone to identify with the legislative analyst's office. After all, it was employed by the legislature to contest with the governor's budgetary experts. The analyst was "their man" in the competition between the branches of government. Legislators might disagree with the information which he dug out, but it was better information than the governor's office came up with initially.

Competition established respect, and the respectable information he found freed legislators from a paralyzing uncertainty resulting from a dependence on a single source.

In a typical case, the legislative analyst was pivotal in repealing the Welfare Relative's Responsibility Law, legislation that had required parents to reimburse counties for any general assistance given to adult children (other than that given to the blind, the totally disabled, and parents of dependent children). The particular hardship that this law caused was infrequent, but it was dramatic when it did occur. When a county placed a lien on the assets of an elderly retired couple whose "good-for-nothing" son, who had long ago deserted them, sought a welfare handout, the law seemed quite unjust. The governor's budget people had always taken the position that the law's repeal would be very expensive. When the analyst's office double-checked their estimates, they found that the state would lose a pittance, at most $2.3 million. Good information like that endeared the office and its methods to legislators.

The analysis made legislators aware of how much there was to learn and at the same time gave them the tools to correct their lack of facts, perspectives, and reasoning.

The analyst's influence was underscored by his presence at the floor debates on the Budget Bill. The Budget Bill was always the final major piece of business to be completed before the one-month summer recess. The analyst sat to the side of and below the Speaker's dais, facing the assembly members. Whenever a legislator made what the analyst thought was a good point or supplied useful information or made explicit the assumptions under which the governor or some legislator was proceeding, the analyst would smile visibly. If a legislator made an unsubstantiated remark or argued *ad hominem* or just made noises with his mouth, the analyst would frown. Like the respected and remote headmaster of a boarding school whose reputation was built on continuous accomplishment, the analyst—both by his actual presence and through the budget analysis—inspired by example and challenged with authority. He did for the legislature what John Stuart Mill declared was absolutely essential in any school of political capacity:

> What is wanted is the means of making ignorance aware of itself and able to profit by knowledge, accustoming minds which know only routine to act upon and feel the value of

principles, teaching them to compare different modes of action and learn by the use of their reason to distinguish the best. When we desire to have a good school, we do not eliminate the teacher.[7]

The work of the legislative analyst set a standard of excellence by which the legislators learned to "distinguish the best" among the lobbyists.

V

But if knowledge was available inexpensively to the legislator, and if he had mentors who showed him how necessary "reason" was to doing the "public business" competently, one still wonders what made the individual legislator desire to become knowledgeable.

Of course, no one enjoyed looking like an ignorant fool in front of constituents or colleagues. And no one liked to feel the loss of control that came from casting an uninformed vote. Yet in other state legislatures it was not difficult to find plenty of individual legislators who took their paychecks and seemed little discomfited by their lack of competency.

I believe that California legislators desired knowledge and were willing to work hard to get it because they had adopted the vocation of politics. They were by ambition and by circumstance professional politicians. In particular, the young men and women in the assembly had a long public career to look forward to, but it was a future full of change and uncertainty. None could reasonably, and few wanted to, count on a dependable future in the assembly. That meant that they had to internalize the benefits of their assembly experience so that they could carry them on to the next stage of their public careers. They had to make the products of their legislative lives portable, so to speak.

Power—influence based on the authority of the legislative vote, bill-carrying privileges, and committee subpoenas—could not be transported outside the assembly. An assemblyman's vote was tied to his seat. Converting the power of the vote directly into wealth, the currency of a venal legislature, was a legal taboo, and, in California's legislature, a moral one, too. Strict disclosure laws, appli-

7. John Stuart Mill, *On Representative Government*, p. 228.

cable to legislators and lobbyists alike, prevented outright corruption such as pay-offs for favorable votes.[8]

Furthermore, the power of the parties was limited: it did not determine political destinies. The party nominees for every elective office in the state were determined not by party leaders but in popular primaries. The parties could not dictate the terms of nomination. Nor could party leaders obtain patronage jobs for loyal and compliant legislative hacks and their families, because there was virtually no patronage system. Civil service was the only route to all but the highest level jobs. There were almost no low-visibility, unimportant, decently paid political plums available to influence the legislators in casting their legislative votes.

Finally, one legislator's votes could not be traded for the votes of another with much certainty, because other legislative members voted on important legislation by their own lights, "on the merits."

There were, however, jobs in and out of government that beckoned to knowledgeable masters of the public business—elective higher offices, high-level posts in state and federal government (including judgeships), positions for politically skillful people in private business. Knowledge was a universally acceptable currency in both the public and private sectors.[9]

8. It is difficult to prove something negative, and to persuade skeptical readers that there was no corruption in the California legislature in the last half of the 1970s requires just that. By chance, however, a parallel (and much more extensive) investigation than my own inquiry into corruption was conducted from 1977 to 1980. An exhaustive probe was undertaken by the Federal Bureau of Investigation as a result of allegations made in 1976. A special federal grand jury reportedly interrogated 130 witnesses in the course of running down charges of legislative wrongdoing in Sacramento. On 21 March 1980, however, the FBI and the grand jury announced that they "had uncovered no crimes and no criminals" (*San Francisco Chronicle*, 22 March 1980, p. 1: "Probe of Legislature Finds No Criminals," by John Balzar). Even some newspaper editors overcame their skepticism to offer their congratulations: "The point is that after three years of looking, the FBI couldn't come up with a single charge. That is commendable, and these legislators are in line for congratulations on their clean bill of health," said the *San Francisco Chronicle* (25 March 1980, p. 42).

9. As Nelson Polsby put it, one of the functions that legislatures perform is "the maintenance of a pool of potential recruits for future political leadership," (Nelson W. Polsby, "Legislatures," in Fred I. Greenstein and Nelson W. Polsby, eds., *Handbook of Political Science* [Reading, Mass.: Addison-Wesley, 1975], v. 5, p. 259). To obtain an idea of how much "political leadership" the California legislature provided, I looked at the careers of 199 assembly alumni—i.e., every member of the lower house elected between 1958 and 1976 who relinquished his or her seat for one reason or another. Among those 199 members there were at least twenty-five United States congressmen, thirty-six state senators, six state officers, six important federal agency officials, and eight judges. In addition, there were several who upon leaving the

By stemming corruption and "spoils" on a broad basis, California had closed old opportunities for advancement based on political pull. At the same time new opportunities based on merit opened up to those with political knowledge of good quality. When partisanship and party discipline broke down in the state, political individuals found they could negotiate a good political career without having to be an unthinking crony. If they took their intellect out of mothballs and put it to work exploiting the educational resources of the assembly, they could go places.[10]

VI

What were the social and moral effects of cultivating the legislators' desire for knowledge? First, it bears repeating that it altered the operation of lobbyists in Sacramento. Crude and ignorant lobbyists purveying unmarked envelopes filled with money began to lose causes they had won before, and lobbyists who could teach began to get their way. The more influence the latter kind of lobbyist wielded, the more the interests in the marketplace began to employ better lobbyists. As mentioned earlier, several oil companies, inexperienced in the legislative ways of Sacramento, hired lobbyists of the old school, and when they lost the contest over oil depletion, those lobbyists were changed for the better. In turn, the more that lobbyists could succeed on the basis of what they knew, the more interested knowledgeable individuals became in careers as lobbyists. Sacramento was a pleasant place to lobby when its ethical practices improved; indeed, working conditions were hard to beat.

As lobbyists improved, one might have expected the passage of better public policy. This did not necessarily follow, however. Many other factors determine the quality of legislation—a state's wealth,

assembly became mayors, county supervisors, and lobbyists. Because I only looked at recent alumni, these figures do not include earlier alumni like Caspar Weinberger, presently United States secretary of defense, and Charles Wiggins, who acquitted himself so skillfully as a member of the congressional Judiciary Committee during the Watergate inquiry. Their last election to the assembly was 1956 or earlier.

10. Why did state legislators want to leave their legislative positions and "go [other] places," particularly to Washington, D.C.? Over and above the possibilities of better salaries and more secure employment, there were two major reasons: the intellectual satisfaction that came from meeting new challenges, and the social pleasure of achieving more personal prestige by performing on the Washington stage. For an explanation of the notion of personal prestige and its functions, there is no more valuable book than William J. Goode, *The Celebration of Heroes: Prestige as a Social Control System* (Berkeley and Los Angeles: University of California Press, 1978).

its political traditions and history, the accident of a good or bad legislative specialist in a particular policy area. Nonetheless, even if one cannot say California's policy was better or produced more happiness, no one could deny that the policy-making process was more energetic and better informed. It set lots of wrongs right.

There was also strong personal identification with California's legislature on the part of the members. They felt a part of the legislature, liked it, defended it publicly. On the stump they did not run against it. Instead of denigrating it and blaming it as the cause of social ills, they celebrated it for its capacity to deal with problems in a democratic way. The congressional scholar Richard Fenno was much troubled by the tendencies of members of the national House of Representatives when he observed them back home in their districts.[11] Rather than explaining the House, they would attack it, placating their constituents by railing against the institution of which they were a part. Generally, that did not happen in California. The members' identification with the assembly was epitomized in a remark made on the assembly floor by a black freshman at the end of her first year: "It has been a most interesting educational experience, and I'm proud to be a member of the assembly." Where there was a sense of personal growth, there followed affection for the institution that made that growth possible. The assembly produced loyal alumni.[12]

There was one final effect. Legislators projected on others their own desire for knowledge. As they became more capable, they assumed that others thirsted for understanding in the ways they had. As a result they expected incoming legislators to want to know the public business. Certain that the freshmen wanted knowledge, they shared their competence in the belief that the favor would be returned in kind. And, by and large, it was.

11. Richard Fenno, *Home Style: House Members in Their Districts* (Boston: Little Brown, 1978).
12. E.g., former Congressman Jerome Waldie of California, upon retiring from the House of Representatives, told reporter Michael Green that he "would model the House after the body he knew [in California where he had been an assemblyman], with all the modern, up-to-date research facilities and other devices . . . introduced to strengthen the Assembly as an independent branch. . ." (Quoted in Bevier, *Politics Backstage*, p. 223).

Six

I talk with people and keep accurate records and make the most of whatever position I'm placed in. I'm seated in the back of the room: people stop by and ask me questions. Then I can be a resource on parliamentary procedure and what have you. That's what's important, that they're turning to you for information. Once that happens, I've got them.

Assemblyman William Thomas, 1977

Some say that the earth has bounty enough for all, and that more for one does not mean less for another, that the advance of one does not mean the decline of another. They say that poor-paid labor means a poor nation, and that better-paid labor means greater markets and greater scope for industry and manufacture. And others say that this is a danger, for better-paid labor will not only buy more but will also read more, think more, ask more, and will not be content to be forever voiceless and inferior. . . . For we fear not only the loss of our possessions, but the loss of our superiority.

Alan Paton, *Cry the Beloved Country,* 1949

Why Resourceful Legislators
Desired to Share Knowledge

I

Before exploring why legislators wanted to share their skills and knowledge with their colleagues, we should review a few elementary notions about reciprocity. The typical regime of reciprocity functions to bring together consumers and suppliers, to juxtapose desires and resources. We could say that such a regime consists in large part of lots of little markets created to facilitate meetings and exchange.

Exchange in kind, the simplest form of exchange, can take place when two parties are one another's merchant and customer. Both parties submit to the desires of the other and require that the other submit in turn. More typically, reciprocity involves more complex transactions than exchanges in kind. Marketplace reciprocity involves a series of one-way exchanges systematically interrelated by currency. The butcher supplies meat to the mechanic, the mechanic repairs the car of the tennis coach, the tennis coach teaches the children of the banker, the banker services a loan to the florist, and the florist delivers roses to the butcher. This chain of unilateral submissions is mediated by money. Money and the requirement that it be accepted as recompense function to bridge the gaps of time and space that ordinarily separate individual supply and need.

The point of reciprocity is that, through in-kind and linked transactions, individuals exchange their abundance for something they are short of. All of this cooperation can be said to be voluntary if the exchanges are fair. The problem is to make the exchange "fair," or nonexploitative, to bring some equality to the "worth" of the mutual submissions. The device principally relied upon by a regime of reciprocity to produce a sense of fairness is competition. Suppliers compete with one another, and their competition functions to reduce the extent to which they will require the consumer to submit. In turn, consumers compete with one another for a particular good and in so doing increase the extent of the submission offered to the supplier. Each member of a regime of reciprocity benefits by competition *for* his business—his resources or his desires—and is harmed by competition *with* his business. From the regime's standpoint, if competition is universal, the individual benefits and injuries offset one another and produce fair exchanges. Conversely, when monopoly occurs, making the supplier or consumer the only one in town, the benefits and injuries are skewed to the advantage of one party and the disadvantage of his trading partner. The assurance of fairness perishes.

From the point of view of each individual, however, both competition and monopoly are advantageous. Each wants competition for his business, yet wants his business to be a monopoly. Conversely, he is unhappy about competition with his business, and equally glum when his business faces a monopoly.

We will use these four notions—of markets, currency, competition, and monopoly—in the remainder of the book. They will first help us understand why resourceful legislators in California wanted to share their abundant knowledge rather than hoard it. It is the latter aspect of the question, of course, that goes to the heart of our inquiry. Why, to paraphrase Alan Paton, did legislators in California feel that the advancement of another colleague's political capacity would not mean their own decline?

II

Let us begin our explanation by examining a specific instance of a resourceful legislator sharing his knowledge. In this unusually vivid example, a member of the assembly created a market and signaled his approachability and his willingness to share the fruits of his unique insight.

In 1975 Assemblyman Bill Lockyer set out to create a market for knowledge about the problems of the poor. We met Lockyer earlier, negotiating the oil depletion tax bill through the author system. As we saw, he was young, ambitious, professional, skillful in legislative politics, ardent to make the world better and to take credit for it.

In his second term Lockyer was offered the chairmanship of the welfare committee. Among the twenty standing committees, welfare was near the bottom in attractiveness. Its low standing was due to its superfluous character. Legislation assigned to it dealt with the poor and the costly welfare programs that served them. Whatever legislation the committee approved or developed, consequently, was reexamined in the fiscal committee and was usually rejected as too expensive, or else was substantially redone. Lobbyists knew that and typically made a minimal effort to educate the welfare committee, focusing their energies instead on the members of appropriations. The poor teaching given the members of welfare affected their sense of responsibility. The absence of good teachers made it difficult to cut through the confusion inherent in the federal structure of welfare with its budget complexities and administrative apparatus produced by the twenty titles of the Social Security Act of 1935 and related laws. The resulting sense of futility tended to weaken the members' desires for an understanding of welfare. As a result they were not competent to do their work well, and even the committee staff ceased to tutor their reluctant charges.

A third factor that contributed to the committee's unattractiveness was its miniscule agenda. Major committees had taken some vital welfare topics away. Unemployment insurance now belonged to the business committee. Medical and mental health care for the indigent was the responsibility of the health committee. The education committee had jurisdiction over compensatory education for the children of the poor. Personnel and labor divided up federally subsidized (CETA) jobs and apprenticeship programs. Public housing was in the domain of the housing committee. And so on. By the time this jurisdictional cannibalism was concluded, the welfare committee was left with welfare money payments, and that subject matter had been virtually absorbed by the federal government.

With a seemingly superfluous task, a decimated agenda, and a staff that was unused to either success or responsibility, the welfare committee was often used by the Speaker (who made committee assignments) as a "dump" committee, to which unattractive members of the legislature could be assigned. Nonetheless, Lockyer jumped at the chance to be its chairman, and with considerable enterprise turned it into a valuable capital resource in the knowledge marketplace of the legislature.

III

With the assistance of the two nonpartisan staff members assigned to him as chairman of the committee, Lockyer assumed a role as one of the legislature's informants about the poor. He directed his staff to draft a series of memos on poverty-related subjects, in plain English, for circulation to other legislators.

The memos dealt with such issues as CETA jobs and food stamps. One was about child care. Child care was concerned with facilities for pre-kindergartners, from infants to five-year-olds, and was a topic of particular interest to single parents, especially AFDC mothers, who constituted the largest class of welfare recipients at the time.

The memo that dealt with child care was twelve pages long. Among the questions it answered were: What were the different child care programs already existing in California? Who took advantage of them? How much money was spent on them? What were some of the problems inherent in them? The questions were not particularly profound, and child care was not a particularly abstruse topic. For many legislators, however, trustworthy answers in this area were elusive, because child-care responsibilities were scattered in little bits and pieces. Each of three different major state departments—Health, Education, and Business—administered child-care programs. Each program was designed with different purposes, serving different clienteles, staffed by different kinds of professionals, and funded variously. To legislators busy with other subjects but barraged by telephone calls from women's groups and desperate mothers, the bits and pieces of knowledge that they could snatch from the various department representatives just did not add up to the whole picture. They could never get a handle on the matter, and they lacked the time to understand the reasons, facts, people, and issues constituting it.

Lockyer knew that, in order to grasp the subject, a legislator had to understand the basic programmatic distinction between the various preschool child-care services: some programs had heavy educational commitments (like Head Start), while others served only to take safe custody of children while their mothers worked. That distinction was a crucial point of departure, because questions of staffing, eligibility, and departmental jurisdiction tended to hinge on it. Educational programs had to be much more heavily staffed than custodial programs, and hence cost more and relied more exclusively on federal funding. The federal connection meant that some programs had to be linked to welfare clientele more exclusively than did others. There was simply less discretion in the eligibility decisions about federally funded child-care programs than with state funded programs.

Lockyer edited the staff's draft so that it taught his colleagues lucidly[1] and spoke to their concerns. He made sure that the memo focused his fellow legislators' attention on the bread-and-butter issue, the sensitive matter of the just distribution of this valuable and expensive service. He gave them a handle of competing principles—the principle of the child's need versus the principle of the mother's need. He wrote:

> The issue of eligibility is: Who should be served by child care if not all can be served? The miserable, mistreated child? The child of the welfare mother who is willing to undertake work? The child of the welfare recipient, whether or not "at work or in training"? The working parents' child? The child who can benefit, or be benefited by the the Program? The child of the mother who wants to go to college? The child of any mother who wants such care? The child of the most politically powerful mother?

Lockyer circulated the memo to all legislators—Republicans as well as Democrats, senators as well as members of the assembly.

To say that the memo was helpful to others, however, would require some qualification. Aside from members of the welfare committee (who discussed it in committee among themselves and with lobbyists from the agencies), perhaps not more than two or three legislators actually read the memo closely. Yet, like a piece of advertising hurriedly glanced at, the memo notified even the most casual reader that a manageable body of knowledge on child care existed, and that Lockyer could supply it for the asking. When the need for that knowledge arose, they would remember.[2]

1. For example, Lockyer provided a dictionary of child-care terms used by the experts. Without a glossary and history of technical terms, the uninitiated legislator would find phrases like "Section 10.6 Funds," "MOE," "Title IV-C WIN," and "AB 99 Centers" about as instructive as Chinese characters. Lockyer's memo defined these phrases and fitted them into a logical and chronological system.

2. Some memos got a more thorough reading than the poverty-related memos, but widespread reading was unusual because the legislature was largely an oral school. One widely read memo, also authored by Lockyer, dealt with public financing of legislative elections. Common Cause had persuaded the Speaker to support a bill calling for state government funding of primary and general election candidates for

Moreover, in writing the memo, Lockyer himself learned the subject systematically and thus could with skill teach it orally whenever occasion demanded it—when the timing was right.[3]

IV

What prompted Lockyer to share his knowledge and to make the effort of advertising his availability for consultation? For one thing, he earned the trust of several fellow legislators, who tested Lockyer's analysis back in the districts or in solving a constituent's problem. If the test was positive, if the analysis "worked," they could be assured that Lockyer's homework had been done thoroughly. In turn, the test in the field convinced a few of them that they might safely share Lockyer's larger assumptions of fact and value regarding child care. Having come to share his outlook, they relied on him for further education. If they had the time, they would catch him in his office to ask him to explain some related bill, soothe some qualms, or find out how to defend a vote. They might raise considerations that Lockyer would accept to improve his own thinking, and the sense of contributing to Lockyer's understanding made them his allies. If they lacked the time for extended discussion, they might simply accept his direction as a bellwether and follow his vote when he cast it in committee or on the floor. In short, by sharing his knowledge with persons who wanted it and could trust it, Lockyer "got them."

---

the state senate and assembly. Lockyer's memo influenced the Speaker to retract his endorsement, and the bill eventually died for lack of an author. The memo consisted of twenty-two separate arguments against the bill, which provided sixty percent public financing for each candidate's campaign, up to a given expenditure limitation, upon the raising of a minimum amount of private funds, with each nonincumbent given more public funds and having a ten percent larger campaign limit than incumbents. Argument no. 19 gives the reader a feeling for the force of Lockyer's argument: "The bill provides an excellent method of torpedoing incumbents; all that's needed is a little in-party organization. For example, the opposition runs four primary candidates. If these four collect the minimum number of signatures, they collect a total of $21,600. If they can raise $9,200 each, they qualify for a total of $147,200. These four pledge to donate at least half of their ad time and space to slamming the incumbent. Assuming the incumbent has no primary opposition, he or she can only collect $7,425 from the state. Thus, the opposition party spends about twenty times as much as the incumbent. Even in the general [election], he or she is still outspent by 10%. It seems to me that this is truly playing with a stacked deck." That is the kind of argument that evokes gratitude from legislative colleagues.

3. Of course, the usual way for a resourceful legislator to create a market for his knowledge was to author a bill. Actual performances before legislative committees were natural advertisements of a legislator's competence.

The implications of being a bellwether developed further. The fact that a bloc of legislators relied on him enhanced Lockyer's attractiveness to lobbyists, who returned to educate him still more. By teaching Lockyer well, they were affecting a weighty vote—one that influenced a number of others. Thus an increase in influence caused an increase in knowledge, which added still more to his influence.

Within a two-year term, Lockyer attained a legislative preeminence in child care that no bureaucrat, lobbyist, or legislator could ignore. He had to be consulted and educated because friendly legislators, like Rosenthal, gave him legislative recognition. They listened to him and had confidence in him as a "good, feeling human being who knows about how you try to help people."

Lockyer, however, did not exact acquiescence as a price for his knowhow. He taught across party and ideological lines, with the foreknowledge that a handle on child care was as useful to the naysayers as it was to the sympathizers.

Especially among his committee members he tried to appear evenhanded to Republicans and Democrats alike. He made it plain that he wanted each legislator to be as knowledgeable as his or her interests and capacities permitted. What he received in return was their willingness to reciprocate by supplying him with a handle on a subject in which they were expert. Because he allowed others to use him, he felt entitled to make a claim on their expertise, wherever it was. He could ask a Republican for a description of the personalities within the Republican delegation. With an opponent of child care who knew about debtor-creditor law, he could ask for an explanation of the fine points of bankruptcy, information he could later share with members of the welfare committee. Information was like currency, a store of credit.

Lockyer could count on the willingness of other members to teach him as part of their end of the implicit bargain they had struck. The first successful act of reciprocity seemed to unclog the relationships between Lockyer and a colleague; subsequent exchanges of knowledge flowed freely thereafter.

Lockyer had no need to fear the loss of intellectual superiority in the child-care area. For one thing, legislators were already too busy with their own specialties to want to encroach on Lockyer's turf. For another thing, Lockyer was less concerned about forever dominating the field of child care (or the field of poverty) than to use the legislative recognition generated by it to broaden his knowledge of diverse fields. His ambition to be a career politician led him to look on preeminence in a specific policy area as a means for attaining political leadership, not as an end in itself. Ambition, under these circumstances, triggered generosity, not the hoarding reflex. It paid to advertise, not to hunker down like a porcupine.[4]

V

But the reason for his intellectual generosity has to be more complicated than mere intellectual and political ambition. The opposing tendency—to hoard what one knew—was so strong, and so dominant in other legislatures, that its absence from the California assembly has to be understood.

Knowledge is power in legislatures. If Lockyer had been the only member of the legislature who understood the existing laws concerning child care, if he had been the only connection between the legislature and the personnel in the agencies, if he had been the only legislative contact with the governor and his budget office, if he had been the only member who grasped the meaning of the budget and could translate it in terms of real-world programs and effects, and if he had been the sole employer of legislative staff whose loyalties were such that they made their researches available only to him—if all this were the case, then no other legislators would be likely to propose legislation in the child-care area, lest they have to confront Lockyer's sophistication and be made to look foolish. Moreover, any proposal Lockyer had to make would be unlikely to be criticized astutely by any colleagues, for they would not know enough.

Having a monopoly on knowledge in a particular area would invariably make it much easier for a legislator to negotiate his program. If Lockyer had kept his grasp of programmatic details and political consequences to himself, opponents of his programs would have had no one else to turn to. Under such circumstances the most they could

4. Youthful ambition cut many ways. The serenity of later life, when the fever of advancement abated and the imperatives of going somewhere else slackened, had redeeming value, as Senator Behr observed: "I'm lucky because I'm not going anywhere. When you want to move up, then things fall out of perspective very quickly. You are always more than you were and less than what you will be, when, in fact, you really don't make much of a difference. There are lots of waves that strike the shore, and while maybe once in a while there is one uniquely large, if different, one, most waves are like the other waves. To remember that is to eliminate a lot of flotsam and jetsam from your thinking. And that's important to do."

have hoped for would have been little concessions in return for their overall passive acquiescence.

If Lockyer's proposals had been good ones, a monopoly on knowledge would have allowed him to get them into law and operation much faster and with much less effort. With no need to compromise with knowledgeable colleagues, he would have been able to realize his policies intact. He would have been a leader without peer or potential peer—a person of dominance and accomplishment. If he endured long enough and if his programs were good enough, opposition in the long run would have died or been modified by the obvious good effects of the legislation. And in the short run it surely would have been more efficient to be the only one who had vision in a house of the blind. Urgent problems would have been dealt with promptly.

To share knowledge indiscriminately, as Lockyer did, was to undermine the advantages to be gained from monopoly. Supplying fact and understanding to the opposition supplied rallying points against Lockyer's own proposals. Lockyer's own intellectual generosity forced him to answer more pointed and critical questions in debate. Informed debate highlighted the "downside" of his own policies, and that might have led to a political impasse. Knowledgeable legislative opposition might force a compromise that, for any number of reasons, might subvert the slightest hope of success for innovative programs. In sum, sharing knowledge vastly complicated things for Lockyer.

Unless the reader appreciates the beguiling attractiveness of a monopoly of knowledge, he will not see the miracle that the legislature's sharing of knowledge really was. What caused California's legislators to be intellectually generous? What prevented secrecy?

VI

The answer is that legislative knowledge was too available. Abundant and inexpensive alternative sources of knowledge rendered monopoly nearly impossible.

We have already discussed the role of the legislative analyst's office. One of its effects was to facilitate a competitor's encroachment upon another legislator's turf. The information supplied by the analyst reduced the costs of building the base of knowledge necessary to make such a claim. Where monopoly was unnatural, where abundance made it easy for competitors to encroach on new policy areas, monopoly was less likely to occur than in situations where it happened by virtue of natural shortages and the high costs of mastering complex subject matters.

Still, intellectual monopoly would have been possible, and even likely in the many areas not conventionally under the scrutiny of the legislative analyst. Since the analyst's major area of concern was the Budget Bill, he knew a lot about state benefit programs but had very little to say about the private sectors that government could or did regulate. The budget analysis therefore had nothing to teach legislators about puzzling and complicated matters like the financial practices of auto dealers or milk pooling or union jurisdictional disputes at farmers' markets. Nor did it have anything to say about newly proposed legislation. Rather, the legislators depended critically on the nonpartisan committee staffs for coherent information about the products of the author system. The role of the staffs was to develop the teaching materials to make each bill comprehensible. Lobbyists, of course, had their expertise to share, but the staffs were vital in maintaining the academic integrity of the legislative learning process.

A committee chairman who wanted to have a controlling say over legislation, however, could try to attain a monopoly of competence on all matters before his committee. He could do so by hiring a closed staff. A closed staff reported only to a chairman and did its work only with regard to his purposes. Such closed, monopolistic practices had occurred in California before, and undoubtedly they occur presently in many state legislatures. In 1975 a procedure was developed in the California assembly to prevent staffs from working in a closed fashion. The procedure was called the Third Reading Analysis (TRA). One of its functions was to provoke competition between committee staffs. Another was to provide competing outlets for lobbyists' expertise.

When the legislature met on the floor to debate and approve bills passed to it by committees, every legislator received a looseleaf volume containing one- to three-page analyses of each bill to be discussed. Each analysis looked much like analyses prepared by committee staffs. It described the problem to be solved; it contained a description of the bill, an examination of its operation on the problem, and a statement of its probable costs and benefits. It also recorded the bill's history: what legislators had voted for and against it in committees and what agencies and groups had taken positions on it. TRAs were prepared by a special, nonpartisan research office on the basis of all the preceding analyses, partisan and otherwise, that dealt with the bill.

Procedures required each committee to forward every one of its staff analyses to the research office (if the state senate were the house of origin on a bill, senate staff analyses were gathered, too). Each lobbyist—each agency involved, each private group remotely interested in the matter—was invited to forward an assessment of bills about which they had commented. If the legislative analyst's office was involved, its work was also forwarded. Then a nonpartisan staff of writers worked up a composite of all this analytic work, framing the issues, arraying the arguments pro and con, systematically discarding the specious, and highlighting the weighty arguments.

It might appear dangerous to concentrate so much responsibility in the office that wrote the Third Reading Analyses. After all, if the legislators actually came to depend upon the TRAs, the office preparing them could, to further its own views, omit troublesome information and publish only the part of the case with which it agreed. Working under egregious time pressures (when legislative work peaked, much of the writing had to be done under conditions that would make a newspaper editor wince) the writers were subject to fatigue and carelessness that could compound any ideological bias.

Nonetheless, to judge from the legislative approval accorded it, the TRA procedure worked. The conscientious, hard-working McAlister said:

> The analyses we get on the floor have worked a great improvement. I used to go out and collect committee analyses often. But now the Third Reading Analysis does that for me. They don't leave out much. They get the pros and cons down. That's been very helpful. Usually they have dissenting votes of committees and sometimes on a close vote even the members who were on the majority. It's helpful to see who the players were, obviously.

Dedicated Republicans commented in a similar vein:

> The Third Reading Analysis has made a difference. It gives the opportunity to know the salient points of the bill. The research office, though it's Democratically dominated, tries to be objective.

It is important to see why the TRA made a difference. It changed entirely the practices of several committee staffs. Before the TRA procedure, it was possible for a committee staff to analyze a bill, consult with the chairman, arrive at a conclusion, and provide virtually no written work for the committee membership. In short, it was possible to have what I have called a closed staff.[5] Under the TRA procedure, however, closed staffs fell victim to the requirement that all committee staff work be divulged in written analyses, to be judged "on their merits" for inclusion in the TRA in competition with the work from other committees, state agencies, proponents, and opponents. The legislators were put in the position of having the staffs compete for their attention. The quality of committee staff work, as a result, improved.[6] Legislators got better educational services. As staff analyses vied for inclusion in the TRA, they began to grapple with the toughest issues; they made explicit the reasons and the facts necessary to reach decisions; they laid out options and compared them; they were written intelligently, simply, and understandably. They were something that, as J. B. Priestley observed elsewhere, "at a pinch could be read aloud in a pub."[7]

5. The converse, and equally insidious practice, was the "capture" of a chairman by his staff. In *Politics Backstage: Inside the California Legislature* (Philadelphia: Temple University Press, 1979), Michael Bevier contends that a highly competent staff member's personal preferences prevented a legislative chairman from hearing all sides of the issue: "But what impressed me the most while working with a state legislature which is a model of reform was the extent to which its strongest feature—a large and competent staff—had insulated the elected representatives from the guts of legislative decision-making" (p. 234).

6. John Stuart Mill once wrote of competition and mankind's tendencies to indolence and narrowness: "I do not pretend that there are no inconveniences in competition, or that the moral objections urged against it by Socialist writers, as a source of jealousy and hostility among those engaged in the same occupation, are altogether groundless. But if competition has its evils, it prevents greater evils. . . . It is the common error of Socialists to overlook the natural indolence of mankind: their tendency to be passive, to be the slaves of habit, to persist indefinitely in a course once chosen. Let them once attain any state of existence which they consider tolerable, and the danger to be apprehended is that they will henceforth stagnate; will not exert themselves to improve, and by letting their faculties rust, will lose even that energy required to preserve them from deterioration. Competition may not be the best conceived stimulus, but it is at present a necessary one. . ." (John Stuart Mill, *Principles of Political Economy*, 7th ed. [London: Longmans, Green and Co., 1929, W. J. Ashley, ed.], pp. 792–93, Book 4, chap. 7).

7. In J. B. Priestley, *Delight* (New York: Harper and Brothers, 1949), as quoted in *The Christian Science Monitor*, 27 November 1979, p. 21: "At the end of a long talk with a youngish critic, a sincere fellow whose personality (though not his values) I respect, he stared at me and then said slowly: 'I don't understand you. Your talk is so much more complicated—subtle—than your writing. Your writing always seems

The TRA procedure was not always flawless, but it was good enough for a human institution. It appealed to the pride of the staffs; it directed them toward a wider audience for their teaching materials; it engaged them in competition; it deprived their chairman of his monopoly over them; it invigorated them and disseminated the products of their intellectual energies. Under the conditions created by the TRA procedure, a monopoly of knowledge, even by the wiliest and stingiest legislator, was made virtually impossible. That was why the TRA "made a difference." It was the Sherman Antitrust Law of the legislature.

VII

The TRA procedure, along with committee staff and the Office of the Legislative Analyst, was the center of the nonpartisan support system.[8] Together, these three mechanisms were the equivalent of Nature in the economist's model, and the packages of information and understanding they generated were Nature's bounty. The support system, by distributing information and perspective disinterestedly, made an intellectual monopoly by a single legislator unlikely, unattractive, and even impossible. In that sense the nonpartisan information system tilted each legislative member away from tendencies of autarchy and hoarding and toward customs of interdependence and exchange.

Yet the support system was peopled by individuals, with their own ideological and idiosyncratic ways. We have already noted the monopolistic powers the research office had attained as a result of widespread legislative reliance on the TRA. Similarly, the legislative analyst's staff resources gave the analyst's office unusual influence in fiscal controversies. What, then, compelled the nonpartisan support system to share fairly its abundance of information?

---

to me too simple.' And I replied: 'But I've spent years and years trying to make my writing simple. What you see as a fault, I regard as a virtue. . . .' Rightly or wrongly, I am not afraid of the crowd. . . . Because I am what is called now 'an intellectual'— and I am just as much 'an intellectual' as these younger chaps—I do not feel that there is a glass wall between me and the people in the nearest factories, shops and pubs. I do not believe that my thoughts and feelings are quite different from theirs. I prefer therefore a wide channel of communication. Deliberately I aim at simplicity and not complexity in my writing. No matter what the subject in hand might be, I want to write something that at a pinch could be read aloud in a pub."

8. Other important parts of the nonpartisan support system were the legislative counsel's office, an auditor general's office, and a long-term research component called the Assembly Office of Research.

The answer is the political parties. The legislators in the assembly were organized into two competing clubs. Members of the same party, though there were wide ideological differences among them, regarded themselves as members of the same team. They expected to have access to the party consultants' staff; to be able to share confidences with each other in the party caucus; and to back one another up if the party leadership or the nonpartisan support system failed to play fair. There was a solidarity among them, not on political issues, but on institutional issues. No party member felt alone if institutional policing was necessary.

Staff was made available to both parties. Party staff members were "slack" resources, in a sense—they were without formally assigned purposes, like a reserve in army maneuvers. As we saw in chapter 3, they normally educated the freshmen on how to proceed through the author system. Yet they could be mobilized to countervail the nonpartisan support system if it failed to be nonpartisan. The Republicans could have put their staff to work to generate "underground" TRAs or analyses of the budget if partisan bias began to infect the nonpartisan research office or legislative analyst's office.

Parties played another important intellectual role. Each was expected to develop knowledgeable specialists who competed with one another with respect to crucial policy areas. The Republican specialists were expected to share what they knew with all the Republicans and any Democrats who were for any reason willing to learn from a Republican specialist. The same was true with Democratic specialists: all Democrats felt entitled to exploit them, and uncertain Republicans could come to them too. If the Democrats had an elementary school financing specialist, it was legitimate for the Republicans to develop one as well. If the Republicans had an excellent mental health specialist, it was perfectly acceptable for a young Democrat to work up a specialty on the same turf.

Of course, the minority party—the Republicans in 1975, but Democrats just six years earlier—labored under greater limitations regarding the number of policy domains they might cover adequately. After all, in 1975 the Republican assembly members numbered twenty-five, and only a handful of them had the inclination or capacity to become specialists. They simply lacked the manpower to mount competition in all the specialties developed by the fifty-five Democratic members.[9] Yet the institution of the assembly, because

9. Party leadership tried to coordinate the members of the political team so that they did not duplicate one another's specialty. Lockyer described a leadership decision

of the two-party system, legitimated and even invited partisan competition among specialists. We thus come to the vital conclusion. In a legislature whose dominant characteristic was its nonpartisanship, the crucial enabling factor was the competitive party system. The threat of resourceful partisan competition kept the nonpartisan support system energetic, careful, and as fair as humanly possible. Nonpartisanship in the California legislature did not mean that competition between parties was or should have been absent. It meant equal access to Nature's intellectual bounty for members of the majority and minority parties alike. Nonpartisanship was the legislature's guarantee against discrimination.

VIII

What were the effects of cultivating the legislators' desire to share what they knew? What resulted from encouraging the resourceful members of the legislature to advertise their understanding of some topic, to take the time to teach it well and recurrently, and to hunt up colleagues who might need it? The most precious result was that it integrated the individual competences of legislators into an institutional competence.

The individual members of the assembly brought impressive intellectual credentials to Sacramento. Almost all had college training at some of the best private and public universities in the country. The eighty members included many with graduate training—a medical doctor, an optometrist, a Ph.D., an architect, two M.B.A.s, and twenty-eight lawyers. Fifteen of them were former educators. The few who did not have a college degrees were impressive in their own right by virtue of a special expertise in farming or ranching or

---

that assigned him rather than another Democrat the oil depletion tax bill: "During this time one of the other members, a freshman, introduced the same kind of measure. The next step was the Democratic caucus where we first took up the question of whose bill would be the first to go forward. Mine had been put in slightly before his, and while that is not always important, it was a factor. The next step would be the assembly taxation committee, and Dan Boatwright, the chairman, had a policy that members of his committee should, where possible, carry major tax bills. It meant, I guess, that there would be a little more sophistication brought to these tax matters and to the committee. Then I talked with the Speaker about which bill to start off with. Mine was a little clearer, a little better written. Besides, the Speaker was worried that a brand-new freshman might make some mistakes that would cost a critical vote or two."

language training, which gave them an advantage over their more academically trained colleagues.

The members were no political innocents, either. At least thirty-five of them had had substantial political and governmental experience before winning a seat in the assembly. Among them were former mayors, city council members, county supervisors, city managers, school board members, and legislative staff.

However, all the individual backgrounds did not necessarily add up to a collective intelligence. The abundant knowledge of farming in one assemblyman's head, for example, was not magically transmuted into an intelligent, well-considered legislative decision about the pricing of dairy products. Knowledge had to be taught and broadcast and learned. The cultivation of intellectual markets for knowledge served to build an institutional competence. Market-building generated information about the intellectual talents and shortcomings of individual legislators. Advertisements guided the needy legislator to willing sources of supply. Moreover, the practices of an open legislature induced legislators to develop a special capacity of their own and teach it.

This open legislature made maximum use of lobbyists, yet discouraged reliance on any one lobbyist. The TRA provided easy, inviting access into the decision-making process for all lobbyists, but their ideas contended against one another and neutralized individual bias.[10] When staffs ceased to be closed, lobbyists of all persuasions deemed them more approachable. Finally, when a tyro legislator needed an understanding of an area, he was likely to know of a legislator who was glad to introduce him to the subject and could provide him with a perspective on the views of the lobbyists.[11]

10. As de Tocqueville remarked, "The ambition and the maneuvers of the one will serve . . . to unmask the other" (*Democracy in America*, v. 1, p. 249). He was talking about the corruption and ineptitude of popularly elected officials and the democratic incentive of their competitors to expose those vices. But the general point applies equally to lobbyists. Competition among a multiplicity of lobbyists exposes the inadequacies of each.

11. Former Assembly Speaker Jess Unruh, the father of the modern California legislature, has written that lobbyists "have influence in inverse ratio to legislative competence. It is common for a special interest to be the only source of legislative information about itself. The information that a lobbyist presents may or may not be prejudiced in favor of his client, but if it is the only information the legislature has, no one can really be sure. A special interest monopoly of information seems much more sinister than the outright buying of votes that has been excessively imputed to lobbyists" (quoted in *The Sometime Governments*, p. 129, from Donald Herzberg and Jess Unruh, *Essays on the State Legislative Process* [New York: Holt Rinehart and Winston, 1970], p. 80).

The personal effects of legislative sharing were also important. The system produced personal habits and attitudes as well as legislation. Among the most important was the habit of openness. By working in an institution where knowledge was exchanged, legislators learned that there was more profit than risk in enlightening others.[12] Sharing knowledge was rewarded with respect. It became the norm of the place. Because everybody did it, so did every entering freshman.

Released from having to hoard knowledge, the legislators talked with each other incessantly, unguardedly sharing this joke, that anecdote, a historical fact, a capsule sketch of someone's personality,[13] a bit of strategy, a statement of the issue, a perspective, a handle on a matter. The place throbbed with talk, activity, intellectual exchange, superabundant energy.[14]

12. Of course, in the marketplace the enrichment of one's customers works a blessing, while enrichment of one's competitors can be very threatening. Similarly, sharing knowledge with a legislative rival might prove dangerous, but sharing one's special expertise with legislative colleagues whose principal interests were very different from one's own might prove rewarding. Peter Blau has explained why someone becomes a competitor or a customer: "Competition occurs only among like social units that have the same objectives and not among unlike units with different objectives . . . whereas exchange occurs only between unlike units" (*Exchange and Power in Social Life*, p. 331).

13. Handles were just as important regarding personalities as with subject matters. Each legislator needed to become astute about the strengths and limitations of each of his colleagues. The late congressman Clem Miller eloquently depicted this part of a legislative education: "The result of these sharp-honed feelings is an enlarged apperception that is used to scrutinize fellow members. While Congressmen are quite ordinary in general outline, their practice of the political art has made them knowledgeable in assessing one another. Their instincts, sharpened by the conflict of the personal and the impersonal, enable them to characterize each other to the finest hair. Thus, each Congressman is given his little pigeonhole, with all his strengths and weaknesses, foibles and tricks, duly noted for use on the proper occasion" (*Member of the House*, p. 106).

14. Compare the California legislative process with Connecticut's as described by David Ogle, in *Strengthening the Connecticut Legislature: A Report of the Eagleton Institute of Politics* (New Brunswick, N. J.: Rutgers University Press, 1970), pp. 3–4: "The major part of important legislative business [is conducted] within the space of a few days in late May and early June during odd-numbered years. The people of Connecticut hear and read of little being done by their legislature during the first three or four months of a legislative session. Then—in the middle of May—the Connecticut General Assembly explodes into the headlines for a few days with stories of important legislation being passed in the early hours of the morning after a continuous ten- or twelve-hour session, of bills being passed only by number or title with just a few leaders being aware of what they provide, of numerous compromises on measures which had previously been stalemated for months, and of important bills mysteriously disappearing, not to be found until after the session has ended."

Seven

The purpose of a member of the legislature is to look for deficiencies to be cured. Either he fulfills his public obligations, or he'll be a freeloader. And I don't think many are freeloaders.
  Assemblyman Frank Lanterman, 1976

Losers hang out with losers.
  Billy Martin, Manager, Oakland A's, 1981

Why the Best Legislators Got to the Top

I

Alister McAlister was a tireless, hardworking legislator—a man of intellect and stern moral convictions, who worked long days and nights for a fraction of the income he might otherwise have enjoyed as a lawyer in private practice. The legislature was a meaningful institution to him. He was enlivened by its problems, big or small, and he was infuriated by any careless lapses perpetrated by its members. He was a stickler for standards of competency and honesty. Partially as a result of his assignment in 1975 as chairman of the business committee, it lost its historical reputation as the "bag committee," one whose members were prone to seek corporate contributions to their own personal and political well-being. The committee's reputation for integrity, in fact, was considerably heightened by the stern manner in which McAlister governed its affairs.

McAlister was a member of the leadership coalition of the assembly. He was a Democrat, a valued supporter of the Speaker, chairman of the most important policy committee, industrious, careful, and intelligent. He had also assumed a variety of responsibilities for specialized subjects: liability insurance, eminent domain, and tort law reforms, for example. In addition, out of his Mormon scruples, he had assumed leadership of the anti-abortion, pro-life forces in the legislature, and he had reasonably severe attitudes about criminal violence, reflected in his authorship of a moderate capital punishment bill.[1] He was also an astute student of politics, prone to read both scholarly and trade books on the subject.

1. A moderate capital punishment bill was one that narrowly defined the circumstances under which the death sentence was permissible.

One evening, in a relatively expansive mood, he began to reflect upon the nature of the legislature as he had experienced it in more than seven years of service:

> I read a book recently, Burnham's *The New Machiavellians*. It was a very good book. In it he summarizes the view of a group of thinkers he called neo-Machiavellians. And he made one point preeminently. Whatever the form of government, even in representative government, only a few people really will ever hold the power and make the decisions. I see that generalization put in practice here all the time. . . . There is a definite structure and hierarchy in a legislature. On the ultimate questions only a few make decisions. But they cannot ignore others. They run the risk of alienation and opposition. They have to maintain the appearance and sometimes the reality that others can participate.

In the California assembly there was, most assuredly, a "definite structure and hierarchy." A small number of legislators were universally respected by their colleagues and seemed invariably to be where the action was. Others were practically invisible and were rarely talked about. The legislature was made up of "big fish and little fish" (as another legislator said); there were upper-class legislators and lower-class ones—and of course there were the inbetweens.

An important series of questions arises from McAlister's observations. Why did only a few people dominate so many decisions? What determined who those few were? And were they among the best or the worst of the individual legislative members?

In a knowledgeable legislature like California's, those who were judged by their legislative colleagues to be the most talented achieved a high status that earned them deference from legislators and lobbyists alike. They could not be ignored on any matter they cared about. These few, however, could maintain their high status only if they continued to win the votes of their many colleagues for the many bills they were required to carry. But in the sense that votes could kill bills carried by notables and nobodies alike, and could turn a notable into a nobody (and vice versa), there was a reality to the participation of "others."

II

Status in the legislature depended upon the members' success in the author system. Thoughtful legislators agreed that "you have to carry legislation to be recognized." The author system was the showplace of a member's competence, and the touchstone of a legislator's status was his or her "batting average." A legislative batting average was the percentage of a member's bills that he got through the legislative process and onto the governor's desk. Every legislator worth his salt had a distinct impression of his colleagues' batting averages, as well as of his own.

Legislative batting averages, like those in baseball, were interpreted with subtlety by the cognoscenti. Every baseball buff knows the necessity of making a mental adjustment of the quotient derived from dividing a player's hits by his "at-bats." A player's true value cannot dependably be determined by his batting average without knowing about other factors. After all, some hits are singles, some home runs. Some hitters with low averages hit well in the clutch, while some high-average hitters never seem to come up with the big hit. Some players compensate for a mediocre batting average by their skill as defensive players. And so on. As a result, the batting champion is not always the highest paid or most highly regarded player. Far down the batting average list are sluggers whom pitchers find more daunting than the apparent batting champion. Nonetheless, batting averages have their place as a convenient index by which to judge which players are premier performers and which are mere journeymen.

So it was in the state legislature. Batting averages were adjusted with equal sophistication by the knowledgeable, but they were computed nonetheless and were considered valuable. The legislative batting average—dividing the bills enrolled (BE)[2] by the bills introduced (BI)—was sometimes discounted for a number of reasons: the meaninglessness of some bills because they were "district bills" or had been so much amended that the original thrust of concern was nullified, or the inability to carry big bills in knock-down-drag-out fights when every vote counted, or the inability to defeat hostile legislation. Conversely, a premium was accorded the batting averages of those

---

2. An enrolled bill could be vetoed by the governor. His veto could be overridden only when two-thirds of the membership of each legislative house voted to do so. Vetoes were rarely overridden.

who put through "good bills," won the close ones, and were formidable opponents.

Let us look at the unadjusted batting averages[3] of the assembly members in 1975–76, the eighty who were originally elected and the two who were elected to fill vacancies halfway through the term. The ratio of bills enrolled to bills introduced, BE/BI, has been carried out to three decimals, which we shall call "percentage points" as in baseball.

Rank	Name	Party	District	BI*	BE*	Pct.
1.	McCarthy	D	18	10	8	.800
2.	Beverly	R	51	24	18	.750
3.	Lanterman	R	41	60	44	.733
4.	Mobley	R	31	45	33	.733
5.	Calvo (x)	D	21	27	19	.704
6.	Chel (x)	D	58	50	35	.700
7.	Knox	D	11	109	76	.697
8.	Lancaster	R	62	24	16	.667
9.	Collier	R	61	3	2	.667
10.	Garamendi (x)	D	7	41	26	.634
11.	Foran	D	16	51	32	.627
12.	Duffy	R	32	61	38	.623
13.	L. Greene	D	6	54	33	.611
14.	Lewis	R	67	45	27	.600
15.	Craven	R	76	62	37	.597
16.	Chimbole (x)	D	34	52	31	.596
17.	Badham	R	74	46	27	.587
18.	Fenton	D	59	36	21	.583
19.	Ingalls	D	68	62	36	.581
20.	W. Thomas (x)	R	33	35	20	.571
21.	Priolo	R	38	23	13	.565
22.	Davis	D	1	25	14	.560
23.	Egeland (x)	D	24	70	39	.557
24.	MacDonald	D	36	65	36	.554
25.	Gualco (x)	D	5	58	32	.552
26.	Berman	D	43	44	24	.545
27.	Burke	R	73	39	21	.538

3. In one case, that of Assemblyman Cullen, I have adjusted his "bills introduced" downwards to eliminate fifty-two bills he apparently introduced at the end of term solely for purposes of distributing printed versions to interested parties for discussion. All other bill loads appeared to comprise bills that the legislator seriously considered moving in the 1975–76 term.

28.	Vicencia (x)	D	54	43	23	.535
29.	Vasconcellos	D	23	62	33	.532
30.	Hart (x)	D	35	55	29	.527
31.	Murphy	R	28	40	21	.525
32.	Fazio† (x)	D	4	50	26	.520
33.	Sieroty	D	44	111	57	.514
34.	Suitt (x)	D	75	55	28	.509
35.	Maddy	R	30	58	29	.500
36.	Deddeh	D	80	65	32	.492
37.	Keene	D	2	98	48	.490
38.	Arnett	R	20	56	27	.482
39.	Siegler (x)	D	8	67	32	.478
40.	Chappie	R	3	106	50	.471
41.	V. Thomas	D	65	30	14	.467
42.	McAlister	D	25	101	47	.465
43.	Papan	D	19	59	27	.458
44.	Boatwright	D	10	55	25	.455
45.	Miller	D	13	31	14	.452
46.	Lockyer	D	14	75	33	.440
47.	Hayden	R	22	37	16	.432
48.	Perino (x)	D	26	65	28	.431
49.	McVittie (x)	D	65	79	34	.430
50.	Brown	D	17	94	40	.426
51.	Montoya	D	60	53	22	.415
52.	Wornum (x)	D	9	54	22	.407
53.	Briggs	R	49	35	14	.400
54.	Z'Berg‡	D	4	67	26	.389
55.	Tucker (x)	D	50	31	12	.387
56.	Mori (x)	D	15	47	18	.383
57.	Rosenthal (x)	D	45	51	21	.382
58.	Thurman	D	27	92	35	.380
59.	Bannai	R	53	46	17	.370
60.	Dixon	D	49	65	23	.354
61.	Nestande (x)	R	70	20	7	.350
62.	Wilson	D	77	66	23	.348
63.	Antonovich	R	41	61	20	.328
64.	Robinson (x)	D	72	58.	19	.328
65.	Goggin (x)	D	66	52	17	.327
66.	Keysor	D	39	106	33	.311
67.	Ralph	D	48	75	23	.307
68.	Alatorre	D	55	66	20	.303
69.	Kapiloff	D	78	99	29	.293
70.	Hughes† (x)	D	47	35	10	.286

71.	Torres (x)	D	56	72	20	.278
72.	Nimmo	R	29	18	5	.278
73.	W. Greene‡	D	47	12	3	.250
74.	Campbell (x)	R	64	45	11	.244
75.	Bane (x)	D	40	58	14	.241
76.	Chacon	D	79	51	12	.235
77.	Cullen	D	57	58	13	.224
78.	Meade	D	12	45	10	.222
79.	Carpenter (x)	D	71	99	19	.192
80.	Cline	R	37	48	9	.188
81.	McLennan	R	63	17	3	.176
82.	Warren	D	46	34	5	.147

(x): Indicates freshman members of the assembly.
* BI = bills introduced; BE = bills enrolled (i.e., bills awaiting governor's signature).
† Fazio and Hughes were elected midterm to fill vacancies.
‡ Z'Berg died midterm; W. Greene was elected to the state senate midterm, thus vacating his assembly seat.

The averages disclose some surprises. For example, Republicans did well in a heavily Democratic legislature. Of the top twenty-one, eleven were Republicans, even though Republicans were outnumbered two to one in the house as a whole. In several cases their bills were lightweight district bills, and this explains their high average. But not in all cases: some Republicans were effective legislators even though their load was large and their bills heavyweight. Another surprise: rookies did proportionately well. Six of the top twenty-four legislators were in their first term. Unlike freshmen congressmen, good rookies successfully carried out substantial responsibilities in the California state legislature.

There are also a couple of anomalies that need additional explanation. The legislator with the worst average was Charles Warren, chairman of the energy committee. He was regarded universally as among the best members and pointed to as a model legislator. He was a redoubtable opponent of others' legislation. Moreover, his "hits"—his five successful bills—were big and meaningful legislation; his timber severance tax, for example, cured a long-standing and serious problem. His misses too were often spectacular: he negotiated a bitterly contested land-use planning bill through three major committees and one house. His low average reflected an unconventional imbalance between big and little bills, with the big bills tilting the scale. One shrewd admirer said of him that he "is a specialist, and he has the greatest latitude." As the specialist in energy, the newest challenging topic of public policy, Warren's batting average was abysmal, although this had no appreciable effect on his reputation. He was the exception that proved the rule, namely, that batting averages were important.

A second anomaly: perhaps the most effective and eloquent legislator, Willie Brown,[4] a black representative from San Francisco, had a batting average of .426, which ranked him in fiftieth place. He had been, however, the principal challenger for the Speaker's seat, and the assembly leadership coalition had subsequently kept a short tether on him. He waged stiff legislative battles without staff and without benefit of a chairmanship and, even when he lost, always came close. Moreover, most of his causes were uphill. He and Sieroty (.514 average, thirty-third rank) were the major protagonists for liberal spending programs in a fiscally conservative regime. No one questioned their effectiveness. In their cases the number of bills they succeeded in enrolling (forty and fifty-seven, respectively) was a more apt measure of their competence than their batting averages.

The Brown and Sieroty anomalies might lead one to mistrust the whole notion of batting averages. One might object that the low percentages in Brown's and Sieroty's cases were simply a function of the number of bills they were asked to introduce. A less active or respected legislator who introduced fewer bills would have a higher average than one who was equally productive, that is, got as much legislation to the governor's desk, but introduced more bills. One might object further that, unlike in baseball, where an at-bat without a hit represents a missed opportunity, a bill not carried forward does not lose ground and therefore should not diminish a legislator's average. Thus the similarity between the activity of a baseball player and that of a legislator is spurious, as are legislative batting averages.

4. Assemblyman Brown had been chairman of the appropriations committee for several years prior to 1975–76. He was a masterful chairman, as is illustrated by a remark made by a lobbyist: "I brought to California to represent Lazard Freres, which was trying to sell some property to the state, this New York lawyer named Bartels, a man seemingly with but one purpose—to protect his client. He would not go into any committee hearings, even on his own bill. He would pace the halls. Finally, I dragged him in to watch Willie Brown handle appropriations. Well, I couldn't get him out of there. He was fascinated by the guy. And now every time he comes to California, he wants to go see Willie."

There is some merit to this claim, and the anomalies of Brown and Sieroty result partly from the fact that among the bills they introduced were contingency or "back-up" bills, that is, bills introduced by way of precaution in the event a parallel bill carried by someone else was killed. The compelling answer to the objection, however, is that bill loads by and large consisted of serious legislation, and in the usual case a bill not carried forward did forfeit valuable opportunities. After all, each group or agency or individual behind a bill had a problem of some kind. A legislator's failure to move a bill cost the possibility of a debate about a social solution to a real problem. In that sense a bill not carried forward did resemble an "out" in baseball.

Furthermore, some legislators carried huge bill loads yet maintained high batting averages, as did Knox, Lanterman, and Chel. More than any other simple index, batting averages were useful touchstones of effectiveness: fallible, yes, but illuminating nonetheless, especially when used in conjunction with productivity (i.e., the number of bills enrolled).

In general, legislators who had high batting averages tended to stand tall in the legislative social system. More significantly, those whose averages were low and were accorded low social status as well. Legislators and lobbyists, in their continual scrutiny of each other for abilities and vulnerabilities, tended to find that the best legislators were among those who batted well in the author system. Those legislators regarded as the worst, in turn, tended to have the lowest legislative batting averages. Certainly legislators and lobbyists looked more seriously at bills carried by legislators who batted .700 than ones authored by .350 hitters. Although a difference of a few percentage points did not matter greatly, it was rare that a poor legislator would score over .450 and it was unusual for a deeply admired legislator to drop below .350.

III

What was the relationship between a member's high batting average and his colleagues' high esteem for him? Were individuals with admirable personal qualities successful legislators because of their admirable qualities? Or were successful legislators admired individuals because they were merely successful? What caused success?

It was not enough to attribute success to the power individuals wielded by virtue of committee chairmanships and the staffs they managed. Some committee chairmen did score high: Knox of local government, Foran of appropriations, Greene of education, Ingalls of transportation, and Mobley of water. Some were remarkably low: Chacon of housing, Keysor of elections, Ralph of rules, Wilson of government operations. Most were in the middle, although some were highly productive, enrolling impressive numbers of bills: Sieroty of crime, McAlister of business, Keene of health, Lockyer of welfare, Deddeh of state employees.

The house party leadership—McCarthy of the Democrats and Beverly of the Republicans—had the best averages, but their bill load was lean. Other party leaders averaged both high and low: neither Dixon, the Democratic caucus chairman, nor Papan, the assistant Speaker, was among the leaders, nor was Campbell, the Republican whip.

Why, then, did legislators have high batting averages or high productivity if party, experience, committee staff, and partisan leadership were uncertain influences? The answer is, they taught well. Those legislators who had batting averages of .600 or better all were accomplished instructors. In hearings where their bills were being assessed, they justified in principled terms the compromises they negotiated between opposed groups; they prepared their witnesses well; they dispersed lobbying forces to tutor large number of legislators on an individual basis; they made systematic presentations; they taught the committee staffs conscientiously, hence the staff prepared good teaching materials for the committee members.

I asked Larry Chimbole, a wise and older Democratic rookie legislator who had long prior experience in local government, to discuss some of the legislators he thought were the best. He thought as he spoke, and as his ideas crystallized, he talked with more force. He singled out three particularly productive members:

> Well, I think that there are a few legislators I would have to put in that category. I would judge a guy like Barry Keene, who has an intense interest in his subject area, that way. He's knowledgeable, convincing. Leroy Greene: he's a student of his area, makes a logical presentation and specializes. . . . Willie Brown: I don't agree with much of his legislation, but he's logical, reasonable, and persistent. Most of them have specialties. They are not noisemakers, not grandstanders.

Chimbole's phrases extolling the legislators he deemed the best were typical of his colleagues' praises: "knowledgeable," "convincing," "a student of his area," "makes a logical presentation," and "reasonable." These were terms one would hear in any academic setting. The legislators with high batting averages tended to be the resourceful ones who had the pedagogical graces of patience and orderliness and a sense of the significant. Those with low batting averages tended not to have such graces.

Good teachers won the votes of their fellows, and their bills passed, raising their batting averages. In turn, their success enhanced their attractiveness to lobbyists, who asked them to carry more bills and promised effective help to pass them. For example, the various agencies of state government gave their important bills only to legislators of proven stature, legislators who had been tried out on the agencies' small bills and who had proved effective. Over time, the good legislative teachers increased their bill load and maintained their high averages. That development meant that they appeared more frequently before committees and spoke more often in the floor debate. A strong legislator like Jack Knox carried 109 bills in 1975–76, received his colleagues' approval to appear sixty-four times in front of an appropriations committee of one house or the other, and in the course of getting seventy-six bills enrolled, taught his legislation 399 times (if we include the seventy-six times a senate colleague spoke for him in the senate after having been coached by Knox).[5]

On the other hand, poor teachers were denied the votes of their colleagues and lost bills. Their low batting average diminished their attractiveness to lobbyists, who gave them few important bills to carry. The bills that the less esteemed representatives got to carry were those that had been rejected by the higher-status legislators: they were the proposals of unattractive interests with questionable solutions, and with small chance of passage. As a result, lower-status legislators had fewer opportunities to appear before their colleagues, and when they did appear, the subject matter was less interesting or appealing. A weak legislator like Doc McLennan carried seventeen bills, appeared in front of an appropriations committee only three times, and, at most, had twenty opportunities to teach his legislation to his fellows.

If one were to glance at the batting average tables, it might appear that some legislators with low averages carried big bill loads. Appearances deceived, however. This might be true for one or two

5. One admiring legislator said of Jack Knox, "He is one of those people that can carry legislation that will do anything."

terms, but over time unsuccessful authors almost always reduced their efforts in the author system to the bare minimum. Among the twenty-nine legislators who introduced more than sixty bills in 1975–76, eight had batting averages below .350—Wilson, Antonovich, Keysor, Ralph, Alatorre, Torres, Kapiloff, and Carpenter. Those eight got strong signals not to aspire to the role of legislative teacher (or, if they were freshmen like Torres, to improve quickly). Sometimes the signal was given humorously by a committee member: "We love you, Joe, but your bills are terrible. You must have someone helping you think up those bills. You couldn't be doing it all by yourself." Sometimes the message was given with cruel sarcasm. To an immoderate legislator whose bullying and ignorant ways with savings and loan associations backfired in his utter defeat at a hearing, the committee chairman said with sarcasm: "Thank you, Mr. Jones. You have given us a good education in the savings and loan industry." A bad teacher's noisemaking simply went unrewarded; the members withheld the resources a bill-carrier had to win to gain permission to continue, namely, their votes. If a legislator who lacked the knack for teaching insisted on authoring bills and taking up valuable time, the punishment could be devastating. A freshman, Carpenter, carried ninety-nine bills in 1975–76. The assembly terminated seventy-two of them, the senate eight more. On only nineteen occasions—many of them early in the term—was he allowed to get his bills to the senate floor.[6]

The important point was that the legislators had a decisive way to pick the colleagues they wanted as their teachers and mentors. They defeated the bills of an incompetent colleague, and a series of

6. Frank Lanterman talked about one member of the assembly (*not* Carpenter) who kept trying to get the legislature's attention when it had decided not to give it to him: "There is one guy on the floor who is an irresponsible idiot. . . . He demands your ear when you don't want to give it. He has an overwhelming desire to get recognition. He had a bill that he had drawn up for him with the notion that it was God's answer to malpractice. We had knocked the bill down in appropriations. Things were pretty tight on that subject. He went to the Speaker and had the Speaker come up to give the word to Johnny Foran [chairman of appropriations]. Eventually he got the bill to be reconsidered and approved by the committee, but I have never seen Foran madder. The bill made no sense. I went to the Speaker and asked him why he had made such a pitch for the bill. . . . Well, the bill came down on the floor, and when this pestiferous pest rose to defend the bill, the members' faces registered, 'You asshole.' With a person like that, I doubt you can cure it, but the house sure can blunt the consequences. He had used undue pressure as a result of persistent obnoxiousness."

defeats alerted lobbyists with any choice in the matter to desist from giving him any legislation to carry.

IV

There was a class system in the legislature. The upper class of mentors had rights and duties appropriate to their status, and the lower class of listeners had their own privileges and obligations. A person in the mentor class was expected to give lessons—accurate, reliable, well-pondered, and well-taught lessons. As Arnett, a highly respected Republican, put it:

> You assume a position of leadership in a field, and you acquire a reputation and people come to you. That's complimentary and good for the ego. And it's a mountain for you to climb.

The expectation that mentors would keep up-to-date, be ready to debate extemporaneously, prepare courses (for each bill was like a course, some big, some small), and be flawlessly accurate was an unrelenting pressure. Such were the daily obligations of the upper class, and they were indeed a mountain to climb.

Aside from personal rewards, the assembly member who was an effective teacher might be awarded the chairmanship of a standing or ad hoc committee by the Speaker. Even minority party members were picked to chair committees if they were good. The benefit of a chairmanship was the nonpartisan, technical staff positions that were attached to it.

Why was it that the Speaker would appoint the best and the brightest as heads of committees? Put another way, what permitted the Speaker to evade the demands of loyal but relatively incompetent cronies for chairmanships of their own? The answer is that, as a rule, only the best legislators wanted to be chairmen. The worst had no desire to assume a chairmanship. Of course, sometimes the Speaker had to appoint relatively ineffective members as chairmen of second-rank committees because the available talent was thin. But the Speaker was not subjected to intolerable pressures to pick incompetents as chairmen.[7] Why that should be so deserves an explanation.

7. Upsetting times skewed even the best of general rules, however. In 1980 the Speaker was severely challenged by a Democratic colleague for the leadership of the assembly. In order to win over a pair of crucial adherents from the challenger, the Speaker appointed them chairmen of two newly created committees with small agendas and a modest nonpartisan staff. The two appointees were among neither the brightest

Imagine a state legislature in which the Speaker could determine the salary levels of the members of the house. Imagine that he could dictate that Assemblyman X would receive twice the pay of Assemblyman Y. To make it more realistic, imagine that the Speaker was permitted to pay the chairman of the appropriations committee twice the salary of a committee member. Holding a chairmanship under such circumstances would assume the proportions of a life-and-death matter. It would determine whether the legislator and his family ate well or not. It would not matter that a member was unqualified to be a chairman, or that he was over his head intellectually or morally: he could not afford to step down from his chairmanship.

In California the Speaker had considerable powers of appointment with respect to his house, but his appointments did not decide a member's standard of living. In salary matters all legislators were equal. The Speaker could provide a member with extra nonpartisan staff, but not extra wages. He could not repay loyalty or hard work with money. His patronage was a resource that was useful only to someone who had a lot of hard legislative work to do. The compliant member, the lazy, the venal, or the indifferent, had no need for a big nonpartisan staff that would pile up the work. For the best legislator, however, the one who wanted to do more than just get reelected, the kind who felt that intellectual mastery of policy areas was important, staff positions were like manna. The best legislators sought them out and were delighted and willing to assume the burden of managing the intellectual enterprises that staff made possible.

The secret of the California legislature's status system was that the Speaker's legislative largesse largely took the form of a currency redeemable only in a knowledge market.

What of the lower class of legislators, the "little fish"? Why might they accept their lesser status willingly, without rancor? For one thing, they often had no choice: as we noted earlier, the outside world of lobbyists ceased to give them legislation to carry. For another, the loss of self-confidence stemming from brutal defeats or "screwing up" an important area of public policy demoralized them, made them fearful of being active again. But most important, in their lower status they escaped a condition of intellectual indebtedness, for the author who was an ineffective legislator found himself asking for more favors than he could return. Because he lacked the

nor the best. The speakership fight, however, made imperative the generation of some additional legislative patronage.

intellectual equipment to win approval on the merits of the matter, he was in the constant position of a supplicant, pleading for a vote that neither his bills nor his presentation of them deserved. As a consequence he felt almost bankrupted by his activity, overextended, unable to return the favors extended to him except by compromising his own sense of self-control.[8] Inactivity brought respite.

If these less effective teachers withdrew gracefully from the action, if they were content with their status as disciples rather than mentors, of vote-givers rather than vote-seekers, then they were treated with generosity and dignity. If they were willing to do their homework, concentrating their energies on committee duties, they received good committee assignments, where they could associate with interesting colleagues and lobbyists and perhaps even have an opportunity to become a petit mentor—a master of a "small" problem area. If they used the talents they did have—of reacting to proposals or of reflecting a significant point of view—they would never be harmed. Members never scoffed at colleagues who worked diligently in committees. No one ever called a plugger a "freeloader" because he submitted so few bills, not only because it would be silly to make needless enemies, but because it would have upset the class system of the legislature. Quite the contrary: pluggers found praises heaped upon them for being so useful. As lower-status legislators retreated from the author system, they found themselves freer to exercise their own independent judgment about the bills of others in the committee system. Members came to appreciate their balance. Because they had no "hidden agenda" behind their votes, no complex trade in which votes on one matter were used as means to get votes in some other area, they were fair. They were appreciated because they gave their votes on the merits. Their status also shielded them from retaliation when they were critical of high-status legislators' bills. Criticism was their status right. The class system resolved for them what the sociologist Peter Blau called the Dilemma of Approval: how to

8. The loss of control experienced by an indebted legislator was palpable. Assemblyman Chel talked about the consequences of indebtedness incurred in another context—getting extra perquisites from the Speaker—but his story captures the widespread dread of the legislative collection agent: "If I took my hat in hand, I could get extra staffing, and extra offices and extra contingency funds. But I know what that means. I know the Speaker or one of his leadership group would be around to collect on it. I like my independence. There have been occasions when I have seen them moving around committees telling members, I expect you to vote no."

be critical and be loved at the same time.⁹ The pluggers kept in touch with one another—their friends tended to be other pluggers. They did not dine or consort with the big men on the legislative campus—the Knoxes, McCarthys, Sierotys, Browns, Keenes, or Lantermans. It did not bother them to keep their distance. Nor did they miss the substantial staffs of nonpartisan consultants that the upper-class legislators seemed to manage so well.

The status system meant a great deal to both classes. Mentors could expect that their intellectual homework would be productive. They could expect that its quality would influence substantial numbers of their colleagues. To the pluggers the status system provided the assurance that they would not be abused by coercion or political skulduggery. They did not have to be preoccupied with politics. For example, it permitted Rosenthal, a good critic of others' legislation, to defend a negative vote and retain the friendship of the author he opposed. He told this story:

"You voted against my loggers," Mrs. Davis said. "Mrs. Davis," I said, "that bothers me. I want you to vote on the merits, not on what went on previously. I know I'm only a freshman here right now, but I'll be here a length of time. You ought to reconsider your concept." A couple of days later she had reconsidered my position and told me so. And I appreciated that. I don't ever remember who gave me votes. I try to forget, and I try to resist the logrolling concept.

He had upheld his end of the bargain by coming to a reasoned conclusion. As a plugger he was under no obligation to accept the "logrolling concept," and it was the duty of master teachers to observe the difference between using intellectual force and political force, and to respect the taboo against using the latter on conscientious lower-class legislators. Status assured the pluggers academic freedom, the latitude to make up their own minds.

There were also duties and rights within a given class. In the upper class any mentor could expect other mentors to argue fiercely on the merits of each case and to test and be tested constantly. Their duty was to debate, not to sit quietly. Among the pluggers, on the other hand, there were duties of social support, especially to come to one

9. Peter M. Blau, *Exchange and Power in Social Life* (New York: John Wiley and Sons, 1964), p. 316: "By offering incisive criticisms, he earns their respect but often also their dislike, since they are predisposed to consider his criticism too severe."

another's aid when their intellectual integrity was under political threat.

V

A regime of reciprocity—be it a marketplace, a liberal civilization, a state legislature, or a schoolroom—always creates a class system. Understanding why differentiated status develops generally may help put the legislative hierarchy in perspective.

Reciprocity supports the successful, the talented, the resourceful, the lucky; it offers rewards to them for being generous, and it generates incentives to empathize with others. For those who have something to exchange, the regime is profitable. For the failure, however, the person who needs more than he can give back, the customer who cannot pay his debts, the good-for-nothing, reciprocity is more problematic.

One might guess that creditors would cease to do business with chronic debtors, substituting other consumers who can pay the asking price for the creditors' resources. But for a number of reasons, dropping customers who are down and out occurs less often than one might expect. Those who hold the resources, unless hampered by seriously straitened circumstances, become generous. They consider inertial factors like affection and fear of the unfamiliar. The outcome is that creditors frequently make heroic efforts to rescue indebted customers. They make yet another loan, or negotiate their prices downward, or make up jobs for the good-for-nothing to do. The paradoxical fact is that it is the failures themselves who are likely to break off a reciprocal association that has become one-way. Instead of being involuntarily replaced, the indebted individuals often voluntarily withdraw. They retreat to their own level.

Let's take the case of a young woman who is smart, kind, and rich. She writes her boyfriend's term papers when he is vacuous, is patient when he is depressed, and comes up with the rent when he is broke. This relationship is in danger, not because she will walk out, but because he will. The anthropologist Elliot Liebow observed the ups and downs of the affectionate relationships between "nice" attractive women (who held paying jobs) and a dozen unemployed vagrants who hung out at Tally's streetcorner in Washington, D.C. Invariably it was the man who broke off the relationship. "For reasons which he did not understand himself,"[10] the vagrant went back to the life of the streetcorner. Liebow described the man's renunciation as a descent to a "sanctuary for those who can no longer endure the experience or prospect of failure."[11] Going back to the streetcorner was a retreat to a status that relieved him of the obligation to make something of himself as recompense for women he liked. He unburdened himself of superabundant obligations.

Why do beneficiaries of "sweet deals" call it quits? Sociologists Blau and Homans attribute the retreat of the less resourceful to their desire for self-respect.[12] So strong is the moral norm of reciprocity ("Today's taking must be recompensed by tomorrow's giving") that it obtrudes even into the hearts of life's losers on skid row. The men of Tally's corner felt demeaned by the abundance with which their women supplied them. The things they took made them feel like moral bankrupts, for their personal resources were inadequate to recompense their "nice" women. The loss in self-respect offset any material or emotional benefits the vagrants derived. They preferred to descend to a less demanding marketplace, the streetcorner, where the shortages were of something they could supply, however meager these personal resources might appear. In a less classy relationship they had the goods to serve the needs of others. Retreating to their own social level transformed them from good-for-nothings to good-for-somethings, and that meant that they regained some power of a reciprocal sort. Winos found other winos with whom to associate and fulfill the golden rule of reciprocity: repay your debts.

In short, reciprocal regimes are likely to stratify. Suppliers and consumers in the same class tend to separate voluntarily from suppliers and consumers of higher standing. Class-consciousness follows in the wake of liberty of contract. These general principles applied in the state legislature with great force. The moral norm of reciprocity suffused the legislative culture, so much so that "pay your debts" might be called the "terms of the legislature." Conversely, just as

---

10. Elliot Liebow, *Tally's Corner: A Study of Negro Streetcorner Men* (Boston: Little, Brown, 1967), p. 160.

11. Ibid., p. 214. Cf. Robert Lane, *Political Ideology: Why the American Common Man Believes What He Does* (New York: The Free Press, 1972), chap. 4, "The Fear of Equality," particularly the discussion of social equality, pp. 73–75.

12. See Peter M.Blau, *Bureaucracy in Modern Society* (New York: Random House, 1956), p. 51; George Homans, "Social Behavior as Exchange," *American Journal of Sociology*, 62 (May, 1958): 597–606: "They could exchange help and liking, without the exchange becoming on either side too great a confession of inferiority" (p. 605).

with the legislatures of James Madison's time, so in 1975 "ingratitude [was] a common topic of declamation against human nature."[13]

It is my impression that the individuals who came to Sacramento as legislators were more than normally animated by obligations of gratitude. Take for example the gentle and straightforward assemblyman John Thurman. Here is how he explained his decision to run for political office to his daughter:

"Well, honey," I said, "it may sound corny as hell, but when your mother and I got married, we wanted to make this ranch work, and the community was very kind; they trusted us for twelve years while we worked to make something of ourselves. I think we've got something to return back to the community."

By and large the people who applied to go to the Sacramento boarding school of politics and were accepted by their constituencies were "corny." They believed seriously that one should always give something back for what was given.

The general norm of reciprocity was continually applied in Sacramento as a standard of fairness. In small discussions and at ceremonial occasions—eulogies for members who died, the annual "debate" at the end of each session over a legislative salary increase, the opening remarks of the Speaker—the legislative culture defined the ways in which a member was expected to return something to the community. The thoughts of Lou Papan, a rough-hewn assemblyman, revealed the moral foundations of the legislative institution:

Legislators can get taught a lot here. Legislators are bombarded with the big picture, and they start asking themselves, what are they doing with themselves? The way I see it, you are a temporary custodian of the public trust. You must use it, temporary though it is. And you use it to help the less fortunate. You've got to grasp that priority, and you've got to weigh what's important.

The legislative favors a member was obliged to return were the lessons that taught how to use the public trust justly and efficiently to help the less fortunate in a free country. Such favors were paid for, at the very least, by intelligent listening and critical learning.

Papan was not an upper-class legislator. He had few strengths as a teacher of his colleagues, and he knew it. He was a loyal crony,

13. *Federalist* no. 57.

a legislative follower of the Speaker. He had learned the norm of reciprocity and had accepted its consequences: that he would work hard, listen critically, and on the big issues defer to those superior members who merited his support in helping the unfortunate. Papan did not always meet such a standard, but he always felt regret when he remembered he had not. The norm of reciprocity and the status system it implied made him feel that he was really doing something with himself.

Eight

The big task is to keep the real hacks out of it.
  Assemblyman Jack Knox, 1978

A school of political capacity . . . is worthless, and a school of
evil, instead of good, if through the want of due surveillance,
and of the presence within itself of a higher order of characters,
the action of the body is allowed, as it so often is, to degenerate
into an equally unscrupulous and stupid pursuit of the self-
interest of its members.
  John Stuart Mill, *On Representative Government*, 1861

Why the Real Hacks Kept Out of the Action

I

The open system of exchange and status created incentives for self-regulation. Legislators cooperated voluntarily. Out of self-interest they taught their fellows, shared information, avoided the appearance (and the practice) of deception, and refined their manners. They tended to empathize with one another. As a result the legislature hummed with energy. The capital seemed to stimulate the legislators' creative instincts, and as a group they looked joyful. They talked as if they felt free and in control of their legislative lives.

In this free regime, however, there was opportunity for misbehavior. So many transactions were built on mutual trust, so many legislative proposals were complex and subtle beyond quick analysis, so much of value often rode on a bill, so often the means by which legislators and lobbyists could legitimately influence one another were left undefined, that the opportunities and the temptations to cheat, deceive, steal, and injure were considerable.

Legislators had chances to sell their votes, the sale price ranging from out-and-out graft to campaign contributions to offers of future employment. Or they could extort favors from citizens by threatening injurious legislation or harassing investigations. They could slyly pass laws and hide the damaging consequences until it was too late to remedy them. They could play the demagogue and deceive the public. Within the legislature they could dishonor their commitments. They could, especially if they were part of the legislative leadership, violate procedures. In short, the members of the legislature could unscrupulously and stupidly pursue their self-interest, exploiting the legislative prerogatives entrusted to them.

Likewise, lobbyists had abundant opportunities to give false information. They could also offer bribes, threaten careers, and even take important legislative proposals hostage and demand unconscionable ransoms for their survival. In short, outsiders could prey on the extreme exposure of the legislators as they did business in the legislature.

All these misdeeds were possible. They were all acts of theft. They denied the moral norm of reciprocity by violating the rule that today's taking must be recompensed by tomorrow's giving. When they occurred, they discredited the legislative institution. They tended further to impede the openness of the legislature and to intimidate the habits of trust upon which its enlightenment depended. The danger posed by acts of thievery, if unprevented or unpunished, was that the exchange of knowledge languished. Legislators, if unprotected from thieves and injurers, tended to become timid and defensive.

The reciprocal controls we have discussed thus far were the primary deterrents of antisocial acts. Legislators regarded with contempt any colleagues they suspected of venality. They cast votes of "no" against the tainted legislation they carried. They put "blocks" on members who deceived or reneged on their commitments, or were remorseless and unconcerned. They could ridicule cruelly the infrequent "pestiferous pest" who was beyond redemption. And if a lobbyist were dishonest or pestiferous, the legislative grapevine carried the news quickly, and doors that had once been open closed in his face. At the same time, the legislative institution offered incentives for bad legislators and lobbyists to clean up their acts. Generous help was proferred those who conducted themselves virtuously.

Nonetheless, reciprocal controls were sometimes insufficient to rectify misconduct. "Real hacks," the thieves of the legislative process, existed, notwithstanding the forces that discouraged legislators from acting like rogues. The hacks were attracted by the riches and the power the legislature possessed in such abundance. Consequently, just as in the larger free society where law enforcement officers are required to deter thieves and agents of violence, so an open legislature like California's depended upon a policeman to observe and catch the real hacks. The unique means available to policemen, whether in the real world or the legislative one, is their legitimate coercive power. While their authority to threaten the strongarm or the cheat is necessary to prevent illegal harm, a police presence nonetheless excites worry. The policeman is the single individual in a community with the legal right to harm others. The possibility is always there that he could become as abusive as the criminals he is supposed to guard against. In his monopoly of authority lies the potential of corruption in the sense of both wickedness and venality. Intellectually, a policeman in a free society is an anomaly, for he embodies the paradox that reciprocal regimes, in which cooperation is achieved without "the whip of authority,"[1] have to protect themselves with a whipmaster.

In the folklore of the conventional school, there is no more tyrannical a figure than the disciplinary dean playing vigilante, bullying the anxious and the free-spirited, often in the name of exorcising cheating, heresy, disloyalty, and ingratitude. In the Sacramento school of political capacity, or at least in the assembly, it was the Speaker who played the policeman's part and was suspected of awful tyranny and abnormal greed.

II

The Speaker had many formal powers. Rule 26 of the Standing Rules of the Assembly set out some of his "duties":

(c) To have general direction over the Assembly chamber and rooms set aside for the use of the Assembly, including the rooms for use by Members as private offices. . . .

(e) To appoint the membership of all standing and special committees, and their respective chairmen and vice chairmen, except as to the membership of the Committee on Rules. . . .

(g) To have general control and direction over the . . . bills of the Assembly.

He thus governed over the committee system by his duty "to appoint" committee memberships and chairmen, and he controlled the author system by his duty "to have general . . . direction over . . . bills." While he lacked the power to appoint the membership of the Committee on Rules, he was empowered to appoint its chairman. Since the rules committee had the responsibility to assign staff and to authorize legislative expenditures, the Speaker had a strong influence on the specialist system with its need for research resources.

1. Robert L. Heilbroner, *The Worldly Philosophers: The Lives, Times, and Ideas of the Great Economic Thinkers*, 2d ed. (New York: Simon and Schuster, 1961), p. 10.

Furthermore, the Speaker served as chairman of the research office (which prepared the Third Reading Analyses), and he appointed many of the officers of the legislature (e.g., the assistant Speaker and the majority floor leader).

These three formal powers—of appointment, bill-control, and legislative patronage—constituted vast coercive capacity. The Speaker could threaten a member's social purposes, constituency, personal education, stature, and personal comforts. He could, and sometimes did, send legislators to the solitary confinement of poor committees, strip them of their respectable legislation, and deny them the intellectual liberties a good staff made possible.

He also had an informal, awkward, and always suspect power: the privilege of dispensing campaign funds. Leo McCarthy, like every other Speaker of the assembly since Jess Unruh in the 1960s,[2] personally raised election funds, not only for his personal district race, but for the campaigns of other party colleagues. He disbursed excess funds to legislative colleagues who were in need, and collected a campaign chest in the neighborhood of $350,000 in 1976 alone. Because the Internal Revenue Code did not count as income the campaign funds he "crosscontributed," he could legally use them as a form of personal political patronage, to be bestowed or denied at his discretion. This resource, therefore, collected and controlled by terms set outside the legislative school, augmented the already considerable institutional powers of the Speaker. Some legislators felt uncomfortable that the Speaker not only played the policeman but also the godfather. That was why admirers as well as detractors were "not so sure all the power should be centralized in one person." As the water specialist Gualco said, "Leo is an honest guy, a hardworking guy, and I've been a recipient of some of the largesse of that power. But I often think, What if he weren't?"

III

There were times, however, when all the powers of the Speaker seemed vitally necessary. Were it not for such powers, the "real hacks" could have worked their skulduggery with impunity. I want

2. Lou Cannon, *Ronnie and Jesse: A Political Odyssey* (Garden City, N.Y.: Doubleday and Co., 1969), pp. 99–100, 113. In the context of the practice of crosscontributions, Unruh's best-known political aphorism has special meaning: "Money is the mother's milk of politics."

to focus on three kinds of misdeeds that were easy to perpetrate in a legislature. I shall call them bullying, shakedowns, and terrorism. Bullying occurred when preeminent legislators dominated other legislators by defying the legislature's general rules of application and procedures. Shakedowns occurred when legislators dominated lobbyists by threats or favors in order to enrich their personal bank accounts. Terrorism occurred when legislators or lobbyists dominated a legislator on an issue by threatening an innocent hostage unrelated to the matter at hand.

These three misdeeds were the techniques of the real hacks. They might be used singly or in combination to perpetrate an illegitimate transaction. For example, a committee chairman might shake down an interested group for the favor of carrying its bill, then abuse procedures to finesse the bill past committee opposition, and finally use terrorism against a colleague to extort a necessary vote on the floor. For purposes of understanding the value of the Speaker's disciplinary powers, however, it will help to take three instances where the techniques were used (or suspected of being used) singly.

Bullying. The procedures of the state senate prior to 1974 required committees to dispose of bills only by roll-call votes but did not stipulate publication of the votes of the individual members of the committee. Under these procedures some formidable committee chairman, like the Democrat Randolph Collier, could defeat bills (or pass them) by announcing at the conclusion of a vote that an insufficient number of ayes (or nays) had been obtained, even if that were not true. The intimidating presence of the chairman, his grasp of the subject matter, and his reputation for severe retribution silenced objections to his lawlessness. After a while, the disappointed committee members lapsed into a condition of passive acquiescence to Collier's defiance of the rules.

There was no easy way to call this legislative bully to account for his misbehavior in the senate. He was a committee chairman in a house whose traditions awarded chairmanships on the basis of committee seniority. It was unthinkable in the senate to strip a chairman of his committee against his will. By design, the senate lacked an official who had the muscle and the will to sack a chairman, whether he was an angel or a bully. Thus in the senate each committee became a little fief, to be governed according to the scruples of its chairman. Single members dissatisfied with Colliers's discriminatory application of the rules of voting (one senator, one vote) were either too weak or too pusillanimous to make an effective correction.

The results of Collier's injustice were predictable. Lobbyists, knowing the reality of Collier's committees, approached only Collier and ceased to teach the rest of the committee membership because Collier's practices had made the others superfluous. Likewise, staff prepared and distributed materials for Collier's eyes only. As his colleagues' ignorance increased through their being neglected, Collier's monopoly of expertise grew unchecked. Without his approval, no legislation ever passed out of his committees; with it, legislation was certain of passage.

The condition was finally redressed in 1974 when the Republican Behr, using the momentum he had gained by defeating Collier over the Wild Rivers Bill, organized a majority to reform the senate procedures. Following the model of the assembly, he altered the senate rules to require that "all roll call votes . . . shall be recorded [and] published."[3]

Like magic, senators ceased to acquiesce to Collier's domination, once they knew their passivity was being made visible for anyone to see. Because their votes were being counted publicly, they took care that the record did not lay them open to criticism from political opponents. Lobbyists then began to direct their persuasive energies to the members because they now counted, and the educational process, so weakened by Collier's old ways, received a dose of reform.[4]

The state senate, unlike the assembly, resembled the United States Congress in its use of the seniority rule and its aversion to concentrated power. By governing itself on the basis of seniority, which meant that chairmen were assured virtual lifetime tenure, however, the senate exposed itself to the dangers of domineering chairmen.

The assembly, on the other hand, did not disperse appointive powers, but rather concentrated them in a single official. When

3. The full text of the assembly rule was: "All roll call votes taken in a standing committee shall be recorded by the committee secretary on forms provided by the Chief Clerk of the Assembly. The chairman of each standing committee shall promptly transmit a copy of the record of the roll call votes to the Chief Clerk of the Assembly, who shall cause the votes to be published in an appendix to the Journal on a weekly basis. . . ."

4. The chairman of the assembly transportation committee commented: "Now, being committee chairman is not so important as it was before they began recording roll call votes. That little change made this place a lot less oppressive a dictatorship."

chairmen misbehaved, the Speaker was the responsible authority to whom an aggrieved legislator or lobbyist could turn. After all, the Speaker had the power to sack a bully. The Speaker, in fact, chose to rationalize the discretion he had been given to discipline his chairmen. He developed written procedures to convey his expectations of how chairmen should behave. That was why the assembly developed the "record-and-publish" rule on committee votes years before the senate had got around to curtailing the mischief of defiant committee chairmen.

Concentrated power, in this case, was a precondition for focusing responsibility. The possibility of being blamed for things he had a "duty" to correct induced the Speaker to curb the unjust application of the assembly's procedures. The legislative bully was tamed because legitimate authority was strong enough and visible enough and obliged enough to bring him under control.[5]

Shakedowns. In any legislature venal members have the opportunity to profit from their bill-carrying authority. The classic method of lining one's pocket is the law-firm referral. Constituents who request legislative help are told by their representative to retain a lawyer (who just happens to share his fees with the legislator) to "draft" the desired legislation. Another classic practice is for a member to author harmful proposals and then accept payment to drop them. In California such exploitation of office was called a shakedown and was considered unethical. Unfortunately, the costs of political life have sometimes made the temptation to be unethical virtually irresistible.

With regard to shakedowns, the conventional wisdom had it that the narrower the scope of a bill, the more vulnerable it was to unethical use. "Little bills," which benefited or harmed only a few rather than a general population, afforded the best opportunities to shake down constituents. To reduce temptation, California's legislature had rid itself of many trivial and specific legislative responsibilities. For example, the legislature had given cities extensive powers of home rule and had assigned to impartial commissioners administrative-

5. Let me reiterate a warning first uttered at the beginning of Part One. Like all procedures in California's legislature, this one—to give the Speaker effective power over committee appointments, but not too much—was not born immaculate or without a history. It evolved from a protracted process of scandal and reform, of venal abuses and revolution; and "revolution, to borrow the words of T. S. Eliot, means to murder and create" (quoted in Louis Hartz, *The Liberal Tradition in America*, p. 65).

type decisions such as location of highways; had it not delegated such authority, the legislature would have been involved in the passage of a lot of little bills.

While the California legislature aspired to deal only with policy matters of general interest, "special interest legislation" still appeared on its agenda. It had not eliminated all opportunities for shakedowns. For instance, the legislature had not established a general ceiling on interest rates, one that would apply broadly to all lending institutions. Rather, there was a particular interest rate schedule for each one of the various segments of the financial community. Banks, savings and loan associations, credit unions, mortgage bankers, pawnbrokers, finance companies, and insurers were each subject to specific regulation of their lending operations, and almost every year the legislature found itself involved in altering each of the various rate schedules. Bills to increase the lending rates of finance companies were classic special interest legislation, and legislators were always taking a second look at any colleague who carried interest rate bills and the possible profit accruing to him.

Another area of special interest legislation was the vulnerable exemption. If an industry enjoyed a special exemption to a tax or regulation of general application, opportunities for political blackmail arose. Exemptions were the ideal hostages: they were highly exposed and hard to defend because they lacked a broad base of support. In 1975 the best known of these vulnerable exemptions was the "home office" property tax loophole. For nearly a century local insurance companies in California had not had to pay a tax on any real estate used as their headquarters. Since these home offices were often massive thirty-story skyscrapers in the high-rent districts of Los Angeles and San Francisco, the home office exemption saved local insurance companies millions of dollars each year. The exemption dated back to a time when California sought to establish home-grown companies to compete with the great eastern insurance establishments. By the 1970s the exemption had outlived its purpose, but its very obsolescence made it a vulnerable stalking horse for greedy legislators. A Speaker who took seriously his responsibilities as legislative policeman kept an eye out for colleagues who stalked the exemption too ardently. The Speaker's suspicions focused on previous insurance company allies who, switching sides, introduced legislation eliminating the loophole. Such erratic and unexplained behavior alerted the Speaker that someone was attempting to turn a personal profit.

Legislative shakedowns brought discredit to the legislature, and it was the Speaker's job to see that they did not occur. In his first year as Speaker, Leo McCarthy encountered a fellow Democrat, a former supporter of the home office exemption, who suspiciously introduced legislation to get rid of it. The Speaker stopped the bill flat, directing it to a committee with instructions to deny it a hearing. He also designated a member of his coalition to author an identical bill, gave him adequate staff to research and publicize the closing of the loophole, and had a sympathetic committee of origin give the matter priority. The Speaker's bill eventually passed, much to the credit of the legislature and to the relief of the Speaker.

The Speaker, however, knew that he had violated two crucial rules of the author system: that every bill would get a hearing and that no legislator would hijack another's bill. Merely on the suspicion of a shakedown, the Speaker had denied a member's rights, and such preemptive police action usually meant trouble down the line. The Speaker, knowing that he had infuriated a member of his own party, expected him to try to get even by withholding support from the Speaker at some crucial time. Dealing with the member's holdout might require the Speaker to meet some extravagant demand.

In fact, events unfolded in just that way. The disaffected member withheld a crucial vote during the budget process and demanded as the price of his cooperation the establishment and funding of a pet project, an *ad hoc* legislative committee to oversee it, and the staffing of the legislative committee with one of his friends.[6] The Speaker

---

6. The budget bill always required two-thirds approval in each house. As Madison warned in *The Federalist* no. 58, extortionate possibilities abound in requirements of extraordinary majorities: "In all cases where justice or the general good might require new laws to be passed, or active measures to be pursued . . . the power would be transferred to the minority . . . to extort unreasonable indulgences." If a legislator was a part of the Speaker's coalition, his sense of team play moderated the temptation to ask "unreasonable indulgences." With outsiders whose votes were needed, however, the demands were often quite unreasonable. However, some demands seemed more exploitative than others. One legislator asked for a chairmanship of an *ad hoc* committee; another asked for approval of a district bill, that would raise bar pilots' fees in San Francisco Harbor; a third sought an additional judgeship for Orange County; a fourth asked for a budget augmentation to a child development program; the Republicans, as a delegation, asked for an increase in public school aid and a procedural change that would assure the defeat of a bill to provide public financing for state legislative elections. Some of these concessions were decisive: the defeat of the public financing bill, for example, did not require the state senate and the governor to cooperate in its defeat. Some concessions were not risky at all: the child-development augmentation, for example, was killed in the state senate, and the extra judgeship was vetoed by the governor. Nevertheless, the passage of the budget was conceded to be a time when outsiders could make some progress.

immediately agreed to the demand and spent his influence with the
senate and the governor to get them to pay the ransom. Afterwards
the member, still bitter about the Speaker's suspicions, nevertheless
expressed a detached admiration for the Speaker's tactics. As he
viewed matters,

> [The Speaker] finally found a way to get to me. He recognized
> that I was interested in something. . . . I found when he had to
> deal, he dealt. When he had to buy, he bought. . . . I
> misjudged him. I didn't think he was that smart.

The Speaker was smart because he had stopped a member in what
looked like a possible shakedown of the insurance companies, then
"bought" the member off from taking revenge and tamed him with
a vested interest in the legislative institution. By giving the member
an *ad hoc* committee to chair, the Speaker had bound the member
to the legislature. It was not a simple act of policing, nor an ethically
unproblematic one. Nevertheless, by allotting a staff appointment,
the Speaker made the member vulnerable to the threat of losing
something he was interested in. Cultivating a hostage—giving one's
adversary something to lose—righted the balance of power between
the two men just when it was dipping in the member's favor. After
all, there was no way to get rid of the member altogether: that task
was up to his constituents, and he seemed to have a lock on them.
The Speaker did not win the member as an ally by establishing the
special project, but he forestalled a lot of counterproductive
harrassment.

The Speaker did not have enough staff positions to squander them
on many suspects.[7] Nevertheless, if the legislative school could be
made so interesting to most of the members that they would resist
the temptation to act suspiciously, then there would not be too many
occasions for this kind of policing. In that case the Speaker would
have enough resources to buy off the few suspicious legislators he
felt he had to "get to."

Terrorism. No misdeed was more troublesome to legislative au-
thorities than terrorism, which was defined as the breaking of a
legislator's resistance to a dubious bill (or to an unmerited defeat)

---

7. Cf. Louis P. Westefield, "Majority Party Leadership and the Committee System
in the House of Representatives," *American Political Science Review* 68 (December
1974): 1593–604: " 'Manufacturing' committee positions, then, is not a suprising
leadership response. . . ."

by threatening harm to a "good bill" the legislator cared about. Terrorism was difficult to police partly because it was difficult to make explicit the line between illegitimate acts of terrorism and the acceptable arm-twisting of routine politics. But it was also difficult because opportunities for terrorism were so abundant. There were so many innocent hostages lying around in a legislature, so many bills being authored, so many specialties being built, that a ruthless member or lobbyist could always find some innocent to slaughter if he wished to do so.

Like pornography, terrorism was hard to define, but legislators knew it when they saw it, and it provoked their greatest outrage. It took courage to stand up to terrorism. An admiring freshman liked to repeat the counsel of then Senator George Moscone, later the mayor of San Francisco (and thereafter an assassin's victim). I first heard the rookie legislator's story in an anecdote about the pressures applied by a notorious senator to relax air pollution standards in the Los Angeles air basin:

> When the vote got close this Los Angeles senator threatened all the holdouts. He threatened to vote against Lockyer's percentage depletion bill (it might have failed for one vote in the senate); he threatened Berman on his public employees collective bargaining bill. He threatened Jack Knox's bills and went right down the line. The only persons he could not threaten were those few who had no bills they cared about. He tried to bully George Moscone, and Moscone threw him out. George told me, "If you let his kind know they can get away with pushing you around, there's no stopping it thereafter. He'll just pick you apart on every matter you care about.

Terrorism was picking someone apart on every matter he cared about. Terrorism posed the ultimate danger to the operation of the legislative school: the specialist, author, and committee systems were so exposed that they could be destroyed by terrorism. When terrorism occurred without control, there could be no independent judgment, no authoring of good bills, no building of good public policy, and no attachment to anything one cared about. Unless the terrorists could be civilized, the legislature could not function as "a school . . . of good."

No one posed the threat of terrorism more seriously than the governor. The governor's destructive capacity was inherent in his power to veto bills and, more important, his power to veto *parts* of appropriations bills. The item veto, as this latter power was called, permitted the governor to eliminate or adjust downwards particular items of expenditure in legislation before he signed it and without sending it back to the legislature for modification.

The item veto had particular consequences for the annual budget bill, which the governor needed to finance his administration. The item veto meant that he could "blue pencil" any element he did not like without cutting his own throat. It also meant that he could veto the pet project of any legislator who had resisted him. The budget, in short, was rife with hostages.

In this the governor of California differed from the president of the United States. If the president did not like a particular item in the budget bill, he could rid himself of it only by vetoing the whole of the budget. The governor of California, in contrast, could throw out the bathwater but keep the baby, and this vastly changed the balance of power between the two branches of government.

Both the item veto and the simple veto could be used to break an individual legislator's resistance. For example, a bill was introduced to forbid school boards from assigning teachers to schools on the basis of a lottery (instead of seniority, merit, or convenience). While couched in universal terms, the bill was really directed at the Los Angeles school board, which had implemented a system to randomize teaching assignments in order to comply with a federal order to integrate school faculties.

The governor had personal as well as politically principled reasons to want to kill the bill before it landed on his desk for signature or veto. His prospects, however, were bleak unless he could turn around certain assembly members already committed to its passage. An astute freshman described how she thought the governor got his way. Speaking of the health specialist Keene, one of several members who changed their votes, she said: "He vowed to Keene that he would kill his right-to-die bill, on which Barry had slaved for weeks and weeks, with no mercy whatever. . . . So he became a 'no' vote." The right-to-die bill was the first euthanasia legislation in the country. It permitted doctors to withhold life-sustaining medicines and treatment from the terminally sick if they had previously indicated a desire to die. This pathbreaking and important bill was an ethical and legal thicket, over which Keene had slaved and which he had negotiated with great sensitivity.

The governor's threat to kill the bill was perceived widely as an act of terrorism. The high quality of the bill made it seem so innocent: it was legislation with statewide consequences, not a mere district bill. The governor was jeopardizing a "good bill," not on its merits but as a harsh example to those who might cross him. There was an imbalance between the harm the governor threatened and the self-interested, seemingly petty objective he sought to gain. There was also no logical relationship between a health bill dealing with old people and a school bill dealing with teachers. The lack of proportion and the lack of connection in the governor's methods stirred anxiety and outrage in the legislature. Keene's case was the more menacing because, as an active, exemplar legislator, he was particularly vulnerable to the governor's tactics. If the governor was so encouraged by the success of his extortion as to continue to apply it, he would have the legislature at his mercy.

The Speaker's "duty" was to play the policeman and to guarantee the collective security of the legislature. His job was to restrain the governor from intimidating individual legislators. He had but two options. He could exact retribution from the governor, or he could enwrap the governor in reciprocal controls so that he would refrain from harming the legislature out of "gratitude" for good deeds done in previous times. In short, the Speaker could extort or exchange.

He exchanged. At least in 1975–76, the Speaker preferred a reciprocity strategy. He never held one of the governor's bills hostage, nor did he try to mobilize the legislature to override a single gubernatorial veto. Rather, he slaved to secure passage of bills of importance to the governor—the agricultural labor relations act, the medical malpractice reform, the civilian conservation corps, and the governor's skimpy, fiscally conservative budget. He cooperated instead of coerced. He let himself be used, in order to stop the governor from terrorizing his legislature.

Getting the necessary majorities needed to support the governor took great persuasion. McCarthy often sweetened matters by dispensing small favors to reluctant legislators. He dispensed patronage because he had patronage to give—not only legislative perks like chairmanships, staff, support on bills, and office space, but campaign funds as well.

A person unfamiliar with California might ask, Why didn't the governor do likewise? Why didn't he intrigue for legislative support by offering little jobs and little favors of his own? If patronage was sometimes persuasive when dispensed by the Speaker, why didn't the governor play the patron instead of the terrorist? The answer is that the governor had little patronage to give. He could nominate a few persons to judgeships, and he had a few well-paying vacancies on commissions. But the little favors were not his to give: civil service and administrative reforms long ago denied a California governor the favors that eastern and southern governors traditionally dispensed in the form of jobs and contracts. He also lacked, perhaps as a consequence, a political party machine to provide the funds and the services necessary to support the legislators' electoral needs. In contrast to the Speaker with his abundant patronage, the governor of California had little to offer.

My guess is that the Speaker saw the natural complementarity between the two offices. The speakership had the little pieces of patronage the governor lacked. By deploying his resources on the governor's behalf, McCarthy insured that the governor would observe the integrity of the legislature, and that any disagreements the governor had would be fought out on the merits of the bills, not on the basis of coercion. The partnership tamed the governor, policed him. At least that was the Speaker's plan.

Some thoughtful legislators, however, did not believe it was necessary to concentrate the power of patronage in the speakership. Bill Thomas, an attentive legislator, remarked:

> I don't buy the conventional wisdom around here that the Speaker's power has to be so absolute as a countervailing force to the governor's power. The legislature on a collective basis could just as well countervail against the governor.

In Thomas's opinion, the legislature would naturally and voluntarily rally to the defense of an intimidated colleague and fight terrorism with terrorism.

Yet if it was indeed necessary to police the governor, the case for the speaker's reciprocating strategy was strong. It did not run the danger of escalating into virtual deadlock—often the result of mutual retaliation. Rather than punishing the governor for harming the Keenes of the legislature, the Speaker set out to inculcate in the governor habits of self-restraint. As a policeman can better influence a wino by giving him pocket money "for a drink" than by threatening

him with arrest once he has gone out of control,[8] so the Speaker
sought to control the governor, by granting him favors and by convincing him that they were dependent on each other.
Did the policing strategy work? On balance, I think it did, largely
because both the Speaker and the governor were thoughtful and
ethical men. But let Speaker McCarthy have the last word:

> I tried to cooperate with the governor . . . because the
> machinery of government is so complex that it defeats most
> efforts to get anything done if it's at all controversial. I guess I
> felt I had to go out of my way to cooperate and to create an
> atmosphere of harmony. I just think that people in this process
> need to accomplish a few things of consequence—a few serious
> accomplishments, not just some press release, but something
> replenishing to the spirit. I'm not certain that it ever worked.
> But my own philosophy is that we are all part of a team. I was
> often accused of carrying the governor's water too often. Maybe
> I did; maybe I didn't. But I did help him in our house and his
> strength here ran over to the state senate. They would not pass
> out legislation to buck the governor because they knew we
> would defeat legislation which he didn't want.
>   I don't remember him threatening unmerited vetoes very
> often in 1975–76. He does it more often now. With a few
> authors, maybe, whom he's asked, and they have always voted
> against him. But, I don't know. He's not that tough. After all,
> he's entitled to do it anytime. And if he's decent to a legislator,
> he ought to collect a chit or two once in a while. . . .
>   But it is pretty easy for the executive to pick off some
> individual legislator to make him beholden to the governor.
> That weakens the legislature. The more cohesive legislative
> leadership is, the more able is the legislature to make its own
> judgments. . . . The power of the governor is much greater
> than the legislature's. He can encourage or mutilate any
> particular program at any time. . . . The governor has
> enormous inherent power. . . . The legislature is a different
> place. Basically, it's a forum for public differences. It's not
> supposed to be one voice. A legislature has to go through two
> phases. Phase number one, it's got to get as much from each
> member individually to offer for deliberation, and phase two,
> after the legislation has been hammered out, it's got to organize

---

8. Cf. William K. Muir, Jr., *Police: Streetcorner Politicians* (Chicago: University of
Chicago Press, 1977), chap. 5, on how policemen patrol skid row.

to group action. If it is weakened by incohesive leadership, it can't compete with the executive branch.

IV

The Speaker had extensive powers—powers "too great" in the minds of many of the most thoughtful legislators. Nearly all the legislators could point to some legislative event that they thought had been misdirected by the Speaker's power. An observant fresh-man complained: "There's an acceptance of the inevitable here, even when things go wrong. The Speaker . . . has so many powers that the general feeling arises that 'it isn't worth it to buck it.' "

Yet an experienced, moderate Republican, known for his honesty and hard work, with a lifetime in politics at the local level before he got elected to the assembly, dissented: "The Speaker's total power does not really bother me." In his mind there were limits on the Speaker's power that were effective in working to reduce the like-lihood of abuses. What were they?

One has to start with the fact that certain things were outside the Speaker's control. One crucial limitation was that he could not fire, nor could he diminish the salary of any member of the assembly. As Alexander Hamilton warned when he urged that Congress should be denied the power to "increase or diminish . . . the compensation of the President during his term of office," "in the main it will be found that a power over a man's support is a power over his will."[9]

There were also procedures that publicly exposed the Speaker's worst machinations. The most important device was the Committee on Rules. Though the Speaker appointed its chairman, each of the parties controlled the appointment of three members. While the Speaker usually played a dominant part in the appointments from his own party, the minority party members owed him nothing. Since the rules committee had to give its consent to the Speaker's decisions on staff and expenditures, they were informed about such decisions and the justification for them. As a consequence, they could reveal any irregularities in the press and other effective channels.

There was, furthermore, a democratic control. The Speaker could be ousted by a majority of the assembly membership at any moment. All of his formal powers depended upon a democratic election in which every member of the assembly had a say. The Speaker was

9. *Federalist* no. 73.

continually obliged to retain the support of forty other members of the assembly. In fact, thanks to the practice that the candidate who could win a majority of the majority caucus would dependably be supported by all the members of the majority party, he needed the support of less than forty members (likewise, a challenger needed only a majority of a majority to depose him).[10]

Keeping the support of a majority of a majority at all times was the fundamental requirement of power. In the term of 1975–76, when fifty-five Democrats and only twenty-five Republicans were in office, the Speaker needed the allegiance of twenty-eight Democrats (including himself) to hold office (that is, half plus one of the majority membership). The twenty-seven members who joined the Speaker were his coalition. To the extent that legislative patronage was available to the Speaker, the coalition had priority in getting it. They were entitled to the committee chairmanships, the seats on appropriations, and the perks of staff, offices, and expenditures.[11] But that coalition, as any Speaker knew, was unstable. Members might not only defect—they might leave the assembly to seek higher political office, to accept appointment to federal or state agencies, to retire, or as the result of electoral defeat.

Nor was there any assurance that the initial coalition would contain abundant talent. In reviewing his coalition to find a good chairman, he might find that some members were too inexpert, too lazy, too discredited, too extreme, too ideological, or too cantankerous to do the job well. In selecting an appropriations committee chairman, for

10. Or so it was thought until 1980, when a member of the incumbent Speaker's own coalition challenged the Speaker and obtained a bare majority of the Democratic majority to support his ouster. The Speaker, however, refused to be deposed and persuaded his own supporters to withhold their votes from the challenger. The Republicans simply abstained from the Democrats' intraparty squabbles, leaving the challenger lacking the formal forty-one votes he needed to unseat the Speaker. Deadlock ensued. Ultimately the challenger withdrew, but a destructive bitterness remained as a result of the fight, the Speaker feeling personally betrayed by a comrade, and the challenger believing that the rules and practice of the game had been violated.

11. A member of the Speaker's coalition described the importance of the Speaker's race in this way: "The contest for the Speaker of the assembly is an unusual event. That's when the house functions as a democracy. It may happen every six months or every six years, but when it does, this house is a democracy. At any other time, it's a benign dictatorship. It's like choosing the emperor in Japan, our shōgun, and it develops in you a powerful loyalty to those who put you there. Your privileges and opportunities, your individual and mutual fortunes, ride on the outcome of that contest. Everything you have depends on the same roll of the dice, so to speak. That develops close relationships."

example, the speaker did not necessarily have the pick of the litter. The most resourceful legislators might be in the opposing coalition or might have to serve as majority leader or might have other preferences. Thus the choice might come down to one between two candidates, neither of whom was desirable.

Over time, therefore, the Speaker necessarily sought to bring into his coalition former adversaries simply because they were competent, yet persuade his loyalists that they were being treated fairly. Thus democracy—the need to maintain a supportive majority day in and day out—played a crucial part in moderating the tendencies to dictatorship.

In the end, however, some informal controls were also necessary to strengthen the formal limitations on the Speaker's powers. The crucial control, I suggest, lay in the intellectual competence of the majority of the members. Many of the legislators did not pander to the Speaker; they dared to be irreverent; they refused to play the sycophant. They dared to assert their dignity because they had the option to "bolt" from the Speaker's coalition or from the legislature and politics itself if the Speaker became intolerable. The education in public affairs they received in the legislature was not attached to their seat in the assembly. It could be taken by the well-schooled member into the private or other public sectors. The legislators had other options than to suffer the humiliations, whims, or abuses of a dictatorship.

Because the educational effects of the legislature were distributed not to a few but to any who claimed them, personal dignity was widespread, the rule, not the exception. And because most of the legislators were accomplished in a specialty, even if it was a minor specialty, they had something of value to give to the Speaker, something that permitted them to hold their heads high and remain free from petty abuse.

The competence of most of the legislators enabled the assembly to flourish despite the concentration of power in a single policeman. The autonomy of each individual was a precondition of the effective use of concentrated power. In this sense Jack Knox's observation took on special significance: "The guy who's dangerous here is the fellow who wonders whether his vote will decide whether his kids are going to eat or not." The fellow dependent upon a government job was dangerous because he had to support the Speaker, no matter how abusive the exercise of power. The autonomous legislator, on the other hand, had the option to withdraw because he was in demand in other quarters. And in a system where the machine of discipline was so formidable, such an option was indispensable.

This discussion has implications for the way we conceive the professional politician in the United States. The person who pursues the vocation of the politician must always retain the confidence that he and "his kids are going to eat" if politics must be left behind. There is a paradox in this—to pursue a political career as a professional, with all one's energies, yet retain the detachment of an amateur to enable one to enter other careers. Knowledge resolved the dilemma. If politicians performed in institutions that educated well, they increased their options because both private and public sectors competed for them.

V

Walter Ingalls was an assembly member of the Speaker's coalition. As chairman of the transportation committee, flattered by the heady responsibilities conferred on him despite his youth, he might properly be suspected as unduly sanguine. A recipient of the Speaker's largesse, he was unlikely to be objective about the system. After all, he was nothing more than a student writing his own report card. Yet when he applauded his house and his Speaker, I think he was right:

> It's the best legislative forum in the world, with the possible exception of the British parliament. It's vastly superior to Congress because of accountability. . . . By accountability I mean that if the assembly does not do something or does something distinctly wrong, the Speaker's got to take the blame. His interest is in the product of the house. It works until the Speaker aspires too high. Often then he wants to become associated with particular legislation. But now, as he sees his job as one of letting the members perform to their best abilities, it is a professional and judicious place, an open and fair process, and the product is good. It's a democratic process.

Nine

The discussion to come will hinge on the assumption that
United States congressmen are interested in getting reelected—
indeed, in their role here as abstractions, interested in nothing
else.
David R. Mayhew, *Congress: The Electoral Connection*, 1974

One wants to know the meaning of his suffering and to learn
how, as a responsible being, he should acquit himself. Should he
commit suicide? If so, why; if not, why not? The search for
meaning becomes supreme.
Gordon W. Allport, 1959

Why Assumptions about Human Nature Are Vital

Legislators needed knowledge about political and governmental matters, and this need brought into focus important and subtle events in the California legislature. One saw the educating effects of the legislative institution, which raised in turn two questions: How good was the legislature as a school? And how did it stimulate and satisfy its members' desires for knowledge?

The argument of the book has been that reciprocity served to create and distribute information concerning the world and ways of improving it. The California legislature functioned well as a school because it provided five conditions that promoted reciprocity: abundance, competition, encouragements, policing, and quality control.

The legislature's abundance consisted in an enormous investment in professional staff that provided a bounty of educational materials and personnel—resources that were available to any California legislator for the asking. The legislative analyst's office, the committee staffs, and the office of research which compiled the TRA (Third Reading Analyses)—all of them nonpartisan—collected knowledge from numerous sources and made it available in accessible terms. Because of the open competition among staffs, they were given the incentive to supply an abundance of high-quality information.

Second, the presence of competing legislative houses and of well-staffed and competing parties within each house made monopoly of critical areas of knowledge nearly impossible. Multiple sources of supply, beyond the control of any one individual or group, dampened any monopolist's hope of restraining the trade in ideas. Once monopoly was precluded, commerce in information began to develop, and it was to each legislator's advantage to find an institutional need for scarce knowledge and fill it.

Third, the author system encouraged legislators to want to become increasingly knowledgeable. Because the public could pick its bill-carriers from the entire pool of legislative members, it functioned in effect to grade the effectiveness and intellectual capacities of the members. The legislators themselves competed to carry the most attractive legislation, which was awarded to those authors with the best developed skills and understanding. At the same time, the status system within the legislature, by which "big fish" and "little fish" legislators alike gained social support and a sense of usefulness from their efforts, prevented demoralization among the losers in the competition, namely, the more limited legislators. The status system generated appreciation for persons who kept on doing their best, whatever their capacity.

Fourth, a system of legislative procedures deterred thievery. The leadership was concerned enough to enforce the rules concerning both public and recorded committee hearings, waiting periods and deadlines, public notice requirements, the quality and access of professional lobbyists, and good (i.e., nonextortionate) manners.

Fifth, the legislature was like a social laboratory, working by trial and error. Legislators employed theories in designing public policy and then tested them in practice, thus making ignorance and error visible. In that way it soon became evident which information and sources were reliable and which counterfeit.

The California legislature was organized to provide a first-rate political education and to discipline legislators to work hard in exchange for it. That is to say, the legislators functioned in a system of internal, institutional incentives designed to make them smarter and better public officials. The committee system (and the votes that committee membership awarded legislators) gave them the intellectual tools to grasp the essentials of particular public policies. The author system (and the bill-carrying license to which election to the legislature entitled each member) provided the exercise in political skills essential to negotiate public policy. The specialist system (and the ability of the subpoena to focus attention) offered the opportunity to learn how to combine intellect and skill to make enduring improvements in society.

There had to be, however, a personal incentive to make the institutional incentives effective. The legislators needed to feel meaningful and valuable, to have a sense that they had done something that would endure. Put negatively, the personal incentive was to avoid not mattering. The California legislative institution gave its members the chance to make the world a bit better. The only condition the legislative institution attached to the opportunity was that the members had to educate themselves in something useful.

Recall the veteran state senator Randy Collier's words to the young assemblyman Jerry Lewis. "I assume you intend to stay around here," said Collier, "and that you intend to do more than just get reelected."[1] Collier, then nearly eighty, was speaking from nearly half a century of political life and was offering advice to a promising member of a new generation of legislators:

> I hope you will select two or three areas which affect your
> district and slowly become the master of them so that you know
> more than some of those smart-ass young consultants of the
> committees. You've got to do some homework over the long
> haul.

The assumption of this book has been that most California legislators were fundamentally interested in the "long haul" and were concerned with whether and why they should stay in the legislature. They thought deeply about the whys and wherefores of their political careers because they had had to sacrifice so much to pursue them. As legislators, they gave up most of their privacy. They denied themselves the respite of home and the gratifications of family life. They lost old friends who wearied of politics, and they recurrently had to ask new friends and acquaintances for reelection contributions. They had little financial security. They were maligned publicly and often unfairly. They rarely had a day off. They exhausted themselves in different public undertakings and then watched projects they had given years to destroyed or frustrated by the complexity of events.

I do not mean to say that there were no benefits to offset the sacrifices—there were indeed. There were people to meet, things to be learned and done, the gratitude returned for big favors and small, the satisfaction of exercising a skill or fulfilling one's duty, the feeling of having done something meaningful, and even the prospects of

1. See Chapter 4.

wealth if and when one left public life and put one's know-how to profitable effect in the private sector. None of these benefits, however, was assured. All depended on one thing: "You've got to do some homework over the long haul." Interesting people ceased to be interested in public officials who knew nothing and could do little. In the political world projects were accomplished only if one had skills in coalition-building and a capacity to anticipate the subtleties of democratic life. The ignorant mucker aroused hate and ridicule, not gratitude.

Knowledge and competence were essential if the benefits of politics were to outweigh its sacrifices. Persons in public life who took neither joy nor pride from it quit sooner or later. If they lacked both interest in their job and the option to give it up, they were soon sapped of the energy necessary to do it, and they withered. Half a century ago, the industrial sociologist Elton Mayo stressed the difficulty of sticking to meaningless work:

> If an individual cannot work with sufficient understanding of his work situation, then, unlike a machine, he can only work against opposition from himself. This is the essential nature of the human; with all the will in the world to cooperate, he finds it difficult to persist in action for an end he cannot dimly see.[2]

To see the purpose in democratic politics while persisting in its practice, a legislator had to develop a political capacity, and the essential ingredient of capacity was knowledge. Without knowledge, he could "only work against opposition from himself."

II

Chapter 5 began with the observation that democracy was *not* sufficient to prod legislators to work hard in the California legislature. To be sure, the incentive to be reelected did make virtually all members responsive to their constituents, but it was the incentive to be respected within the legislature that made them hard-working and responsible in carrying out their legislative duties. Responsiveness— the trips back home to the district, the careful responses to individual constituents, the curing of a bureaucratic snafu, the burden of carrying "district bills," and the endless public appearances—stemmed from the electoral connection between legislator and voters. On the

2. Elton Mayo, *The Human Problems of an Industrial Civilization* (New York: Macmillan, 1933), p. 119.

other hand, responsibility—the effort necessary to read countless bills, effect enduring improvements in the general welfare, foster cooperation among networks of citizens, and study society continually—was evoked by the internal system of incentives in Sacramento. At least, such was the belief of the men and women who held seats in the California legislature. Democracy was good for responsiveness, but not for responsibility.

David Mayhew, in *Congress: The Electoral Connection*,[3] tries to imagine what legislative assemblies would be like if there were no internal incentive structures but only external, electoral incentives for legislators. What would it be like if they were "interested in nothing else" but being reelected?[4] Under such conditions, Mayhew argued, legislators would assume positions on symbolic issues to please their constituents, but, because few voters ever know or care about legislative effectiveness, legislators would not take the time to get their positions adopted into law. At the same time they would seek to plunder the public purse and deliver the booty as election bribes to any attentive and organized group of constituents. The result would be a legislative institution incapable of governing. Legislators would be unwilling to do "grueling and unrewarding legislative work."[5] Majorities would not be mobilized to pass meaningful legislation to help the poor and the unorganized working class.[6] The only lawmaking to get done would be the squalid and "runaway" distribution of spoils to the greedy and powerful.[7]

If the electoral connection is inadequate to instill a sense of responsibility, then there is a need for what Mayhew calls "institutional maintenance arrangements" that would control the effects of legislative overresponsiveness.[8] As examples, he identifies three committees in the House of Representatives. They are made up of responsible legislators who prevent the rest of their colleagues from having an effect on tax-setting, expenditures, and the legislative agenda. Mayhew argues that members of the three "central committees"[9] would have to be influenced to act responsibly not by the

3. David R. Mayhew, *Congress: The Electoral Connection* (New Haven: Yale University Press, 1974).
4. Ibid., p. 13.
5. Ibid., p. 141.
6. Ibid., pp. 115, 163.
7. Ibid., p. 158.
8. Ibid., pp. 146, 180.
9. Ibid., p. 147.

electoral connection, but by "selective incentives." He begs the question of what would make the committee members interested in what he calls the "internal currency" of Capitol Hill—respect and power within the society of legislators.[10] Since the controlling assumption of his analysis is that legislative members have an interest in nothing but reelection, his invocation of institutional maintenance arrangements might strike one as insupportable in theoretical terms.

Nonetheless, Mayhew's book, if taken as pure speculation and not as a description of reality, is an interesting exercise. It illuminates the limitations of external, electoral controls and therefore highlights the critical importance of incentives built into the legislative institution.

The shortcoming of the book is that it does not solve a theoretical problem: if one grants that an internal structure of incentives is necessary to neutralize the irresponsibility of popularly elected legislatures, there is no way to make any conceivable system of internal incentives effective so long as one assumes that legislators are interested only in reelection. Mayhew's assumption about legislators as human beings boxes him in, and he all but concludes that Congress is no longer capable of governing.

III

Mayhew's despairing conclusions seem artificial, however, for they stem from artificial assumptions. He assumes that United States congressmen are not interested in being responsible and concludes that Congress is irremediably irresponsible. The conclusion is as despairing as it is logical, given the premises. The premises, however, are faulty, for Mayhew denies legislators—"for analytic purposes," as he puts it[11]—the essence of their humanity: their need to feel meaningful.

The psychologist Gordon Allport has addressed the problem of starting with faulty assumptions about human nature. Let me quote him at length, for he makes an instructive point.[12]

The behavioral scientist seems committed to study men more in terms of behavior than in terms of experience; more in terms of

10. Ibid., p. 146.
11. Ibid., p. 17.
12. Gordon W. Allport, "The Open System in Personality Theory" (1959), printed in Hendrik M. Ruitenbeek, ed., *Varieties of Personality Theory* (New York: Dutton, 1964), pp. 149–66, quoted at pp. 155–56.

mathematical space and clock time than in terms of existential space and time; more in terms of response than of programming; more in terms of tension reduction than of tension enhancement; more in terms of reaction than of proaction.

Now let us leap our cultural stockade for a moment and listen to a bit of Hindu wisdom. Most men, the Hindus say, have four central desires. To some extent, though only roughly, they correspond to the developmental stages of life. The first desire is for pleasure—a condition fully and extensively recognized in our Western theories of tension reduction, reinforcement, libido, and needs. The second desire is for success—likewise fully recognized and studied in our investigations of power, status, leadership, masculinity, and need-achievement. The third desire is to do one's duty and discharge one's responsibility. (It was Bismarck, not a Hindu, who said, "We are not in this world for pleasure, but to do our damned duty.") Here our Western work begins to fade out; except for some pale investigations of parental punishment in relation to the development of childhood conscience, we have little to offer on the "duty motive." Conscience we tend to regard as a reactive response to internalized punishment, thus confusing the past "must" of learning with the "ought" involved in programming our future. Finally, the Hindus tell us that for many people all these three motives pall, and they then seek intensely for a grade of understanding—for a philosophical or religious meaning—that will liberate them from pleasure, success, and duty. (Need I point out that most Western personality theories treat the religious aspiration in reactive terms—as an escape device, no different in kind from suicide, alcoholism, and neurosis?)

Allport here cautions against making adolescent assumptions about human nature, assumptions that exaggerate concerns for pleasure and success and exclude an inherent yearning for duty and commitment.

Allport's caution seems particularly apt when applied to the study of the California legislature. The legislative reality of 1975–76 quickly made adolescent assumptions seem trite. To encounter the eighty-year-old Senator Collier was to see the philosophical meaning with which he invested his work. Watching the development of Assemblyman Lewis, as he carried out his "damned duty" to master the air pollution problem of the Los Angeles basin, destroyed any simplistic assumptions that legislators were interested solely in reelection. James Madison knew, of course, that "men called for the most part from pursuits of a private nature" might, because of their inexperience, initially think that getting reelected was the be-all and end-all of their personal success. But at the same time he assumed that most of them would develop beyond this adolescent stage once they attained office. In contrast to Madison's developmental assumptions, Mayhew's axiom is static and fixed. It denies the "existential clock" that seemed to govern the individual members in the California legislature and that compelled emotional and intellectual change.

All theory depends on basic assumptions, and theory is crucial to illuminating reality. A theory can probe the darkness of the human condition and light up a tiny piece of it for meticulous examination. But a theory based, as Mayhew's is, on arrant assumptions is like a beam of light pointed witlessly, implying that there is no there there. When theory points nowhere, life appears a void. An analytic theory that takes as axiomatic that legislators fix upon getting reelected—and nothing else—is faulty, or so it strikes me. At the very least, analytic assumptions about politics must presuppose that human beings govern their lives by self-conscious standards of meaningfulness. No matter how such assumptions cloud analysis, political scientists must posit that men and women want to count for something. The fact that scholars have assimilated the study of politics to the natural and physical sciences must not blind them to the unique quality of the subjects of their study. Human beings generally want to know the meaning of things, the whys and wherefores of their being. The need for meaning prods legislators to be something more than freeloading hypocrites.[13] If legislators actually do care about the meaning of what they are doing, then solutions to legislative breakdown more readily suggest themselves. We shall now turn to the matter of effective legislative reform.

13. For readers interested in descriptions of how legislators learn their profession, I suggest four books in particular: James David Barber, *The Lawmakers: Recruitment and Adaptation to Legislative Life* (New Haven: Yale University Press, 1965), on Connecticut state legislators; Robert A. Caro, *The Power Broker: Robert Moses and the Fall of New York* (New York: Knopf, 1974), chap. 7, on Al Smith in his learning years in the New York state legislature; Richard F. Fenno, Jr., *Congressmen in Committees* (Boston: Little Brown, 1973), on United States congressmen who care about making good public policy; and Frank Smallwood, *Free and Independent* (Brattleboro, Vt.: S. Greene Press, 1976), on a political scientist's experience as a Vermont state senator.

Ten

When in that House M.P.'s divide,
　If they've a brain and cerebellum, too,
They've got to leave that brain outside,
　And vote just as their leaders tell 'em to.
But then the prospect of a lot
　Of dull M.P.'s in close proximity
All thinking for themselves, is what
　No man can face with equanimity.
　　W. S. Gilbert, *Iolanthe*, 1882

We had a few successes, but mostly a lot of losses. . . .But
whenever I get discouraged by the results, I just step back and
look at the process, and I marvel. You know, I go around to the
legislatures of almost every state in the Union, and I tell my
colleagues how things work out here in California, how the
legislators here almost always try to listen to all sides with a
certain amount of fairness, and all my colleagues can say is,
"Marv, you're putting us on." But I'm not.
　　Marv Brody, UAW Lobbyist, 1976

Why Legislative Reform
Comes Hard and Is Worth It

Americans have long been discontent with their legislatures. No doubt much of their unhappiness has been justified. There has indeed been a problem with the condition of our state legislatures.

Perhaps no writer has better expressed outrage about the incompetence of state legislatures than Willie Morris. A former editor of *Harper's*, Morris earlier wrote for the weekly *Texas Observer* about the politics of Texas. In his autobiography, *North Toward Home*, Morris reflected on how the Texas legislature operated in 1960:[1]

> I was simply not prepared for it. It is difficult to convey exactly the way I reacted those first days there, but I remember it as a kind of physical sickness, the result of a continuing outrage, for which even writing was no outlet. I do not think this could be attributed to any moral righteousness, nor to an undue naivete. I knew my Lincoln Steffens, and I had more than a passing knowledge of the Whig House of Commons, which appealed to my decadent Mississippi instincts; I had always had a curious liking for politicians, and if the preference were between a sanctimonious old bastard with the right ideas and a politician with none at all, I would not have hesitated. Despite all this, I remained in a state of unusual anger. I would spend most of a working day wandering around the floor of both houses, eavesdropping on the big lobbyists, interviewing the strategists behind the legislative monstrosities which passed as conserva-

1. Willie Morris, *North Toward Home* (Boston: Houghton Mifflin, 1967), pp. 204–5.

tism, and drinking interminable beers with the representatives of what the *Dallas Morning News* called the "liberal-leftist axis." And then he wept.[2]

The loss to Texas of its natural heritage, sold for pottage, had been one of the great shames of a state in which social services contrast so dramatically with basic economic wealth. If an enlightened tax program had been applied to oil and gas two decades ago, Texas in the 1960s might have had the best and most progressive state government in America. It was in this perspective that the constant destruction of decent appropriations took on deeper shades of meaning than in the legislatures of other, less endowed states. The reformers in the Texas legislature never missed an opportunity to argue that theirs was a state which ranked first in the nation in oil, with about half the nation's underground reserves; first in gas, with over 45 percent of the nation's underground reserves; first in cattle, first in cotton, first in everything from livestock and mohair to goats and pecans. Yet in basic social services the State of Texas ranked first in caseload per state social worker; 41st in old-age pensions; 40th in public assistance programs in general, with almost three-quarters of these funds from the federal government; 40th in literacy; 42nd in aid to dependent children; 50th in vocational rehabilitation for injured workers; and close to the bottom in educational services. Despite its impressive beauty, its state parks were a travesty, and it could be judged nothing less than criminal in its neglect of the mentally ill.

Such arguments, made almost in desperation, were greeted, depending on the moment, with smugness, high hilarity, inattention, or a simple lack of intelligence. On the *Observer* we were sometimes overcome with futility and anger, the flaws seemed too great to be measured in terms of our own private contempt, and the sheer enormity of the task of reform from within the system made our occasional optimisms seem a waste of good energy. "If Texas won't," it was said bitterly, "then Washington will."

The 1960 Texas legislature was far worse than the average state house. Nevertheless it stands as a useful symbol of the consequences of institutional neglect. The Texas state legislators, in large part, were smug, inattentive, uninformed individuals, taught by the "big

2. Ibid., pp. 208–9.

lobbyists" how to resist change, and serenely incompetent to design the laws and the most basic social services to enable the "have-nots" to become productive individuals. They knew no better than to sell their natural heritage "for pottage" and to plead penury for the illiterate, the injured, and the unlucky. Unable to protect the most needy, the Texas state legislature became contemptible and rendered itself superfluous: "If Texas won't . . . then Washington will."

But if Texas had a bad legislature, what would a good legislature be like? What would make one work well? How would it overcome the legislative problem of incompetence?

One way to consider these questions would be to identify a successful legislature and examine it closely. This book has taken just this approach. Scholars, legislators, and lobbyists alike have declared California's state legislature the best. To a striking degree, they have shared the sentiments of Marv Brody, the former lobbyist for the United Auto Workers: "I . . . look at the process, and I marvel."

What, then, was the California legislature? In a nutshell, it was a gathering of political representatives, most of whom were energetic, attentive, and informed individuals, learning from the best of its membership within a fair and versatile system the skill of coalition-building and the competence to govern a free people under law. Senator Behr characterized it more tentatively but far more eloquently as

> a group of persons operating under a body of rules which attempts to develop laws, hopefully based on an approximation of the types of conduct which accord with the mores to which people are willing to conform; hence, the laws are easy to enforce and difficult to disobey.

It would be hard to define better the competence required for governing a free people. Of course, Behr was not saying that legislation could not change mores or even improve them. Rather, he expressed the fundamental imperative that persons who were elected to the legislature should learn how to enlarge their talents for teaching, negotiation, compromise, coalition-building, and mastering abstruse and intellectually difficult subject matters. For only if they did, could they—should they—be able to convince a free people to accept laws on their merits. A good legislature educated its membership to become competent public leaders of the American democracy.

II

To recognize the inadequacy of state legislatures and to propose remedies to it are two quite separate tasks. It is far easier to know that an institution is not working well than to know how to make it better. Without some understanding of how a good legislature actually did overcome the legislative problem of incompetence, proposals for reform might appear to make good sense, yet might not speak to the basic problem—or worse, even aggravate it.

Let us look at eight reforms frequently urged in scholarly circles or in the popular media. They strike me as misdirected, in large part because they stem from faulty assumptions about the human nature of legislators. (Many of these reforms presently have the approval of Common Cause, a public interest association dedicated to making legislatures govern better. In the future these same proposals will undoubtedly have new sponsors, but they will be no less erroneous.)

One reform frequently advanced for improving state legislatures is to "discipline" the legislative parties, by which is meant that the members should cast their votes according to the commands of their respective party leaderships. The theory of the reform is responsiveness: the parties being more enduring and visible to the electorate, discontented voters could focus their blame more accurately if they could treat their own respresentatives as surrogates for the party leaders. By knowing whom to blame, the electorate could make the legislative leadership more accountable.[3] It would be hard, however, to imagine a proposal more likely to dampen the energies of the individual representatives. Requiring legislators to cast their votes according to the whims of their party chairmen would simply blunt their keenness and depress their morale. It was the personal responsibility for measuring the merits of bills against conscience and constituency that animated the California legislators and sent them scurrying about to develop an intellectual handle on specific problems. By disregarding the very factor that challenged legislators to learn about areas of public policy, the disciplined parties proposal would simply enervate the individual members. As Gilbert and Sullivan pointed out a century ago, there is something ludicrous about requiring legislators to leave their "brain outside, / And vote just as their leaders tell 'em to."

3. E.g., the Committee on Political Parties, American Political Science Association (E. E. Schattschneider, chairman), "Toward a More Responsible Two-Party System," *American Political Science Review* 44 (September, 1950), supplement.

A second proposal often heard is that legislative districts should be made as "competitive" as possible, in other words to increase uncertainty regarding the outcome of each election. The theory is that fear is an effective prod in making legislators attentive and responsive to their constituents. Each member, therefore, should be placed in a state of extreme peril.[4] Unquestionably, marginal districts may increase the responsiveness of legislators. California legislators from marginal districts, unless they were so demoralized by the certainty of defeat that they stupidly pursued self-interest, never neglected their "district" business. Those most imperiled—the Democrats elected from well-to-do Republican districts and the Republicans from working-class communities—returned home faithfully for social functions and strongly advocated their constituents' rights to share the wealth of the state treasury. But electoral competition did not promote legislative responsibility. In fact, electoral anxiety probably distracted these legislators from the work that had to be done in Sacramento. They could not afford to master a statewide specialty nor examine carefully the merits of their colleagues' legislation. Thus worried about the significance of every constituent's vote, they paid attention to insignificant things, "to everything except what was important," as one member said. Continual concern about the competition at the next election and carrying heavy legislative responsibilities were not, in theory, antithetical, but in reality they often seemed mutually exclusive.

A third proposal would limit the legislators' familiarity with lobbyists. The rationale, of course, is to prevent the buying of votes, but the limitations often suggested are so pervasive as to indicate a more subtle purpose. By distancing lobbyists from legislators, the proposals would prevent lobbyists from conveying the kind of detailed knowledge that helps legislators to be sympathetic to the lobbyists' arguments. The intent of the proposals is to blunt the informational advantages that the politically strong have over the mute and impotent poor.[5] Yet if representatives are frightened into

4. E.g., Joseph S. Clark, *Congress: The Sapless Branch* (New York: Harper and Row, 1964), pp. 212–15.

5. Common Cause has pressed for a comprehensive lobby disclosure bill to require all organizations that do a significant amount of lobbying in Congress to register and report their efforts to influence legislative decisions, including the disclosure of large contributors to such organizations and of all efforts to stimulate grass-roots lobbying. Mike Cole, a Common Cause lobbyist, justified the cumbersome and extensive disclosure provisions as follows: "It bothers me [that 'lobbyists' is considered a shameful

closing their doors to lobbyists and isolating themselves in the capitol and in their district offices, they have no choice but to rely on staffs with particular biases and predilections.[6] The knowledge of California staff members was largely vicarious. They were frequently limited to what was earlier called "first-degree knowledge," shallow information rife with the mistaken notions that come from theories untested by the real world. No legislator in California could have been truly informed had he been afraid to consort with lobbyists and their clients among the citizenry. It was the openness of the legislative institution that made for intellectual excitement.

A fourth proposal would limit the number of bills an individual legislator could introduce. Here the theory has been that legislatures could develop better legislation if their agenda were under better control. Because of the pressure of too many trivial and distracting proposals, legislatures have made important policy poorly and failed to detect insidious legislation. The bill-limitation reform would cure the mischief by a uniform limitation on the frequency with which each member could enter the author system.[7] But the California legislature imposed much more severe and effective restrictions on its worst legislators than could have been mandated by some general procedure. On the other hand, the status system in the California assembly encouraged its best legislators to run with as many proposals as they could manage competently, at the same time demanding of them scrupulous conduct, unimpeachable veracity, and lucid presentations. Bill limitations in California, therefore, would have been unnecessary to discipline the worst legislators and would have seriously impeded the performances of the best.

---

word by many people] because in recent years lobbying has become a much more professional occupation—less dependent on what's been called 'booze, broads and bribes.' Those things are more and more a thing of the past. But because so little light is shed on current lobbying practices—those of all sorts of groups, environmentalists, senior citizens, corporations and labor unions—the stereotype of the corrupt lobbyist persists. It's one reason Common Cause would like more light shed on lobbying by helping to enact a new law" (*In Common: The Common Cause Report from Washington* 9, no. 4 [Fall 1978], "Obstacles to Lobby Reform," pp. 22–23).

6. Michael Bevier, *Politics Backstage: Inside the California Legislature* (Philadelphia: Temple University Press, 1979), p. 234: "staff . . . had insulated the elected representative from the guts of legislative decision-making."

7. E.g., California Assembly Concurrent Resolution No. 3 (1979) would have amended the California legislature's Joint Rules to limit the number of bills a member of the assembly could introduce to twenty-five bills in the first year of a legislative session and fifteen in the second year; a state senator would be limited to forty and twenty-five, respectively.

A fifth proposal suggests that state legislatures should be unicameral (like most city councils) or do most of their work in joint committees, so that legislation would only have to run through a single legislative house, not two as in California, where both the assembly and the state senate must approve a given measure. The theory is that negotiating good legislation twice, through two policy committees, two appropriations committees, and two bodies at large, is too time-consuming and gives too many opportunities for special interests to defeat good measures. The assumption is that simplification of the process would make it easier to pass legislation.[8] I think a good case can be made to the contrary: that bicameralism facilitated rather than impeded the passage of good legislation in California. The ability to choose the house of origin offered groups with problems a degree of political leverage they would have lacked had only a single legislative house existed. But, more importantly, bicameralism was a crucial factor in the legislators' willingness to lodge formidable disciplinary powers in the Speaker. I maintain that it would be unthinkable to concentrate authority in the Speaker if the assembly were the only legislative body. However, with a bicameral system the Speaker's power extended only to a limited domain—the senate always remained outside his jurisdiction. The Speaker could be given effective police powers over others' misdeeds because the state senate stood as sentinel against the possibility of his own misdeeds. Thus bicameralism reduced the risk of so much concentrated power and at the same time encouraged its use to neutralize legislative bullies and to make the process fair in other ways. Like a car that can handle a powerful engine because it has powerful brakes, a bicameral legislature could accommodate a strong disciplinarian because it could redress abuses.

A sixth proposal is that legislatures be reduced in size, which means that representatives would have more constituents. The hope frequently expressed is that financial savings would accrue as a consequence. A larger theory animating the reform is Madisonian: in a large district a representative could not be "kept" by a single

---

8. Jefferson B. Fordham, *The State Legislative Institution* (Philadelphia: University of Pennsylvania Press, 1959), pp. 31–35. Former Speaker Jess Unruh once also made a similar proposal for a unicameral legislature in an address before the 78th National Conference on Government of the National Municipal League, Minneapolis, Minnesota; it was reprinted in Eugene Lee and Larry L. Berg, eds., *The Challenge of California*, (2d edition) (Boston: Little, Brown, 1976), pp. 151ff.

dominant interest, because there would be so many interests counteracting one another.[9] While the proposal would not apply to California (its relatively small legislative houses probably approximate
the reformers' ideals), one has to recognize that in California the
talent "ran a bit thin," as the dour McAlister liked to say. That is,
given the typical distribution in any legislative population of mentors
and pluggers, there were too few potential specialists to fill the many
needs of a modern legislature. In California, with an assembly of
eighty members, most of whom were working to the best of their
abilities, there were still some policy areas left uncovered—private
health insurance and real estate, to mention two of the most important gaps. (In the senate, with only forty members, the unmet needs
were even greater.) There were also many policy areas without competing specialists: higher education, public housing, and bilingual
education were among those public policy areas in which the ill
effects of monopoly had begun to be visible. A good legislature could
deal with a diverse agenda because it divided its labors among competent specialists. A drastic reduction in the legislative population
would diminish its ability to deal with many topics well. Within
important limits, the principle of "the larger the faculty the broader
the curriculum" applies to a legislature as much as to conventional
academic institutions.

A more abstract proposal is that state legislatures should somehow
do more things and do them faster. The theory behind the suggestion
is that inaction is harmful, that debate, reflection, and compromise
are injurious to the body politic.[10] The wisest course, according to
James Thurber, is, "Don't get it right, just get it written."[11] Policy
solutions should be legislated as soon as a problem is recognized.
Any change is better than the status quo. But laws by themselves
are often insufficient to change the status quo. In California it was

9. *Federalist* no. 10.
10. E.g., George Galloway, *The Legislative Process in Congress* (New York: Thomas
Y. Crowell, 1955) has suggested such congressional rules as a rule of relevancy in
United States Senate debate, joint hearings on similar bills, majority cloture in the
Senate, and so on (p. 667). He gives the other side its due, however, by invoking the
late senator Wayne Morse's warning that "what is needed is not greater speed . . .
but more thorough consideration of legislation, . . . that there should be some place
where the merits of a measure may be thoroughly threshed out in debate and where,
through such debate, the public may receive education regarding the desirability of
proposed action. . ." (p. 557).
11. James Thurber, *Fables for Our Time and Famous Poems Illustrated* (Garden City,
N. Y. : Blue Ribbon Books, 1943), "The Sheep in Wolf's Clothing," p. 39.

legislative debate and the popular discussion prompted by it that served to rally people to want effective laws. Because of the openness of the legislative process to deliberation and persuasion, the laws resulting from that process were seen to be necessary, fair, and effective. Legislators brought people along in the discussions of the policies they were considering, even though valuable time was lost. They did not jam laws down the throats of the unwilling, if only because resistance was sure to undermine the laws' effectiveness. Time was necessary to build the political support that would protect the laws after they went into effect—to assure their funding in subsequent years, for example. It took patience to build enduring coalitions, to arouse the public, to focus popular energies, to bring "all parties on board" (in the legislative parlance), and to adjust old habits and attitudes to future prospects. Passing legislation was a part of a process of moral change that involved the whole society— an essential element, but not decisive by itself. Moral change takes time to debate and accommodate.

An eighth and final proposal holds that legislative seats should turn over more frequently.[12] Radical reapportionment schemes and public financing of campaigns have often been suggested, with a view to replacing the incumbents. The theory is that incumbents are conservative and settled in their ways, while their free-spirited and younger challengers will bring change and new ideas. But in the California state legislature, although there were some incumbent do-nothings, there were some younger ones who did nothing as well. While some freshmen were quick learners and achieved legislative recognition of their competence, the most resourceful legislators were likely to have been reelected from safe districts as many as eight times (e.g., Knox) or thirteen times (e.g., Lanterman). In fact it took years for legislators to become truly competent. And the more competent they became, the more they bubbled over with ideas. Some experienced and talented legislators, having grown weary of

12. A major theme of Common Cause proposals for public financing of campaign expenditures has concerned dulling the incumbent's "edge" in obtaining private campaign support. The unspoken premise of Common Cause appears to be that a defeat of a congressman by *any* challenger is a good thing. See, e.g., a Common Cause (California) pamphlet entitled "Campaign Finance Reform: The Second Chance of a Lifetime" (1975): "Back in the 1870's, at least 50% of the members of the House of Representatives were newcomers; today the figure is 10%. In California the trend is even more disheartening. In the 1974 legislative elections, the percentage of winning challengers was .0975."

their specialties, instead of expanding their talents into new areas, quit the legislature to take up new endeavors elsewhere. But their departure was not a cause for celebration—it was like losing a valuable faculty member to early retirement.

III

Although each of the eight reforms looks sensible out of context, none appears so when put into practice. While it is necessary to a certain degree to have some partisan discipline, electoral competition, restraint on lobbyists' practices, restrictions on agenda, simplification of process, limits on size, quickness of response to problems, and turnover of membership, it is fallacious to think that more is better. In general, the object of each of these reforms is to nurture competent individual legislators who worked hard. Yet I doubt whether any of these reforms would have accomplished that goal in California.

There were features of the California legislature, however, that might well serve as models for reform in other state legislatures. The strength of California's institution lay in its procedures, defining that term in the broadest sense to include not only rules but the system of support that made abundant information available on a nonpartisan basis. The obvious centerpiece of the support system was the nonpartisan staff—at the committee level, in the legislative analyst's office, and in the research office where the Third Reading Analysis was developed. The most important rules were those requiring publication of committee and floor votes, the thirty-day rule (no bill could be heard for thirty days after its publication), the four-day rule (no bill passed out of committee could be debated on the floor without a lapse of four days), mandatory disclosure of lobbyists' campaign and personal contributions to legislators, required attendance on the floor, and the rule requiring that conference committees work publicly. Further, the leadership vigorously upheld several vital understandings not actually formalized into rules, for example, that every bill would get a serious hearing (the key to the author system), that bills could not be amended on the floor, that legislators would be polite, and that the formal rules would not be suspended capriciously.

These procedures—support systems, rules, and understandings—turned the California legislature into a superb school of political capacity. They forced lobbyists to become good teachers, served as a rein on their eagerness to convince, forced them to be accurate, encouraged them to be active, absorbed their rich resources of information into the nonpartisan intelligence system, and rewarded them for improving the communication of their ideas. The procedures, in short, encouraged lobbyists to take principles, reasons, and facts seriously. Because the legislators relied so heavily on the intellectual retrieval system that the procedures created, the lobbyists were obliged to couch their pleas in retrievable form. If they could not, they were ignored.

On the other hand, the procedures of the author system permitted the lobbyists to honor the most qualified legislators. Because the lobbyists had free choice of authors, because they were not required to depend on a member who was incompetent, they could reward legislators who improved their teaching capacities. Thus the secret of part of the success of the California state legislature was the system of mutual accountability that existed between legislators and lobbyists. Each group had the means to force the other to maintain high standards.

Procedures, however, did not work in a vacuum. They were set in a social context. It is important to note that one critical circumstance was necessary to assure good learning. Virtually all ideas and perspectives in the larger society had to be represented in the ranks of the legislature's lobbyists. Otherwise there would be a bias in what was taught and understood. If some segments of the population had no spokesmen, the integrity of the legislative process would be jeopardized, no matter how benign the procedures.

Not many years ago a state legislature like California's would have suffered from an imbalanced corps of lobbyists. As the economist Anthony Downs has inferred deductively[13] and the political scientist Grant McConnell observed empirically,[14] the poor and the disenfranchised simply cannot afford to send lobbyists to teach in the legislature. The producers of the world, however—the farmers, the automakers, the truckers, the financiers, and so on—invariably organize to promote their interests.

In California, by 1975–76, that condition no longer applied. The presentation of the case for the lower classes was routinely provided

13. Anthony Downs, *An Economic Theory of Democracy* (New York: Harper and Bros., 1957), pp. 254–57.
14. Grant McConnell, *Private Power and American Democracy* (New York: Random House, Vintage, 1970), p. 349.

by legal aid lawyers—California Rural Legal Assistance, San Francisco Neighborhood Legal Foundation, and the Western Center for Law and Society, among others (collectively known as "the brown bag lobby").[15] Their salaried personnel were responsible for acting as the underdogs' advocates. Though they were lawyers trained to inhabit the judicial process, not the legislative one, they were obliged to carry out their advocacy for the poor in the state legislature. After all, it was the legislature that held the purse strings, not the courts. Poor people needed money, and poor people's lawyers needed to go to the legislature. Thus the legislature began to get a more balanced picture of the world, one in which rich and poor were treated with equal sympathy.

IV

The curious fact about procedural reform, however, is that talented legislators had no incentive to bring it about. For one thing, the procedures were expensive and subject to criticism from the media. But, more important, a talented individual was likely to be far more powerful as a leader in an inadequate legislature than as a leader in a good one. In an institution in which most of the legislators were apathetic, ignorant, and docile and surrendered their votes for "pottage," the going was a lot easier for dominant legislators. The talented legislator was a single star in a black night, and his reputation was likely to be considerable. Assuming that his legislative proposals were sensible and meritorious, the odds were that his legislation would be enacted far sooner than equally sensible and meritorious proposals of the leadership in a good legislature.[16] It therefore was against his narrow self-interest to improve legislative procedures.

On the other hand, if a good member in an inadequate legislature might do one thing better and quicker, he would necessarily do fewer

15. For a detailed example of successful lobbying on behalf of poor people in California, see Mark Neal Aaronson's description of Ralph Abascal (of the San Francisco Neighborhood Legal Foundation) and his role in influencing the shape of the California Welfare Reform Act of 1971, in Aaronson's unpublished dissertation, "Legal Advocacy and Welfare Reform: Continuity and Change in Public Relief" (University of California, Berkeley, 1975).

16. While California has often been credited for its innovative legislation, I would argue that innovation is a spurious measure of a legislature's quality. In fact, the reverse might be the case. An innovative legislature, one that rushed to get its solutions into print, might in fact be the most enervated, uninformed body, too pusillanimous to resist one or two brilliant members. The no-fault insurance legislation first implemented in Massachusetts would be a case in point, in my opinion.

things than a whole legislature of competent members.[17] A legislative institution where most members wasted their talents simply lacked the collective vitality and versatility of a legislature like California's. Even more important, from a larger point of view, was the activity generated by competent legislators outside of the legislature itself. The capable members of the California legislature, full of knowledge and the confidence that mastery instilled, triggered action in their communities and in the institutions to which their political vocations later led them.

Reform was a puzzle. If the most competent legislators had no desire to develop a competent legislature, where would the impetus for reform come from? In large part, the risks of legislative reform had to be undertaken by leaders as an act of selflessness, for the honor of it. The example of California shows that the cost was worth it. Equally important, it shows that reform is possible. The most implacable resistance to change usually rests on the certitude that it can't be done. But, at least in 1975–76, the necessary procedural reforms had been accomplished and were in place in California. And what has been done once can be done again. Not a bad monument for a free people learning how it might govern itself well.

John Stuart Mill warned that developing the intellects of legislators was not the only matter of importance. A legislative institution did

17. Those who admire Alexis de Tocqueville will recognize my paraphrase of his appraisal of the advantages of democracy: "When the opponents of democracy assert that a single man performs what he undertakes better than the government of all, it appears to me that they are right. The government of an individual, supposing an equality of knowledge on either side, is more consistent, more persevering, more uniform, and more accurate in details than that of a multitude, and it selects with more discrimination the men whom it employs. If any deny this, they have never seen a democratic government, or have judged upon partial evidence. It is true that, even when local circumstances and the dispositions of the people allow democratic institutions to exist, they do not display a regular and methodical system of government. Democratic liberty is far from accomplishing all its projects with the skill of an adroit despotism. It frequently abandons them before they have borne their fruits, or risks them when the consequences may be dangerous; but in the end it produces more than any absolute government; if it does fewer things well, it does a greater number of things. Under its sway the grandeur is not in what the public administration does, but in what is done without it or outside of it. Democracy does not give the people the most skillful government, but it produces what the ablest governments are frequently unable to create: namely, an all pervading and restless activity, a superabundant force, and an energy which is inseparable from it and which may, however unfavorable circumstances may be, produce wonders" (Alexis de Tocqueville, *Democracy in America* [New York: Random, Vintage, 1945], Phillips Bradley, trans., v. 1, pp. 261–62).

not exist solely to educate its members well in statecraft, important as that function was. A legislature also had to set public policy, the legal foundation upon which society is based. Perhaps, however, it is now plain that schooling good leaders and making good laws are not incompatible. Quite the contrary. The procedures, staff, and manners that are vital to a good legislative school can also enable a legislature to govern competently.

The sheer quantity of new public policy generated in California each year was impressive. Whether it was better policy than that of other legislatures must be a matter of debate. No one has yet devised a convincing grading scale for public policy. But neither has the public policy of California ever been declared a failure. California's policy has often been imitated by Congress (air quality legislation comes most quickly to mind). The junior college system, the agricultural labor relations law, the legislature's own budget analyst's office, the state freeways, the public defender system, solar energy programs, medical care for the "medically indigent"—all have been emulated or seriously considered by other states.

Whether or not it is hard to judge the quality of California's laws, however, it is considerably less difficult to appraise the process that made them. Here, the California legislature must be placed in the front rank among the world's lawmaking assemblies for its ability to recognize problems and to mobilize support around their solution. The very procedures that enabled it to nurture good public policy makers appeared naturally to constitute a desirable and democratic policy making process.

Appendix: A Typical Committee Bill Analysis

AB 2147—Boatwright (As amended June 6, 1975)

AB 2147 would require auto insurers to disregard on-the-job accidents of a Transportation Department maintenance or tow truckdriver when establishing the premium of his personal auto insurance ("the Caltrans Exception").

The Problem of Superrisk

Caltrans employees who drive tow trucks or operate maintenance vehicles allege that they are more likely to be involved in highway accidents because they are required to expose themselves on their jobs to unusual highway hazards: they sometimes drive extremely slowly on freeways; they sometimes drive the wrong way down one-way streets; they sometimes stop in perilous spots; they sometimes propel snowplows through drifts which conceal abandoned vehicles; and so on. Under merit-rating practices of most (perhaps all) auto insurers, *any* accident, whether on- or off-the-job, affects the driving record of an insured and leads to increased premiums for personal auto coverage. AB 2147 would require auto insurers of State tow truckdrivers and State maintenance vehicle operators to disregard on-the-job accidents in evaluating their driving records.

Exemption Begets Exemption

1. *The Merit Principle:* Auto insurers presently reduce the cost of car insurance for drivers with meritorious driving records: "meritorious" means a record with virtually no *accidents* (no matter how caused) or *traffic violations*. Insurers have adopted the Merit Principle

for two reasons: as an *incentive* to good driving in the future and as a *reflection* of low-cost experience in the past.

2. *The Principle of Overexposure:* AB 2147 undoes part of the Merit Principle for some Caltrans drivers. The distant ancestor of the Caltrans exception is Section 488 of the Insurance Code. This Section, known formally as the "professional driver exception," requires insurers to disregard on-the-job *traffic violations* of a driver "operating a motor vehicle for compensation." This exemption, created in 1969, is sometimes called "the Teamster Exception" and is based on the Principle of Overexposure: namely, an abnormally high ratio of "on-the-job" miles to total miles distorts an individual's record of private law-abidingness, to which his insurance rates are partly geared.

3. *The Principle of Superrisk:* The Teamster Exception did *not* require disregard for on-the-job *accidents*, but legislation was passed in 1973 to change that state of affairs for policemen and firemen. The Police and Fire Exception, being narrower, was founded on the also narrower Principle of Superrisk: namely, an abnormally high ratio of "superrisky" miles materially distorts an individual's record of private accident-proneness, to which his insurance rates are also partly geared.

4. *The Caltrans Exception:* AB 2147 is an obvious application of the Principle of Superrisk. The State tow- and maintenance truckers argue that they undergo superrisks similar to the ones to which policemen and firemen are exposed, and, therefore, they deserve similar personal insurance treatment.

5. *Future Begettings:* Doubtless, in the future other groups of drivers will claim their just and even-handed deserts under the Principle of Superrisk: *e.g.*, city street maintenance workers, private tow-truckers, ambulance drivers, bus drivers, taxi drivers, salesmen, deliverymen—in short, "the professional drivers."

6. *Parity:* The future extension of the "professional driver exception," beyond disregarding only traffic violations to on-the-job traffic accidents as well, will depend on the argument that disparate treatment of violations and accidents makes little sense.

7. *Operational Details:* Some mechanism is necessary in AB 2147 to notify insurers that a particular accident is a "disregardable" one: *i.e.*, an on-the-job accident of an affected Caltrans driver. The easiest mechanism may be for Caltrans to submit to the insurer a written declaration under penalty of perjury that the applicant or insured

was, at the time of the accident, operating a towtruck or highway maintenance vehicle during the hours of his employment.

8. *Wilful Accidents:* Under the "professional driver exception" for traffic violations, certain egregious violations, like homicide, reckless driving, driving under the influence, and leaving the scene of an accident, are *not* disregarded. Similarly in AB 2147 certain accidents might be treated as particularly egregious: *e.g.*, ones that resulted from driving recklessly or under the influence might be treated as wilful accidents and, hence, *not* disregarded by insurers for purposes of increasing the premiums of an insured's personal coverage.

KNOWN SUPPORT: California Transportation Department.

KNOWN OPPOSITION: Association of California Insurance Companies.

Index